The Anthropology of

From khat to kava to ketamine, drugs are constitutive parts of cultures, identities, economies and livelihoods. This much-needed book is a clear introduction to the anthropology of drugs, providing a cutting-edge and accessible overview of the topic. The authors examine and assess the following key topics:

- How drugs feature in anthropology and the work of anthropologists and the general role of drugs in society
- Comparison between biochemical and pharmacological approaches to drugs and bio-socio-cultural models of understanding drugs
- Evolutionary origins of psychotropic drug sensitivity and archaeological evidence for the spread of psychoactive substances in pre-history
- Drugs in spiritual and religious contexts, considering their role in altered states of consciousness, divination and healing
- Stimulant drugs and the ambivalence with which they are treated in society
- Addiction and dependency
- Drug economies, livelihoods and the production and distribution segments of drug commodity chains
- Drug policies and drug wars
- Drugs, race and gender
- The future of the study of drugs and anthropological professional engagements with solving drug problems.

With the inclusion of chapter summaries and many examples, further reading and case studies – including drug tourism, drug industries in the Philippines and Mexico, Afghanistan and the 'Golden Triangle' and the opioid crisis in North America – *The Anthropology of Drugs* is an ideal introduction for those coming to the topic for the first time, and also for those working in the professional and health sectors. It will be of interest to students of anthropology and to those in related disciplines including sociology, psychology, health studies and religion.

Neil Carrier is Associate Professor in Social Anthropology at the University of Bristol, UK. He has conducted much research into the production, trade and consumption of khat in Kenya and beyond, as well as further research into the theme of drugs, including a current project on cannabis in Africa. Wider interests include film, photography and urban development in Kenya.

Lisa L. Gezon is Professor and Chair of the Department of Anthropology, University of Alabama at Birmingham, USA. She has studied political ecology and protected area management in Madagascar. She developed an interest in the production, trade and consumption of khat in northern Madagascar because of its perceived threat to the protected forest. She has also studied multiple subjects related to health and wellness on topics such as tourism, yoga and exercise on a bicycle-pedestrian trail.

The Anthropology of Drugs

Neil Carrier and Lisa L. Gezon

Routledge
Taylor & Francis Group

LONDON AND NEW YORK

Designed cover image: Clemence Rusenga for the project *Cannabis Africana: Drugs and Development in Africa*.

First published 2024
by Routledge
4 Park Square, Milton Park, Abingdon, Oxon OX14 4RN

and by Routledge
605 Third Avenue, New York, NY 10158

Routledge is an imprint of the Taylor & Francis Group, an informa business

British Library Cataloguing-in-Publication Data
A catalogue record for this book is available from the British Library

Library of Congress Cataloging-in-Publication Data
Names: Carrier, Neil C. M., author. | Gezon, Lisa L., author.
Title: The anthropology of drugs / Neil Carrier and Lisa L. Gezon.
Description: New York, NY : Routledge, 2023. |
Includes bibliographical references and index. |
Identifiers: LCCN 2022060510 (print) | LCCN 2022060511 (ebook) |
ISBN 9780367625245 (hardback) | ISBN 9780367625269 (paperback) |
ISBN 9781003109549 (ebook)
Subjects: LCSH: Drug addiction. | Drug utilization. | Ethnology.
Classification: LCC HV5801 .C337 2023 (print) | LCC HV5801 (ebook) |
DDC 362.29–dc23/eng/20230417
LC record available at https://lccn.loc.gov/2022060510
LC ebook record available at https://lccn.loc.gov/2022060511

ISBN: 9780367625245 (hbk)
ISBN: 9780367625269 (pbk)
ISBN: 9781003109549 (ebk)

DOI: 10.4324/9781003109549

Typeset in Sabon
by Newgen Publishing UK

Contents

Acknowledgements   *ix*

1   Introducing *The Anthropology of Drugs*   1
    Beyond Pharmacology 2
    Defining Drugs 6
    Drug Studies in Anthropology 8
        'Premodern Quasi-Ethnography' and Early Anthropology 8
        Alcohol Studies 10
        'Street Ethnography' and Addiction 11
        Drug Use in Global Contexts 12
    Onwards to the Book 13

2   Anthropological Themes and Approaches in the Study
    of Drugs   17
    Functionalism, Social Integration and Ambivalence 17
    Cultures, Meanings and Values 20
    Power and Intersecting Inequalities 22
        Critical Medical/Health Anthropology 23
        Focus on the Margins? 25
    Crops, Commodities and Illicit Flows: The Social Life of Drugs 26
    Materiality, Pharmacology and Agency 27
    Methods and Ethics 30
        Ethnography 30
        Ethical Considerations 32
        Postcolonial Perspectives 33

3   Drugs in Archaeological and Historical Perspective   39
    Drugs and Human Transformation 39
    Drugs in Deep Time 41
    Drugs, Domestication and the Coming of Inequality 45
    Ancient Literature 47

Early Modern and Modern History 51
Histories of Prohibition 54
History and Anthropology 57

4   **Food of the Gods? Psychedelics, Spirits and Healing**   62
Hallucinogens, Psychedelics and Entheogens 62
  Definitions 62
  Pharmacology 63
  Ethnobotany and Anthropological Connections 63
  A Note on Shamanism 64
  Old and New World Hallucinogen Use: 'A Statistical
    Question' 65
Psychedelics in Cultural Contexts 66
  Iboga(aine) 66
  Mushrooms 66
  Mescaline 68
  Tobacco 69
  Ayahuasca 71
  Synthetic Hallucinogens 73
Psychedelics and Social Movements 73
  Counterculture and New Age Contexts 73
  Anthropology Meets Counterculture: Carlos Castaneda 74
  Globalisation and Change: New Religious Contexts 75
    Native American Church 75
    Santo Daime 76
Drug Tourism and Recreational Contexts 76
Drug Studies and Psychedelic Psychotherapy 78
Anthropology and Psychedelics 81

5   **Stimulating Sociality**   86
Pharmacology and Toxicology 86
Everyday Highs: Stimulants in Context 87
  Stimulating Culture 88
  Stimulants from Ritual to Everyday Practice 89
  Drugs as Identity 91
  Stimulating Sociality: Community and Inequalities 93
    Building Community 93
    Inequalities and Disintegration 94
The Need for Speed 95
  Stimulating Labour: Disciplined Bodies 95
  Stimulants and War 97
Stimulants as Pleasure 98

Everyday Lows: Relieving Stress 99
   Cultural and Social Contexts of Drinking 99
   Drinking and Identity 100
   Drinking and Conflict 101
Anthropology and Drug Harms 103

6   **Perspectives on Addiction in Anthropology**   108
   Agency and Power: The Notion of Addiction 109
   History of 'Addiction' 110
   Complicating Addiction 114
      Neurobiological/Disease Models 114
      Cultural Meaning and Social Interaction Model of Addiction 116
      Structural/Political-Economic Model of Addiction 117
   The Anthropology of Addiction 119
      Ethnographies of Addiction 119
      Political Economies of Addiction 121
      Addiction and Treatment as Cultural Constructions 122
   Case Studies 123
      Khat 123
      Tobacco 124
      Opioids 125
   Anthropology and Drug Potency 126

7   **Drug Economies, Livelihoods and Development**   131
   Drugs as Crops and Commodities 131
   Dangerous Commodities? 133
   Drugs and Livelihoods: Economic Development and Its
      Alternatives 134
   Case Studies 136
      Tobacco 136
         Legal Status and Public Health 136
         Tobacco Farming 137
         Profitability and the Global Capitalist Economy 139
         Risks and Opportunities for Livelihoods 141
      Khat 141
         Production 142
         Trade and Trust 143
         Risks and Opportunities 145
      Opiates and Opioids 146
         Eradication 147
         Risks and Opportunities 148
   Review of Production and Distribution Issues: Risks and
      Opportunities 149

8   **The Drug War and Its Effects**   155
Introducing the 'War on Drugs' 155
Anthropological Approaches 159
   Drug War as a System of Meanings 159
   Drug War as Assemblage 160
   Drug War Ethnography 161
      From Global to Local 161
      Drug Commodity Chains 162
      Drug Production 163
      Drug Trade 164
      Drug Consumption 165
      Who Pays the Price? Violence, Structural Violence and
         Marginality 166
      Studying Up 168
A Failed War? 169
Countercurrents: Anti-War on Drugs 169
Conclusion: Summary and Future Directions 172

9   **Postlude: Engagements and Future Directions**   178
Why Study Drugs? 178
Engaged Anthropology 179
Current and Future Directions: Topics and Approaches 182

Index   185

Acknowledgements

We would like to thank many people who have supported and inspired us while we have written this book. Neil Carrier thanks all his students at Bristol who have taken the Stimulating Anthropology: Drugs and Society unit over the years and who have taught him much on the theme of drugs and much else besides. He thanks Rae Hackler in particular, one of the first students on that course who is now studying a PhD on tea and diaspora at Bristol, and who contributed research to the book project. He would also like to thank all his friends in Kenya with whom he has worked on projects related to khat and cannabis, especially Nico M'Mucheke and Gordon Omenya, as well as UK-based colleagues, especially Gernot Klantschnig. Thanks to Amber for all the encouragement, and Sylvie and Emile for being wonderful distractions. Lisa L. Gezon thanks her student assistants who have far exceeded expectations in their determination to find and cite every source: Brianna Leigh Carlisle (University of Alabama-Birmingham) and Alexa Quarles (University of West Georgia). She also thanks her students in Drugs, Culture and Society in the Fall of 2021 at the University of West Georgia for their engagement in helping develop the directions we took in the book. She thanks Louis-Philippe d'Arvisenet, who introduced her to the world of khat in Madagascar, and she thanks the khat farmers, traders, and chewers she met along the way for their gracious hospitality and willingness to share. Finally, she thanks Will Kaufmann, Evan and Adam Block, and all the friends, family members and colleagues who patiently listened to her talk about all the fascinating things she was learning while researching the book.

1   Introducing *The Anthropology of Drugs*

Why have a whole book on the anthropology of drugs? What have drugs got to do with the discipline of socio-cultural anthropology? What can the discipline bring to the study of drugs? What impact can anthropological insight into drugs have beyond the discipline? Such are the questions we attempt to answer in this book with a look at key research and key themes in the anthropology of drugs. We make the case that anthropology has a crucial contribution to make in studying substances often glossed as 'drugs', whether those substances be tea, coffee or crack cocaine. Or whether the substance is khat, something that we both have researched in our anthropological careers (e.g. Carrier 2007, Gezon 2012), and a fascinating substance whose social lives we continue to track, and which will feature throughout the book as a key case study.

Khat consists of the stems and leaves of the shrub or tree *Catha edulis* that are generally consumed by chewing, inducing a sense of wakefulness, sociability and euphoria through compounds that resemble amphetamine in effects. Khat is very popular, although controversial, throughout a wide geographical area from Yemen to Kenya to Somalia to Madagascar and several other countries besides. It has also 'gone global' with the spread of a Somali diaspora in the wake of civil war in Somalia in the 1990s. In the hands of these migrants, the civil war spurred the growth of trade routes taking khat produced in Kenya and Ethiopia to places as far afield as Australia and New Zealand. The substance and the cultures of consumption around it, as well as its production and trade, continue to fascinate both of us. Partly this fascination emerges from just how varied are the meanings and associations that khat evokes in different people. For example, for many Meru of the Nyambene Hills in central Kenya where much khat is grown, it is a key source of pride as both a successful commodity (one that makes more money than 'respectable' crops such as tea and coffee) and culturally valued item of consumption, one traditionally used to bring people together at important times in life, for example when negotiating marriage. Such positive validation of khat is very different from other perceptions of it, including that of Somalis living in the United Kingdom (UK) who campaigned for khat

DOI: 10.4324/9781003109549-1

to be banned on the grounds that it is a harmful 'drug' that breaks up families and causes unemployment. Understanding how positive, negative and ambivalent perspectives on the same substance can emerge requires engaged research into how such a substance is used, and how it links into far wider socio-political, economic and political contexts. For example, understanding negative perspectives on khat in the UK requires understanding how the substance fits into a context of migration and marginality compared to those in East Africa and the Horn of Africa, where it has been used for generations.

Placing a drug like khat into these contexts is a key approach of modern anthropology. It is an approach that allows for in-depth understanding of aspects of a drug's production, trade and consumption, as well as wider societal attitudes towards it and the social effects of drug policy. This is partly to do with the principal method of the discipline – *ethnography*. There are many different techniques used in ethnography, but almost always it involves interacting with people, usually over an extended period of time, as they go about their daily lives – the classic 'participant observation' technique – in combination with interviews and occasional surveys. While this approach can sound woolly to quantitative researchers keen on surveys and numbers, ethnography ideally has the great virtue of foregrounding the 'emic' perspective, that is to say, foregrounding the voices and experiences of the people among whom anthropologists are working (in contrast with an 'etic' perspective, which focuses on the perspective of the researcher and is often comparative or theoretical in nature). Quantitative research in the social sciences can bring much insight through breadth, involving as it does usually large samples, yet ethnographic approaches generally have the advantage of depth. In drug research, entering the everyday – and not so everyday – lives of people through ethnography can be vital in getting beyond much of the sensationalism that revolves around these often-demonised substances, and can humanise their consumers, producers and traders, people often stereotyped in unfortunate ways in popular culture.

We will discuss methodological approaches that anthropologists take to drugs later in this book (Chapter 2), and these certainly offer powerful tools for going beyond one-dimensional understanding of drugs and those whose lives they affect. However, more than this, anthropological – and other social science – approaches to drugs are also important given how their very effects are mediated by the cultural meanings that swirl around them, as well as by the socio-political factors that can influence whether drug use is harmful or otherwise. This book will argue that drug effects are very much mediated and formed in social and cultural contexts, and in this regard, anthropology can help us understand drugs *beyond their pharmacology*.

Beyond Pharmacology

Pharmacology and the practice of pharmacy have brought great advances in understanding how particular chemical compounds have particular effects upon us, and how these effects can be used in medicine. They have also decisively influenced how we view and interact with drugs, both as pharmaceutical compounds and as psychoactive substances. A key historical moment in the history of pharmacology and humanity was the isolation of morphine from opium by German pharmacist Friedrich Sertürner in 1804 (for a history of morphine's isolation, see Schmitz 1985). Isolating such a compound led to very different ways of viewing how the likes of opium achieved their effects on us, and it encouraged further research into the chemical building blocks of drug effects and the further isolation of active compounds, such as cocaine from the coca plant later in the nineteenth century, and ethanol from alcoholic beverages. This isolation spurred a global market in pharmaceuticals, with companies in Germany – site of Sertürner's innovation – leading the way in marketing an ever-expanding range of medicines (Stephens 2022).

Many such pharmaceuticals have important therapeutic uses. However, given the link of the likes of heroin and cocaine with problematic consumption and addiction (and the concept of addiction developed into its contemporary form around the same time), many perceived such compounds as bearing much responsibility for these problems: they became seen as evil compounds capable of ensnaring people in relations of dependency. While problems with such substances were – and still are in many ways – previously seen as the fault of the consumer in making bad and immoral choices, with the rise of pharmacology, drugs themselves – and in particular their active ingredients – began to be perceived as the source of associated harms, a perspective known as *pharmacological determinism* in the drug literature (Reinarman and Levine 1997). Fears that, for example, just one hit of heroin, crack or even cannabis could induce addiction are born of the notion that harms related to such substances are innate to their pharmacology: the portrayal of cannabis in the notorious – and much lampooned – film of 1936 *Reefer Madness* owes much to this perspective.

While in some ways, the idea that it is less the drug user and more the substance that should be blamed might be progressive and led in some cases to more sympathy for those seen as addicted, *pharmacological determinism* is a very inadequate and reductionist way of understanding drug effects on individuals and society. And social scientists – socio-cultural anthropologists included – played major roles in demonstrating how much more complicated are drug effects than just functions of pharmacology. Sociologist Alfred Lindesmith was a pioneer in this regard, writing a sociological theory of addiction in 1938 based on interviews with 50 heroin users in the United States (US) (Lindesmith 1938). Lindesmith saw that understanding addiction as a biochemical process was insufficient, and he emphasised the need to take seriously the meanings drug users ascribe to drug experiences and addiction, meanings which very much mediate the experience. In his perspective, becoming an addict was a very social process of learning, and hence much more complicated than addiction was commonly portrayed at the time he was writing. His approach was very influential in sociology, and it inspired later research by another American sociologist, Howard Becker, on cannabis use (1953). Becker's work also highlighted that becoming a regular user of a drug was a learning process, showing how even sensations of drug intoxication are mediated by this social learning: for example, sensations of drugs like cannabis are often not obviously positive, including feelings of dizziness. Validating such sensations as positive involves learning from others what the effects should be and that they are to be enjoyed.

Around the same time that Becker was writing, an anthropologist – Dwight Heath – would also disrupt ideas of a simple relationship between chemical and human response, this time through a focus on alcohol. Heath had been conducting research in Bolivia among a people called the Camba on the theme of land reform, but a serendipitous encounter with alcohol researchers who were interested in different drinking patterns among people of different ethnic origins in the US led him to question the drinking patterns he had observed among the Camba (see Gladwell [2010] for a popular account of Heath's research). He wrote (Heath 1958) how the Camba regularly drank a fearsome alcoholic liquor in great quantities, yet apparently this did not result in alcoholism or all the harms associated with alcohol in the West, including violence and anti-social behaviour. This went against the idea that alcohol worked on all human bodies alike as a *disinhibitor*, something that removes social and cultural restraints on our behaviour. Yet the Camba case spurred research into how even extreme drunken behaviour is moulded socially and culturally; indeed, the Camba drank in very ritualised ways with distinct expectations of what being drunk means. Drunkenness, in short, was a sociocultural phenomenon as much as a biochemical one. Other anthropologists (e.g. MacAndrew and Edgerton 1969) would also explore how being drunk differs around the world.

Further work in the wider social sciences would complicate simple notions of drug effects and addiction. This famously included research (Robins et al. 1974) on US soldiers serving in Vietnam, many of whom had taken up the cheap and readily available heroin while on active duty and were seen as addicted. There were great fears that soldiers returning to the US would bring this addiction to heroin with them, leading to a heroin epidemic at home. However, the research showed that few soldiers maintained heroin use upon their return from Vietnam or showed signs of addiction. This study was highly influential (for an overview of its influence, see Hall and Weier 2017) in showing how addiction to such an apparently addictive substance as heroin owed much to contextual factors well beyond pharmacology. Leaving a stressful context – a conflict far from home where heroin use could give relief of various kinds – took away many of the spurs to continued heroin usage. Psychologist Norman Zinberg drew on this study in his work *Drug, Set and Setting* (1984) which showed that many people can use substances like heroin in controlled ways, and he sought to understand what social and other factors produced such controlled usage. The triad in the title of the book is famous in drug studies, encapsulating how in understanding forms of drug use, the 'drug' (its pharmacology and other material qualities, as well as mode of consumption), the 'set' (the psychological state of the consumer – 'mindset') and 'setting' (the complex socio-cultural contexts in which consumption occurs) all have to be considered.

The earlier research showed how socio-cultural context weighed heavily on how people experienced drugs, and on whether drug use would become problematic or not. That drug effects should be soaked in the socio-cultural is perhaps unsurprising given widespread awareness of such phenomena as the placebo effect, whereby research has long demonstrated that inactive medicines given in trials can induce therapeutic effects. Daniel Moerman wrote a book analysing the placebo effect from an anthropological perspective (Moerman 2002) in which he argued for the power of cultural meanings in influencing medicinal efficacy and experiences. He argued that pharmaceutical companies have long had awareness of how the colour of pills and other factors apparently superficial compared with the active compounds are important in how customers judge their potential efficacy. Most people are also aware of how expectations of feeling certain effects from drugs can partially induce those effects even before consumption: feeling more awake through the anticipation of drinking the brewed coffee, or the switch to a more relaxed and jovial frame of mind as the cork is pulled on a bottle of wine before a drop has passed the lips. Given all this, it is clear that pharmacology can only take us so far in understanding drugs, and this book makes a case for anthropology being a key discipline in going *beyond pharmacology* in their study.

However, this is not to say that we should dismiss pharmacology – nor wider medical scientific approaches – in our anthropological endeavours. Indeed, the active compounds of these substances are clearly critical in drawing people towards them, while the likes of withdrawal symptoms are important in understanding why people might find it difficult to cease consuming a particular drug. Cultural meanings do not determine a drug's effects: pharmacological compounds can overwhelm even without expectations of feeling certain effects, as evidenced by the practice of spiking drinks (often involving adding sedatives to someone's drinks without their knowledge to incapacitate them). Drugs are *biosocial* entities: their pharmacological actions, the practices surrounding them and wider socio-cultural factors, mesh together in complicated fashions leading to particular outcomes. Understanding drugs involves grasping the *assemblages* in which they are enmeshed and gain their significance. Assemblage is a concept drawn from the writings of philosopher Gilles Deleuze and is now much used in anthropology to highlight how varied types of things – material objects, concepts and ideas, relations between people, and so forth – come together in intricate ways and configurations in our world. And this concept is suggestive of the complexity in which drugs gain their effects and efficacy, and people gain benefits or harms from them. Anthropology and the ethnographic method, we argue, can contribute well to understanding such complexity through work both local and global in of drug use, the 'drug' (its pharmacology and other material qualities, as well as mode of consumption), the 'set' (the psychological state of the consumer – 'mindset') and 'setting' (the complex socio-cultural contexts in which consumption occurs) all have to be considered.

The earlier research showed how socio-cultural context weighed heavily on how people experienced drugs, and on whether drug use would become problematic or not. That drug effects should be soaked in the socio-cultural is perhaps unsurprising given widespread awareness of such phenomena as the placebo effect, whereby research has long demonstrated that inactive medicines given in trials can induce therapeutic effects. Daniel Moerman wrote a book analysing the placebo effect from an anthropological perspective (Moerman 2002) in which he argued for the power of cultural meanings in influencing medicinal efficacy and experiences. He argued that pharmaceutical companies have long had awareness of how the colour of pills and other factors apparently superficial compared with the active compounds are important in how customers judge their potential efficacy. Most people are also aware of how expectations of feeling certain effects from drugs can partially induce those effects even before consumption: feeling more awake through the anticipation of drinking the brewed coffee, or the switch to a more relaxed and jovial frame of mind as the cork is pulled on a bottle of wine before a drop has passed the lips. Given all this, it is clear that pharmacology can only take us so far in understanding drugs, and this book makes a case for anthropology being a key discipline in going *beyond pharmacology* in their study.

However, this is not to say that we should dismiss pharmacology – nor wider medical scientific approaches – in our anthropological endeavours. Indeed, the active compounds of these substances are clearly critical in drawing people towards them, while the likes of withdrawal symptoms are important in understanding why people might find it difficult to cease consuming a particular drug. Cultural meanings do not determine a drug's effects: pharmacological compounds can overwhelm even without expectations of feeling certain effects, as evidenced by the practice of spiking drinks (often involving adding sedatives to someone's drinks without their knowledge to incapacitate them). Drugs are *biosocial* entities: their pharmacological actions, the practices surrounding them and wider socio-cultural factors, mesh together in complicated fashions leading to particular outcomes. Understanding drugs involves grasping the *assemblages* in which they are enmeshed and gain their significance. Assemblage is a concept drawn from the writings of philosopher Gilles Deleuze and is now much used in anthropology to highlight how varied types of things – material objects, concepts and ideas, relations between people, and so forth – come together in intricate ways and configurations in our world. And this concept is suggestive of the complexity in which drugs gain their effects and efficacy, and people gain benefits or harms from them. Anthropology and the ethnographic method, we argue, can contribute well to understanding such complexity through work both local and global in

As Sherratt suggests, seeing drugs as substances without nutritional value is a very Western way of categorising substances, and also a way of categorising that quickly runs up against problems. For example, substances like beer, khat and coca – generally considered psychoactive substances – also possess nutritional qualities, even if these are not in the forefront of consumers' minds. Stephen Hugh-Jones writes in the same Sherratt edited volume of how Western categorisation of psychoactive substances is very different from indigenous categorisation in South America (Hugh-Jones 2007). He studied the use of coca, tobacco and a hallucinogen called *yagé* (also known as ayahuasca) in the Amazonia region, showing how the category drug scarcely does justice to indigenous categorisation of such substances. These are highly complex, nuanced and contextual, incorporating divisions in society relating to hierarchy and gender, and opposition between 'food' and 'non-food'.

It is certainly important to avoid the assumption that 'drug' is a universal category, although it is now a highly globalised term despite its original emergence in Western Europe. Indeed, it or cognate equivalents are found used in most countries, including in Kenya, where Carrier found great curiosity in whether khat could be categorised a 'drug' or not, as if being a 'drug' would give it a special power to harm (Carrier 2008). The internationalisation of drug policy and ideas about drugs in the twentieth century certainly spread the term far and wide, leading to expectations about the effects of 'drug' substances.

There are several alternative terms that are used in the literature, partly as a counter to the loaded nature of 'drug', although these all have their own problems and ambiguities. One such term is 'entheogen' (Ruck et al. 1979). This term was coined from ancient Greek, which means something that causes divine or spiritual inspiration. It was coined for the class of drugs known as hallucinogens, which we will look at in Chapter 4. This term was designed to give more respect to indigenous and other practices that involved the spiritual use of drugs. As well as itself being infused with moral judgement (albeit more positive than that surrounding 'drug'), it is not a term that can pull together the full range of substances that we cover. Speaking of which, the term 'substance' is used a lot in reference to drugs, and in context can be a useful, neutral way of referring to drugs, although often tinged with a moralising edge in 'substance abuse'. However, as Page and Singer point out, 'most substances are not drugs, but all drugs are substances' (2010: 5). Often 'psychoactive' is appended to 'substance' to be more precise, and this can be a useful term emphasising that the substances in question are those that affect our perception or moods. However, in some senses, all substances can be psychoactive, as, for example, food can affect us psychologically through its socio-cultural meanings, and it can even affect our neurochemistry: sugar is interesting in this regard, as a food considered by some a 'drug' capable of leading to addiction. Anthropologist Anita Hardon and her team conducted fascinating work on how youth in different parts of the world use chemicals – not just 'drugs', but also the likes of make-up and hormone treatment, showing how all such substances play a role in 'altering states' (Hardon 2021).

We use a mix of terms throughout the book, and as the title suggests, we do not shun the term 'drug' itself. We apply it equally to illicit substances as well as the licit. Indeed, while the likes of alcohol and tobacco were categorised differently for much of the twentieth century compared to other drugs (reflecting their respectable status in Western society), we find it useful to treat the legal alongside the illegal as this can highlight how arbitrary some of these distinctions can be. We follow other anthropologists in urging dangerous substances like tobacco and alcohol to be brought into the same types of analysis (Hunt and Barker 2001). Overall, we find that the term 'drug' comes with much analytically useful ambiguity that forces us to keep in mind the power of such terms to influence debate and opinion. While it does have baggage, we feel it a useful term to use, even if it has to be used with much caution.

Drug Studies in Anthropology

'Premodern Quasi-Ethnography' and Early Anthropology

There have been many accounts of drug use by travellers and explorers over the centuries that might be what Page and Singer (2010: 27) considered 'premodern quasi-ethnography'. That is to say, they are filled with detailed observation of drug use in particular socio-cultural settings. These include Greek historian Herodotus writing in the fifth century BCE of apparent cannabis use by Scythians, Spanish explorers writing about the use of intoxicants in the 'New World' and Richard Burton writing about a range of substances from cannabis to khat that he came across in his travels in Arabia and Africa. As Page and Singer relate, Engels writing about opium use by factory workers in the industrialised Manchester of the nineteenth century might also be seen as proto-ethnographic. Drugs have clearly long had power to fascinate, perhaps especially drug use by those from different cultural backgrounds, their drug use sometimes serving as a marker for their difference or 'otherness'.

However, drugs are rather a recent thematic interest in the history of anthropology as a discipline. They played some cameo roles in early ethnographies of the twentieth century, a key period in the consolidation of anthropology as a professional discipline, and in the development of its ethnographic methods with the influence of the likes of Bronislaw Malinowski, whose book *Argonauts of the Western Pacific* (first published in 1922) set an early template for how ethnographic research should be conducted and analysed. Psychoactive substances were mentioned in such texts, though mainly in passing. For example, betel nuts (referring to the seeds of the Areca palm that have some mild psychoactive effects and are consumed by chewing) feature briefly in the latter work where Malinowski describes preparations for a *Kula* expedition.

The *Kula ring* is a ceremonial exchange network connecting several islands in the Trobriand archipelago in which bracelets and necklaces circulate in different directions, exchanged by men who embark on intrepid journeys to do so. This is one of the most famous pieces of ethnography in anthropology that has been endlessly revisited and reanalysed and has been critical to anthropological interest in forms of exchange. In the Trobriands, betel chewing is very common, and there is even a picture of Malinowski himself holding a pot of powdered lime used in betel chewing to activate the active compounds (reproduced in Young 1998: 55), though it is unclear whether he himself chewed. Malinowski describes in great detail the preparations undertaken in Kula expeditions, including those related to preparing canoes for the voyages. One stage of these preparations involves laying plaited mats known as *yawarapu* upon the canoe, at which point a spell is made, the first line of which is: 'Betel-nut, betel-nut, female betel-nut; betel-nut, betel-nut, make betel-nut; betel-nut of the ceremonial spitting!' (Malinowski 1922: 198). Malinowski explains that betel is referenced as it is something that men expect to receive during Kula exchanges, and something that is also given in the hope that the betel will induce someone to exchange with them (ibid. 199). Thus, although only mentioned once in the book, betel nut was appreciated by Malinowski as socially and culturally important, an importance he would later return to, describing how before tobacco rivalled it, 'betel-nut was the typical gift offered at all social gatherings' (1935: 301).

This was rather typical of ethnographies of this era, where the likes of betel briefly come into focus in more holistic overviews of the small-scale societies then predominantly studied by anthropologists. However, one substance came into sustained focus in American anthropology in the early twentieth century: *peyote*, the cactus *Lophophora williamsii* consumed in northern Mexico and the US for its visionary properties. In the late nineteenth century and early twentieth century, peyote was spreading quickly among Native Indian groups of the Plains as part of religious practices drawing both from indigenous traditions and Christianity. Anthropologists quickly saw the significance of this practice and a large literature built up focused upon it, including by James Mooney (1897). Later on, a key figure in the history of the anthropology of drugs, Weston La Barre, would write a comprehensive study of what he termed the *peyote cult* (1938). We look more closely at peyote in Chapter 4, but for now it is important to note that anthropologists such as Mooney and La Barre played important roles not only in documenting peyote practices but also in supporting the rights of *peyotists* (as some termed those Native Americans practising rites involving peyote) to use the cactus as a religious sacrament in the face of concerted campaigns to prohibit the substance in various US states and at the federal level. The partially successful role of anthropologists in countering peyote prohibitionists is described in detail by Aurelien Bouayad (2019).

Anthropological attention was drawn to other peyote-like substances through the emergence of the sub-discipline of ethnobotany, which drew greatly in the twentieth century on the work of Richard Evans Schultes (1915–2001). Schultes conducted several expeditions throughout Central and South America studying known psychotropic plants (especially coca) and in search of hallucinogens and medicinal plants undocumented by Western scientists, funded by such organisations as the National Research Council of the US. In his search for hallucinogenic plants, he sought not merely to identify and name them but to understand their place in the lives of the people who used them. This included studying with shamanic healers to learn their often-complex preparations of the drugs. Schultes learned that, for the Colombian Kofán people he lived with, the hallucinogen known as ayahuasca (see Chapter 4), or *yagé*, 'is far more than a shamanic tool; it is the source of wisdom itself, the ultimate medium of knowledge for the entire society' (Davis 1996: 226). Schultes left a huge legacy in his writings as well as in his enormous collection of botanical specimens. Through his writings on the likes of ayahuasca and other hallucinogens, Schultes' work became widely known and disseminated in the 1960s counterculture movement, as mostly young Westerners incorporated these substances into their social practices alongside increasingly popular substances such as LSD. We return to the history of anthropology's influence on the counterculture and New Age movement in Chapter 4.

Alcohol Studies

As might be expected, alcoholic beverages permeate many anthropological works of the early to mid-twentieth century, sometimes in full focus, and other times in cameo roles. It includes an important ethnographic work by the likes of Audrey Richards – a British anthropologist famous for field-work in the early 1930s among the Bemba people of Zambia (then Northern Rhodesia). She was a pioneering scholar of nutrition and conducted detailed research on Bemba diet, as well as other aspects of their society (see, for example, Richards 1939). As in many other societies in Africa and beyond, beer was of great importance nutritionally and socially for the Bemba. Known as *ubwalua*, Bemba beer was principally made from millet. It was not especially potent in terms of alcohol content, and in some regards more resembled porridge than what some might regard as typical beer, but it lay at the heart of much Bemba sociality as Richards described (1939: 76–81). Drinking parties brought people together from different villages and, in Richard's analysis, were governed by strict 'rules of etiquette' (ibid. 81) that structured drinking sessions in terms of who got to drink and when, generally reflecting seniority. Like other anthropologists of that era, Richards drew a sharp distinction between the 'traditional' drinking of the rural Bemba that was controlled and generally unproblematic, and drinking by Bemba in the new urban settings of the era where this traditional control was lost and young men could be seen frequently drunk. Such a distinction was particularly prominent in *functionalist* analyses of drinking, a theoretical approach of the early to mid-twentieth centuries that we will return to in Chapter 2.

The literature on alcohol grew rapidly from mid-century, with more focused work such as Donald Horton's (1943) comparative overview of alcohol's role in many small-scale societies. Alcohol sparked reams of ethnographic writings, especially driven by questions of how harmful alcohol was among people such as Native Americans (as we will discuss in Chapter 2). Anthropologists often countered arguments that non-Western people were more susceptible to alcohol problems. The work of the likes of Dwight Heath (1958), which we covered earlier, was also critical in highlighting the power of anthropology to shake universalist theories of drug effects. Famous anthropologists such as Gregory Bateson (who wrote an insightful analysis of the efficacy of Alcoholics Anonymous in treating alcoholism [1971]) and Mary Douglas (whose edited volume *Constructive Drinking* [1987] explored the social and ritual significance of alcoholic and other beverages) were drawn to the substance too. As Mac Marshall (a key figure in the anthropology of alcohol) put it: 'The cross-cultural study of alcohol presents a classic natural experiment: A single species (Homo sapiens), a single drug substance (ethanol), and a great diversity of behavioural outcomes' (Marshall 1979: 1).

'Street Ethnography' and Addiction

Meanwhile, other drugs were coming more into anthropological and ethnographic focus, partly in response to social concerns in countries such as the US. Indeed, 'street ethnography' in US cities such as New York and Chicago would be much used from the mid-twentieth century onwards to study what was seen as the growing problem of urban drug addiction, focusing in particular on use of heroin, crack cocaine and, more recently, methamphetamine. It was sociologists such as Bingham Dai (1937) who would pioneer ethnographic methods in the study of addiction in such cities, often initially with a problematic focus on drug users as part of 'deviant' subcultures, then a prominent conceptual focus of sociology. Anthropologists would become more involved in this 'street ethnography' as the discipline moved away in the later twentieth century from a primary focus on the so-called exotic and began working in Western urban settings that were previously seen as the territory of sociologists in an old disciplinary division of labour. Classics that we will return to later in the book include Preble and Casey's article 'Taking care of business' (1969) about the life and livelihoods of heroin users in New York, and Michael Agar's studies of cultures around heroin, such as his study of the Lexington Kentucky Narcotics Hospital (Agar 1973).

While funding for such research would fluctuate along with changing politics, especially in the US, public health crises such as the HIV/AIDS epidemic of the 1980s (which can spread through needle sharing) spurred further anthropological engagement, as did concerns of 'new' drug epidemics, such as the rise of crack cocaine, also in the 1980s. Much of the work in this era and into the present was highly critical of the underlying political and economic context that led to some people in society being especially vulnerable to addiction. This critical force became evident in the work of the likes of Merrill Singer who has long shown the need to bring in global political economy into analyses of drug harms (and who pioneered the Critical Medical Anthropology approach we will discuss later). Philippe Bourgois – an anthropologist based at UCLA – has produced vivid ethnographies of the lives of drug traders and users in both New York (Bourgois 1995), and San Francisco (Bourgois and Schonberg 2009), demonstrating lucidly how drug use and trade cannot be separated from the wider structural inequalities that blight so many lives the world over. Anthropologists have also widened the regional focus in studies of addiction to the likes of heroin and cocaine: important work includes that of the late Susan Beckerleg who worked with heroin addicts on the Kenyan coast, showing how heroin shipped from Asia to Europe through East African ports spilled over into use by people living in Kenyan towns such as Malindi and Watamu (Beckerleg 1995). Similarly, Henrik Vigh has conducted research in Guinea-Bissau and Portugal among cocaine smugglers and users. Guinea-Bissau in West Africa gained notoriety in the 2000s for becoming a hub for cocaine shipped from South America to Europe, and once again consumption spilled over into Bissauan society (Vigh 2019). The work of Maziyar Ghiabi in Iran is another example of ethnographic study of addiction in contexts beyond those of the West (2019).

Drug Use in Global Contexts

As the earlier examples from Kenya, Guinea-Bissau and Iran suggest, anthropologists and ethnographers were still doing important work on drugs in other places and contexts, however, and in the later decades of the twentieth century, a range of substances came into anthropological focus. This included coca in South America, the source plant of cocaine whose leaves are also chewed for their mild stimulant effects. One fine example of this is Catherine Allen's ethnography, *The Hold Life Has* (1988), that built on her long-term field engagement with an indigenous community in the Peruvian Andes. Her work used the ever-present *hallpay* (coca-chewing in the Quechua language) in that community as a prism on the 'webs of significance' that bind people together with each other and with the spirits of the land and the dead whose presence is felt deeply. While focused on that Andean community, the wider national and global context of coca and cocaine was very much present in the book as people navigated change. More recent anthropological work on coca in South America explores the local and global politics of production, for example, Thomas Grisaffi's work on coca in Bolivia (2019) that explores a union of coca growers that came to prominence in the election of its leader, Evo Morales, to the Bolivian presidency in 2006.

Other regions and other substances also came into focus too. These included kava, a beverage made from the plant *Piper methysticum* that is popular for its mild sedative effects in the South Pacific and Melanesia, among other regions. Ron Brunton made an important study of its changing significance and social history in Melanesia (Brunton 1989). Cultural institutions built around consumption came into focus too, for example the famous tea ceremony of Japan which was studied by Jennifer Anderson, herself a practitioner of *chanoyu* as the ceremony is known in Japanese (Anderson 1991). The stimulant drug khat – the stimulant leaves and stems of *Catha edulis* which we ourselves have studied in Madagascar, Kenya and the Somali diaspora in the UK – drew anthropological attention to it in the 1980s, first being studied anthropologically in Yemen (Weir 1985, Kennedy 1987). Khat research has taken a journey mirroring that of the plant itself: first focusing on its production and use in its home regions (after Yemen, there have been studies of it in Ethiopia [Gebissa 2004], Kenya [Hjort 1974, Goldsmith 1994, Carrier 2007], Madagascar [Gezon 2012] and Uganda [Beckerleg 2010]); next on its use and trade in diaspora contexts (Anderson et al. 2007, Ermansons 2022); then on the transnational dynamics as people from the diaspora return to countries such as Somaliland with attitudes to khat shaped in the diaspora (Hansen 2013).

Onwards to the Book

As this short and far from comprehensive survey suggests, the great socio-cultural, political and economic importance of drugs ensured they came at least partially into focus for anthropologists in earlier decades, while more recently they have become a central focus for many. The study of drugs provides a window into understanding many topics of contemporary focus, including cultural and historical contexts of meaning-making, the development of sociality surrounding drug use, the agency of material substances and power dynamics that affect access to and consequences for using drugs. Chapter 2 will elaborate further on these themes.

Works Cited

Agar, Michael. 1973. *Ripping and Running: A Formal Ethnography of Urban Heroin Addicts*. New York: Seminar Press.

Allen, Catherine J. 1988. *The Hold Life Has: Coca and Cultural Identity in an Andean Community*. Washington, DC: Smithsonian Institution Press.

Anderson, David M., Susan Beckerleg, Degol Hailu, and Axel Klein. 2007. *The Khat Controversy: Stimulating the Drugs Debate*. Oxford: Berg.

Anderson, Jennifer L. 1991. *An Introduction to Japanese Tea Ritual*. Albany, NY: State University of New York Press.

Bateson, Gregory. 1971. "The Cybernetics of 'Self': A Theory of Alcoholism." *Psychiatry: Journal for the Study of Interpersonal Processes* 34: 1–18.

Becker, Howard S. 1953. "Becoming a Marihuana User." *The American Journal of Sociology* 59 (3): 235–242.

Beckerleg, Susan. 1995. "'Brown sugar' or Friday Prayers: Youth choices and community building in coastal Kenya." *African Affairs* 94 (374): 23–38.

———. 2010. "'Idle and Disorderly' Khat Users in Western Uganda." Drugs: Education, Prevention and Policy 17: 303–314.

Bouayad, Aurelien. 2019. "The Cactus and the Anthropologist: The Evolution of Cultural Expertise on the Entheogenic Use of Peyote in the United States." *Laws* 8 (2): 1–22.

Bourgois, Philippe I. 1995. *In Search of Respect: Selling Crack in El Barrio.* Cambridge: Cambridge University Press.

Bourgois, Philippe, and Jeffrey Schonberg. 2009. *Righteous Dopefiend.* Berkeley, CA: University of California Press.

Breen, Benjamin. 2022. "New Imperial Drug Trades, 1500–1800." In *The Oxford Handbook of Global Drug History* edited by Paul Gootenberg, 113–132. New York: Oxford University Press.

Brunton, Ron. 1989. *The Abandoned Narcotic: Kava and Cultural Instability in Melanesia.* Cambridge: Cambridge University Press.

Carrier, Neil. 2007. *Kenyan Khat: The Social Life of a Stimulant.* Leiden: Brill.

———. 2008. "Is Miraa a Drug?: Categorizing Kenyan Khat." *Substance Use and Misuse* 43 (6): 803–818.

Dai, Bingham. 1937. *Opium Addiction in Chicago: A Dissertation.* Shanghai: The Commercial Press.

Davis, Wade. 1996. *One River: Explorations and Discoveries in the Amazon Rain Forest.* New York, NY: Simon & Schuster.

Ermansons, Guntars. 2022. "'If There Was No Jaad': Poetics of Khat and Remembering the Future in a London Somali Community." *Journal of the Royal Anthropological Institute* 28 (4): 1290–1308.

Gebissa, Ezekiel. 2004. *Leaf of Allah: Khat and Agricultural Transformation in Harerge, Ethiopia 1875–1991.* Oxford: James Curry.

Gezon, Lisa L. 2012. *Drug Effects: Khat in Biocultural and Socioeconomic Perspective.* Walnut Creek, CA: Left Coast Press.

Ghiabi, Maziyar. 2019. *Drugs Politics: Managing Disorder in the Islamic Republic of Iran.* Cambridge: Cambridge University Press.

Gladwell, Malcolm. 2010. "Drinking Games." The New Yorker, 7 February.

Goldsmith, Paul. 1994. "Symbiosis and Transformation in Kenya's Meru District (Unpublished PhD Thesis)." University of Florida.

Grisaffi, Thomas. 2019. *Coca Yes, Cocaine No.* Durham, NC: Duke University Press.

Hall, Wayne, and Megan Weier. 2017. "Lee Robins' Studies of Heroin Use Among U.S. Vietnam Veterans." *Addiction* 112 (1): 176–180.

Hansen, Peter. 2013. "Khat, Governance and Political Identity among Diaspora Returnees to Somaliland." *Journal of Ethnic and Migration Studies* 39 (1): 143–159.

Hardon, Anita. 2021. *Chemical Youth: Navigating Uncertainty in Search of the Good Life.* London: Palgrave Macmillan.

Heath, Dwight B. 1958. "Drinking Patterns of the Bolivian Camba." *Quarterly Journal of Studies on Alcohol* 19 (3): 491–508.

Hjort, Anders. 1974. "Trading Miraa: From school-leaver to shop-owner in Kenya." *Ethnos* 39 (1–4): 27–43.

Horton, Donald. 1943. "The Functions of Alcohol in Primitive Societies: A Cross-Cultural Study." *Quarterly Journal of Studies on Alcohol* 4(2): 199–320.

Hugh-Jones, Stephen. 2007. "Coca, Beer, Cigars, and Yagé: Meals and Anti-Meals in an Amerindian Community." In *Consuming Habits: Drugs in History and Anthropology*, edited by Jordan Goodman, Paul E. Lovejoy and Andrew Sherratt, 47–66. London: Routledge.

Hunt, Geoffrey and Judith Barker. 2001. "Socio-cultural anthropology and alcohol and drug research: toward a unified theory." *Social Science and Medicine* 53 (2): 165–188.

Kennedy, John G. 1987. *The Flower of Paradise: The Institutionalized Use of the Drug Qat in North Yemen*. Dordrecht: D. Reidel Publishing Company.

La Barre, Weston. 1938. *Peyote Cult*. Norman, OK: University of Oklahoma Press.

Lindesmith, Alfred R. 1938. "A Sociological Theory of Drug Addiction." *American Journal of Sociology* 43: 593–613.

MacAndrew, Craig and Robert B. Edgerton. 1969. Drunken Comportment: A Social Explanation. London: Thomas Nelson and Sons.

Malinowski, Bronislaw. 1922. *Argonauts of the Western Pacific: An Account of Native Enterprise and Adventure in the Archipelagoes of Melanesian New Guinea*. London; New York, NY: Routledge..

———. 1935. *Coral Gardens and Their Magic*. London: Routledge.

Marshall, Mac, Genevieve M. Ames, and Linda A. Bennett. 2001. "Anthropological Perspectives on Alcohol and Drugs at the Turn of the New Millennium." *Social Science & Medicine* 53 (2): 153–164.

Marshall, Mac. 1979. *Beliefs, Behaviors, and Alcoholic Beverages: A Cross-Cultural Survey*. Ann Arbor, MI: University of Michigan Press.

Moerman, Daniel 2002. *Meaning, Medicine and the Placebo Effect*. Cambridge: Cambridge University Press.

Mooney, James. 1897. "The Kiowa Peyote Rite." *Der Urquell* 1: 329–333.

Page, Bryan J., and Merrill Singer. 2010. *Comprehending Drug Use: Ethnographic Research at the Social Margins*. New Brunswick, NJ: Rutgers University Press.

Preble, Edward, and John J. Casey. 1969. "Taking Care of Business – The Heroin User's Life on the Street." *International Journal of the Addictions* 4: 1–24.

Reinarman, Craig, and Harry G. Levine. 1997. *Crack in America: Demon Drugs and Social Justice*. Berkeley, CA: University of California Press.

Richards, Audrey. 1939. *Land, Labour, and Diet in Northern Rhodesia: An Economic Study of the Bemba Tribe*. London: Oxford University Press for International Institute of African Languages.

Robins, Lee N., Darlene H. Davis, and David N. Nurco. 1974. "How Permanent Was Vietnam Drug Addiction?" *American Journal of Public Health* 64 (12): 38–43.

Ruck, Carl A. P., Jeremy Bigwood, Danny Staples, Jonathan Ott, and Robert Gordon Wasson. 1979. "Entheogens." *Journal of Psychedelic Drugs* 11: 145–146.

Rudgley, Richard I. 1998. *The Encyclopedia of Psychoactive Substances*. London: Little, Brown.

Schmitz, Rudolf. 1985. "Friedrich Wilhelm Serturner and the Discovery of Morphine." *Pharmacy in History* 27: 61–74.

Sherratt, Andrew. 2007. "Introduction: Peculiar Substances." In: *Consuming Habits: Global and Historical Perspectives on How Cultures Define Drugs* edited by Jordan Goodman, Paul E. Lovejoy and Andrew Sherratt, 1–10. London: Routledge.

Stephens, Robert. 2022. "Germany's Role in the Modern Global Drug Economy." In *The Oxford Handbook of Global Drug History* edited by Paul Gootenberg, 389–407. New York: Oxford University Press.

Vigh, Henrik. 2019. "Life in the ant trails: Cocaine and caustic circuits in Bissau." *Focaal* 85: 15–25.

Weir, Shelagh. 1985. *Qat in Yemen: Consumption and Social Change*. London: British Museum Publications Limited.

Young, Michael. 1998. *Malinowski's Kiriwina: Fieldwork Photography 1915–1918*. Chicago, IL: University of Chicago Press.

Zinberg, Norman. 1984. *Drug, Set, and Setting: The Basis for Controlled Intoxicant Use*. New Haven, CT: Yale University Press.

2 Anthropological Themes and Approaches in the Study of Drugs

Anthropology has long been a diverse discipline in terms of theoretical approaches and thematic concerns, and it grows ever-more diverse as new theoretical currents wash over the discipline. In what follows, we give an overview of some of these currents relevant to the study of drugs, linking them to the wider intellectual history of the discipline. In doing so, our principal focus in this chapter is on socio-cultural anthropology, although we give coverage to archaeology in Chapter 3. Anthropology is often considered a four-field discipline (constituted by socio-cultural, linguistic and biological anthropology, as well as archaeology), so this is inevitably a partial theoretical and thematic overview. We begin the chapter with a look at a theoretical toolkit that anthropologists can apply in the study of drugs, giving some historical background too for these approaches; while some are more fashionable in contemporary anthropology than others, all have potential to bring insight. We turn at the end of the chapter to ethnography, the main methodological approach that anthropologists use, and a key part of the strength of anthropology in researching drugs.

Functionalism, Social Integration and Ambivalence

From the 1940s, alcohol came into close anthropological focus, with the work of Ruth Bunzel on the role of alcoholism in Central America (Bunzel 1940). Its study was quickly adopted into theoretical frameworks of that era, one being a *functionalist* approach. Functionalism in anthropology came in different forms, but the most influential was A.R. Radcliffe-Brown's 'structural functionalism'. It focused on how parts of society served to reproduce the social structure of that society. His variety became the key approach in mid-twentieth-century British anthropology, inspiring much important work in regions such as Africa on kinship, lineage and social structure (Fortes 1949, Radcliffe-Brown 1952). Functionalist approaches, while varied, all generally neglected historical studies of how particular societies came to be, focusing instead on how their current forms are replicated and reproduced. They also generally treated the kind of small-scale societies they focused

DOI: 10.4324/9781003109549-2

upon as bounded entities that could be studied holistically. Functionalism would later be heavily critiqued in the discipline for being ahistorical, for being intimately connected with the colonial project (functionalist accounts of African and other societies being used by colonial administrators), and for this treatment of societies as bounded wholes, insulated from outside influences.

Functionalist approaches have nevertheless been influential in how the discipline engaged with psychoactive substances, alcohol in particular. One of the earliest works in this regard was Donald Horton's comparative overview of alcohol's role in many small-scale societies (Horton 1943), building up an argument that alcohol's key function in general terms is to reduce anxiety. While dated in many regards, Horton made important critical points regarding received wisdom about alcohol and small-scale societies, including pushing back against a common idea of the early twentieth century that there were underlying racial differences affecting how people reacted to alcohol. This idea mostly portrayed people such as Native Americans as being racially susceptible to ill effects of alcohol, unlike whites who were seen as capable of holding their liquor (Horton 1943: 204). Horton drew on the work of influential anthropologist Franz Boas who demonstrated a physiological unity of human beings, so countering the idea of their being racialised differences to how people responded to alcohol. He also made a clear statement of how an anthropological approach to drinking alcohol would differ from that of other disciplines that often focused on problematic aspects of drinking, such as volatile drunkenness and alcoholism. Later, scholars would point out that social and historical factors are better explanations than genetic disposition to chemical abuse. For Horton, anthropologists should focus on the 'normal' drinking of the majority rather than the pathological drinking of the minority (Horton 1943: 212).

This focus on more-or-less unproblematic 'normal' consumption would become a hallmark of anthropological work on alcohol in this era. Earlier anthropologists had a functionalist interest in how drinking maintained societal cohesion and so reproduced society in a particular form. An interesting example of this is the work of Monica Wilson, an influential South African social anthropologist who worked with the Nyakyusa people of southern Tanganyika (now Tanzania). Her research (1951) drew sharp contrasts between pre-colonial and colonial-era Nyakyusa society. In the former, she highlighted how Nyakyusa society was a *gerontocracy*, a society in which power is held by the elders. For the Nyakyusa, according to Wilson, society was held together by the goodwill of the elders, and this was secured by their communal drinking practices. Wilson reported that in pre-colonial times, beer was strictly the preserve of the elders, younger generations not being permitted to drink.

With the coming of the colonial era and the market economy that came with it, however, society was fundamentally transformed, and elders' power waned as younger generations accumulated wealth in this new economy.

Symbolic of this new transformation was how younger generations now also drank beer. In various parts of East Africa – where societies regarded as gerontocracies were common – similar discourse exists that beer (as well as khat in the case of the Meru of Kenya [Carrier 2005], and cannabis among groups such as the Luo [Shipton 1989]), was restricted in pre-colonial times to elders. How much this discourse actually reflected pre-colonial life for people such as the Nyakyusa has been nuanced by the historian Justin Willis (2002) who argues that this notion of beer drinking as a formerly unproblematic practice that helped integrate society is likely idealised. However, Wilson's analysis is emblematic of the functionalist approach that saw consumption of alcoholic drinks as integrated into societies before disintegrating through the impact of colonialism and capitalism. This functionalist approach to the study of drugs has continued to characterise many studies in anthropology, including those that relate the consumption of drugs to the need to adjust to the pressures of contemporary life (see Chapter 5).

This focus on alcohol and its functional role in integrating societies into cohesive wholes came under increasing attack from the 1980s. In part this stemmed from the presentation of alcohol (and in some cases, other substances) in the anthropological literature as unproblematic. This positive valuation was critiqued heavily in a key article by alcohol researcher Robin Room (1984). In the article, Room argued that ethnographers (principally anthropologists) consistently underplayed the problems associated with alcohol, even while members of local communities would describe how alcohol use was causing severe problems. He accused anthropologists of 'problem deflation'. Clearly something was lacking in anthropological approaches if they appeared so out of step with the views of community members among whom they studied. This critique certainly had a potent effect on the anthropology of alcohol, spurring renewed interest in more harmful aspects and forms of alcohol consumption. Seeing alcohol as mostly working to integrate societies lost its impetus, especially as 'functionalist' became a term often used to dismiss older approaches as obsolete and old-fashioned.

Of course, societies are usually highly ambivalent about alcohol and other substances, and most people are aware of dangers of overconsumption. Indeed, there can hardly have been a society in human history where alcohol was used where such dangers were not known, and literature from Classical times onwards is filled with references to this ambiguity. A good example is a poem by the Roman poet Horace, who wrote an ode addressed to a wine jar (Commager 1957) that recounted its power to bring both merry jest, yet also arguments and complaints. Societies such as the Nyakyusa mentioned earlier also were aware of the capacity of beer not just to bring society together through the goodwill of the elders, but also to bring social harm, hence the many restrictions on who could consume.

Ambivalence and ambiguity are now common themes in anthropological writings about not just alcohol but also other drugs too. This is certainly the case with khat, for example, praised much for an ability to generate sociability and so strengthen networks; yet also seen by some as a factor in social rupture, especially in contexts such as use by the Somali diaspora in the UK, where it was seen as generating social harms among a community attempting to integrate into UK society (Anderson et al. 2007). Clearly sharing drugs of whatever type can bring people together and generate forms of social cohesion: for example, work such as that by Philippe Bourgois and Jeff Schonberg (2009) on homeless heroin users in San Francisco shows how shared heroin can generate social bonds, albeit ones that can perpetuate dangers and harms. In this sense, the functionalist focus on social cohesion (albeit a much more ambivalent understanding of this social cohesion) is not necessarily obsolete. Indeed, works such as Mary Douglas' *Constructive Drinking* (1987) continued the functionalist trend in focusing more on the positive social roles alcoholic and other beverages could play in society.

Cultures, Meanings and Values

While social structure became a key focus of British *social* anthropology in the twentieth century, US *cultural* anthropology under the influence of Franz Boas and others had 'culture' as its key concept. In anthropological usage, this term came to have a broad meaning of shared patterns of behaviour, values, meaning systems and symbols that people learn growing up in or adapting to particular societies and social settings. A related concept was that of *cultural relativism*, which continues to be much debated today. This is the idea that many things – ideas, practices, etc. – that might be seen as universal for all humans are actually not universal at all, but *relative* to a particular culture or society. Boas and his students went to great lengths to demonstrate this, most famously Margaret Mead who argued that adolescence was not universally a time of hormone-charged trauma and stress in people's lives, as generally considered in the West, using a counter-example of Samoan society where girls apparently had a comparatively stress free adolescence (Mead 1928).

In relation to drugs, another of Boas' students, Ruth Benedict, argued in *Patterns of Culture* (Benedict 1934) that while the Pueblo people of the Southwest US value moderation and shun excess (ibid. 56–57), they were surrounded by other Native American societies, ones who valued excess. This excess was evident in the value they ascribed to intoxication and the visions certain substances such as peyote could bring. For example, the Pima people of the region equated the intoxication generated by cactus beer with religion according to Benedict: 'Intoxication, in their practice and in their poetry, is the synonym of religion. It has the same clouded vision and of insight. It gives the whole tribe, together, the exaltation that it associated with religion' (1934: 61).

There has been much ink spilled debating cultural relativism over the years (Geertz 1984), and the concept has even become caught up in culture wars as for some it represents woolly social science thinking as contrasted with the hard sciences. Some conflate it with moral relativism, the idea that there is no foundation for morality beyond that of our culture or society. Within anthropology itself, the concept is treated with great ambivalence, with some arguing that it gives too much coherence to 'cultures' as integrated wholes, ignoring internal diversity. Some accuse it of overplaying 'differences between societies' and underestimating 'the possibility of transcending these differences' (Brown 2008: 371). Still others caution that it is apolitical and precludes the criticism or even condemnation of practices that violate human rights. As a discipline, the American Anthropological Association first issued a statement on human rights in 1947, in response to and critical of the United Nations Universal Declaration of Human Rights (UDHR), which was established in 1948. Authored by Melville Herskovits, it cautioned against the possibility of a truly universal code and cautioned against its potential use in support of imperialist and Western individualist agendas.

Later, anthropologists began human rights advocacy for 'vulnerable indigenous populations' and developed a revised statement in 1999.[1] In a different stance, the new statement implores anthropologists to 'protect existing human rights as defined at the interfaces among international conventions and local meanings and struggles and to enlarge the public understanding of human rights based on anthropological research'.

Recognition of human rights does not make cultural relativism obsolete, however. Anthropologists remain committed to understanding local perspectives – or the 'emic' approach. In an approach called *methodological relativism*, anthropologists seek to understand people's motivations and beliefs by suspending their own biases before making a judgement. This is important in drug studies, where moral panic can cloud perceptions. Before condemning drug dealers such as those presented in Philippe Bourgois' (1995) classic ethnography, *In Search of Respect: Selling Crack in El Barrio*, for example, an analyst would want to suspend judgement to learn about the political and economic contexts surrounding decisions to sell. There is much to be said for using the approach cautiously 'as a rule of thumb or intellectual tool' (Brown 2008: 372) as it can push us to see past what we may take for granted.

Some have criticised the concept of culture itself – not just *cultural relativism* – for suggesting that people live within static, homogenous cultural worlds, ignoring diversity and change. Yet anthropologists still find much value in the culture concept, recognising that life is lived *culturally* – that is to say, we are all enmeshed in systems of symbols and meanings, and that values people hold can vary much across cultural contexts. Linguistic anthropologist Alessandro Duranti (1997: 38) proposed that culture is important for understanding 'similarities and differences in the ways in which people around the world constitute themselves in aggregates of various sorts'. He proposed thinking of it as a 'framework for participation'. More recently, the term *assemblage* has been borrowed from philosophy (Deleuze and Guattari 1987) and ecology (Tsing 2015) to conceptualise the intricate relationships between components that come together in particular environments at particular times. The term avoids some of the over-determinacy of the culture concept while providing an alternative that includes non-human actors.

A strong anthropological focus on meaning and symbols is associated with the work of Clifford Geertz, who urged that anthropology's great task is generating *thick descriptions* of cultural practices and beliefs in order to interpret meanings (Geertz 1973). Focusing on meanings and values associated with drugs can help us understand attitudes towards and practices of drug production, trade and use. Catherine Allen, for example, examines the cultural meanings and social significance of coca for a community in the Andes. She found that the cultural practice of chewing coca leaves has vastly different meanings than the practice of consuming cocaine, the alkaloid derived from coca (Allen 1988). In another example, Bourgois' (1995) book brings out the meanings and values attached to the social world of cocaine (crack cocaine in particular) in Harlem, New York City, especially the key value of 'respect' among its traders. As we will discuss, Bourgois also puts the lives of these traders into a much broader political-economic context: understanding these meanings and values is crucial in understanding why people's lives come to be so entwined with such drugs.

Also, as well as considering cultures of consumption associated with drugs, a useful approach in our historical moment is to think about the cultures of prohibition that surround many such substances. Bryan Page and Merrill Singer have brought this out well in their book *The Social Value of Drug Addicts* (2014) that shows how popular culture and media portrayals of drug users as deviants acting outside the law generate many of the associations linking drug users with crime and anti-social behaviour, often forming crude stereotypes that can be harmful to people already suffering from addiction. Such meanings and associations of drugs can also be useful to a wide range of people with vested interests, for example, those profiting from the so-called prison-industrial complex of the US, where high rates of conviction for drugs help keep prisons full and profitable. Politicians often also leverage the meanings and associations of drugs and drug users for political gain, notably Rodrigo Duterte of the Philippines, whose brutal 'war on drugs' has been used to shore up his power (Holden 2021).

Power and Intersecting Inequalities

From the 1960s on, anthropologists integrated the theme of *power* into concepts of culture. That period was a time of great change for societies around the world – with independence for many former European colonies in Africa and elsewhere, as well as counter-cultural revolutions, and the growing strength of the feminist movement – and these changes had huge implications for anthropology as a discipline. Its origins as a professional discipline at the height of European colonialism led to much critique of this colonial legacy (Asad 1973) and has today led to a robust development of postcolonial anthropology, which studies the material, social, and cultural consequences of colonial rule and deconstructs Western and colonial ways of knowing (*epistemologies*) and being (*ontologies*). Feminist anthropologists pointed out the erasure of women's place in societies (Rosaldo and Lamphere 1974). The influence of Karl Marx's thinking also began to loom large in the discipline (having been relatively neglected previously in contrast to other big names in Western social thought such as Emile Durkheim and Max Weber). Structural Marxist and political-economic perspectives were concerned with uneasy and unequal relations of production and with the class stratification of societies. Analysis of power and wealth differentials became prominent in European and American anthropology (for an overview, see Ortner 1984).

Scholars explored how power works in contemporary societies. French philosopher Michel Foucault became highly influential in the discipline, proposing that power works less through overt coercion, and more through self-discipline as people absorb potent norms such as those emanating from Western medicine. He uses the term *biopower* to refer to the ways that forms of governance (including political and medical) regulate life and create subjectivities. An example related to drugs would be how the institutionalisation of resources and sanctions reinforces and creates cultural construction of drugs. For example, Bergschmidt (2004) argues that heroin users obtain subjective moral labels as criminals or as patients as heroin use is either punished through the institution of laws and the criminal system, or treated through medical facilities such as methadone clinics.

Critical Medical/Health Anthropology

With its focus on power, anthropology became ever more concerned with inequalities within and between societies. An approach known as Critical Medical Anthropology (CMA), or Critical Health Anthropology, has been developed to draw attention to how poverty and inequality impact people's health. This approach examines how meanings and lived experiences are shaped within political and economic systems. It pairs *emic* accounts with *etic* analyses of the conditions that constrain and frame decision-making. This approach is in line with public health approaches that seek to identify social determinants of health by understanding not only the ways individual behaviours influence health outcomes but also how behaviours are constrained within contexts that shape and limit choices. These include the political and economic structural conditions that shape the availability of and access to healthcare. American anthropologist and medical doctor Paul Farmer (2004) has used the term 'structural violence' to refer to the systemic lack of will to treat such preventable diseases as tuberculosis, HIV and diseases of malnourishment. In the context of drugs, structural violence has been noted in the ways social arrangements put people at risk of harmful effects of drug use, including not only vulnerability to adverse effects of taking drugs but also risks of incarceration and fines for possessing them created by cultures of prohibition through law enforcement (Tyndall and Dodd 2020). From a lived experience, Bourgois notes that people take drugs as they strive 'for utopian dreams and social solidarity, even as [illegal drugs] expose us to the brutal reality of the vicious depths of human greed and self-interested cynicism' (Bourgois 2018: 386).

To understand how poverty in particular leads to health inequities, we can identify several factors. For one, higher incomes increase access to all forms of healthcare and the likelihood of living in a safe, clean, drug-free environment, as well as having access to healthy food and social services. Also, higher levels of education facilitate access to health information. In addition, the poor are more likely to suffer from what Singer has called *syndemics*, or suffering from multiple co-present diseases, including HIV, tuberculosis, hypertension and obesity. Some of these are exacerbated or caused by drug use: intravenous drug use is associated with HIV/AIDS, which is associated with tuberculosis. Tobacco is one of the biggest global killers, as its use exacerbates diseases that are the leading causes of death in the world today, including lung and mouth cancer, and respiratory and vascular disease. The WHO reports that 'tobacco kills more than 8 million people each year. More than 7 million of those deaths are the result of direct tobacco use' (www.who.int/news-room/fact-sheets/detail/tobacco). Instead of blaming individual users, Singer points out connections between tobacco use and poverty. He writes that: 'rather than being separate and independent factors, poverty, poor neighbourhoods, prisons, disease, and drugs constitute an intertwined complex' (2008a: 23).

The CMA approach highlights that one of the reasons for drug-related problems is higher exposure and access to drugs. Studies have shown, for example, that tobacco and alcohol advertising has targeted low-income communities and communities of colour (Singer 2008b, Marshall 2013). Alcohol problems among Native American indigenous communities have been tied to Europeans colonists, who established a demand for highly potent distilled spirits by using them as a medium of exchange in trade, reminiscent of the demand the British created for opium to balance trade with China in the 1800s. Additionally, European colonists sought trade deals advantageous to themselves by plying the Native Americans with alcohol during trade negotiations. Before colonisation, most Native Americans only consumed weak fermented beverages, and almost exclusively in ceremonial contexts, and so did not have social and cultural controls in place to monitor drinking behaviours (Beauvais 1998). According to Beauvais, the colonists also provided a cultural model for drinking behaviour in their own extreme intoxication (1998: 253).

CMA certainly represents the critical focus on power that has come to dominate anthropology in recent years and shines much needed light on how problems connected to drugs relate to much wider structural issues that blight so many lives. However, it has been critiqued for being too focused on a macro-level of national and global political economy, and not giving enough attention to the micro-level contexts in which lives are led: we should not just focus on the macro-level structures, but also how people respond to them, sometimes with great difficulty, and often in creative ways. In this regard, it is important to remember the multiple social dynamics and identities that can make people more or less vulnerable. These of course include not only class dynamics but also ethnicity, gender and age. All these forms of social inequality intersect (see the concept of intersectionality coined by Crenshaw [1989]) as they are not isolated from each other, often multiplying vulnerabilities (or, looked at from the other side, multiplying privileges). In the study of drugs, gender and race in particular have come under the spotlight in this regard (McDonald 1994, Muehlmann 2018), generating much insight into how harms of drugs – and the often harmful effects of drug policy – intersect in damaging ways.

Focus on the Margins?

Focusing on the harms is part of what Sherry Ortner refers to as 'dark anthropology' (Ortner 2016), the tendency in recent decades for anthropologists to study hard lives lived at the margins of the global economy. Certainly, much anthropology of drugs in recent times is 'dark' in this way, and while analysing important issues, this can be critiqued for obscuring other important dynamics. While there are many horrors associated with drug addiction and the drugs trade (and levels of violence related to the drugs trade are very high in far too many places), there is much that is relatively unproblematic in drug production, trade and use, even in the case of illegal drugs. Indeed, the notion of 'drugs' brings to mind sensationalised images of harm and horror, and drugs come to seem extraordinary things, causing what some have called *problem inflation* (Hunt and Barker 2001: 169). While not downplaying problems, a focus on the *everyday* (the mundane or quotidian) can bring some balance here (Ghiabi 2022). Exploring everyday interactions people have with substances helps elucidate the varied roles and meanings drugs come to have in people's lives. It can reveal where this everyday use might be harmful through patterns of addiction and violence, or it may expose relatively innocuous patterns of use and trade that minimise risks and harms. Studying everyday use in specific contexts also brings important focus on micro-level patterns, albeit ones intertwined with wider structural contexts. Exploring the everyday has also long been a key strength of anthropology and its ethnographic methods.

Finally, in relation to questions of power and anthropological approaches, the discipline's usual focus on the marginalised in relation to drugs is problematic in that many important aspects of contemporary drug cultures and policies get missed out, especially as much consumption is at quite elite levels of society, while policy is usually formulated at elite levels too. In this regard, Laura Nader long ago encouraged anthropology to 'study up' (Nader 1972) and bring light to the social worlds of people who often are in positions of power.

Crops, Commodities and Illicit Flows: The Social Life of Drugs

Much recent work in the anthropology of drugs is concerned with *flows*: how drugs as commodities flow across space and time in networks of production, trade and consumption, reflecting starkly anthropology's move away from the kind of static, functionalist approaches of the past. It is not just drugs themselves that flow through these often-transnational networks, however, but also ideas and ways of thinking and treating drugs and drug users (see, e.g., Raikhel and Garriott 2013). Transnational flows involve the movement of people too: those transporting the drug across borders, consumers who travel with the goal of consumption, and even producers. An example of the latter is that knowledge of growing particular strains of cannabis was brought to Ethiopia from the Caribbean when Rastafarians were allowed to settle in Shashamane in the 1960s (Carrier 2021). These strains are now exported in large quantities in the wider East Africa region where they are much in demand. Anthropologists do not just work in particular places but also often conduct multi-sited fieldwork (see later) to track these flows.

The now classic volume *The Social Life of Things* (Appadurai 1986) spurred research on exchange, encouraging anthropologists and others to track the changing meanings and values, as well as the changing political economy of these goods, as they follow particular trajectories from production through exchange to consumption. This led to more research tracking goods as they criss-cross often very different contexts, including on a global scale, linking to another critical theme in late twentieth-century anthropology: globalisation.

Such a focus on exchange has guided much anthropological work on drugs. Within societies, drugs are things exchanged both as gifts – often in set patterns, as in practices of 'buying a round', or in offering beer or khat to elders in some East African societies – and drugs are some of the key commodities of our contemporary world. Indeed, historian David Courtwright (2001) argues that certain drugs have played a key role in the making of our modern world through their growth into dynamic commodities demand for which binds many parts of the world together in often uneasy relationships (see Chapter 3). Sidney Mintz – an anthropologist – also wrote an important study on sugar (itself sometimes seen as being drug-like and linked to addiction), which explored how it became an everyday commodity in Europe that linked consumers in that region to slave plantations in the Caribbean (Mintz 1986).

Tracking *illicit flows* that form what van Schendel and Abraham refer to as the 'dark side of globalisation' (2005) has also been a key approach in the social study of drugs like cocaine. This can reveal how laws and statutes surrounding drugs *underdetermine* how they are perceived and treated by people: while drug illegality can reinforce a sense of these substances as linked to immorality and wrongdoing, such laws can be contested where communities benefit from drugs socially, culturally or economically. In the terms of van Schendel and Abraham, such substances might be illegal according to the state, but they can still be *licit* for these communities. There is much ambiguity surrounding drugs and the law that anthropologists and others probe and explore (e.g. Carrier and Klantschnig 2018).

Of course, the trade of drugs has strong associations with violence in certain contexts, although these associations should not lead us to prejudge that violence always accompanies such trade. However, cases like that of Colombia in the 1980s and northern Mexico more recently highlight how violence in these contexts can be scarily *everyday* and all-too-ordinary. Anthropologists have done much to explore these contexts and can serve to dispel stereotypes of cartels and *capos* through close ethnographic work that can humanise people often demonised in popular culture and media (see, e.g., the work of Howard Campbell [2009] on cross-border trade between Mexico and the US).

Anthropologists have also paid much attention to drug production, much of which occurs in the Global South (see Chapter 7). This has driven anthropological interest in another theme, namely that of *development* and the role drugs play in promoting or hindering economic development. Merrill Singer has done much work in this regard (2008b), showing through the CMA framework how drugs and their cycles of production, trade and consumption bring the most harm to those already living in poverty. More recent work shows the ambiguities in links between drugs and development in contexts such as rural Africa, where cash crops like khat and cannabis have supported livelihoods for many decades now, although this kind of economic development would be seen as dubious by some being based on *drugs* – although development based on the coffee, tea or wine industry (legal drugs) would be seen as legitimate (Carrier and Klantschnig 2016). In this regard, drug production and trade can provide an interesting lens upon how development is perceived and the normative values that underpin it, so linking also to critical work in the anthropology of development by the likes of Arturo Escobar (1995). However, drugs do link to issues of sustainability and the environment in important ways: for example, khat and other crops have been associated with forest degradation in places like Madagascar (Gezon 2012).

Materiality, Pharmacology and Agency

Materiality also looms large as a theme in the study of drugs. By the *materiality* of drugs, we refer to their various 'thing-like' qualities as objects: their chemical properties, their physical forms (whether pills, leaves, liquids ...), their sensory qualities (smell, taste, texture ...) and also the *material culture* that surrounds them (all the objects associated with their use such as pipes, drinking vessels, artwork ...). Miller (2005) has written much on materiality in general and been an important figure in a so-called material turn within anthropology over recent decades, as the role of material objects in our lives has been greatly theorised. Some of this draws on the work of Karl Marx, who put much emphasis on the material bases of our lives and relations built around their production in his analysis.

Material culture was very much a key focus of nineteenth- and early twentieth-century anthropology, as anthropologists of that era reckoned that objects related to particular cultures could tell much about their pasts and how certain cultural forms *diffused* throughout particular areas (the so-called diffusionist school of anthropology). This focus on such objects and their collection led to the creation of ethnographic museums such as Oxford's Pitt Rivers Museum that were filled with examples of objects from all over the world and which often contain items related to drug consumption, for example paraphernalia related to betel consumption.

Contemporary work emphasises the agency of material objects themselves: that is to say, rather than objects being simply a passive presence in our social lives, they have active potency. The work of Alfred Gell on the agency of art objects (1998) is a recent classic of this approach, looking at how art objects become 'agents' that can set in train various social consequences. The late Bruno Latour is a hugely influential figure in this regard too, especially in connection with Actor Network Theory (ANT) that dissolved agency away from the human actor into the networks in which people's lives intertwine with multiple non-human things as well as other people: from this perspective, things can themselves be *actants* capable of generating change in these networks (Latour 2007). Given that drugs are often represented as extremely potent things – ones with even the capacity to enslave us as ideas of addiction can suggest – they seem to lend themselves well to an analysis that considers the impacts of animate and inanimate human agents, sometimes referred to as 'new materialism' (Fox et al. 2019).

Specifically, we can attest to the variable potency, and toxicity, of different kinds of substances (Nutt et al. 2010). One distinction between psychoactive substances is that some chemical compounds are found in nature, and others are synthetic – made in a laboratory, albeit based on compounds found in nature. Many of the everyday stimulants people take are naturally occurring in plants and may not even seem like drugs to people. These include coffee, tea and even chocolate and sugar. Nicotine is also a stimulant found in the tobacco leaf. Everyday naturally occurring stimulants popular in other parts of the world include khat (originally in East Africa and parts of the Middle East), betel nut (originally in Micronesia and Asia), kola nuts (originally from West Africa), coca leaves (originally in Andean South America), yerba mate (native to South America) and guarana seeds (Amazon basin in South America). Some stimulant plants are primarily consumed locally in the places where the plants are native. Others, like tobacco, coffee, tea and cacao (chocolate), have been central players in processes of globalisation since the 1500s, with demand for these products fuelling slavery and colonialism (see Chapter 3), which in turn have shaped our contemporary global economy where some nations and players have vastly more power and control than others.

The chemical compounds in these plant substances, which are unprocessed or minimally processed, have weaker effects than ones that are either processed natural substances (such as cocaine, heroin or tobacco in cigarettes) or made in a laboratory (such as methamphetamine, mephedrone or pharmaceuticals, including those for Attention Deficit Hyperactivity Disorder). Toxicologists identify strength of drugs by talking about 'toxicity', or how likely a substance is to harm someone. An important way of measuring this is through the effective dose to lethal dose ratio, which identifies the relationship between how much of a substance you need to feel an effect and how much of it will kill you. More toxic drugs are those with a thinner margin between effectiveness and lethalness – less room for error. Heroin (a processed, naturally occurring opiate), for example, is one of the most toxic drugs, where the lethal dose is just five times the effective dose, making it easy to overdose. Fentanyl, a synthetic opiate, is many times more potent than heroin. Note that the way people take a drug (called route of administration) affects its toxicity. Eating or drinking a substance is generally less toxic than snorting, smoking or injecting it, for example. Even alcohol has been found to be one of the more toxic drugs, with the lethal dose just ten times more than the effective dose – the same as methamphetamine. Compare that with cocaine (1:15) and caffeine (1:50).

Some of the least toxic substances are psilocybin (mushrooms) and LSD, where the lethal dose is about 1000 times the effective dose. For cannabis, there are debates about whether it is possible to overdose from ingesting it. Note that these assessments are about physiological harm and do not speak to potential mental health side effects. Some food substances such as chocolate and sugar do not even fall on the WHO list of psychoactive substances. The amount of caffeine in chocolate is minimal. While sugar is rarely thought of as having psychoactive properties, pharmacological studies show that it releases dopamine and opiates into the system (Avena et al. 2008) and there are debates about the extent to which it can have stimulant effects.

Often, synthetic compounds can be and often are made to be stronger, thereby having more intense effects and a higher effective to lethal dose ratio – or higher toxicity. Imperialism, colonialism and globalisation have been mechanisms for making more highly processed and toxic drugs, including high-proof alcohol and tobacco with additives, increasingly available. Bourgois (2018: 385) also pointed to the political and economic facet of toxicity, writing that 'ever since the rise of merchant capitalism and the expansion of European colonial conquest, the trafficking of industrially produced pleasurable substances has often wreaked havoc'.

In sum, toxicologists would argue that the drug substance, combined with the way someone takes it, makes some drugs more physically dangerous, or more toxic, than others. The effects of drugs are a nuanced combination of chemical compounds, cultural and individual expectations about effects, and contexts of use.

It is indeed the case that 'there is no pure (pharmaceutical) object that precedes its socialization and interpretation' (Hardon and Sanabria 2017: 118). We must examine substance use in historical, local, global and intersectional frameworks (see Andrew Russell's [2019] work on tobacco and its place as an actor in local and global contexts for a case in point). We must pay attention to class, ethnicity, gender and other factors that shape and differentiate drug experiences and effects. Nevertheless, there is no denying that chemicals have actions of their own.

Methods and Ethics

Ethnography

Perhaps the strongest anthropological approach of all lies in its ethnographic method. While anthropological theory is now – as Ortner described it in the 1980s – a 'thing of shreds and patches' (1984: 126), there is still much unity around the importance given to ethnography as a set of techniques for getting deep knowledge of people's lives and the influences upon them. And ethnography has brought much to the study of drugs – their production, trade, use and even policy – as Page and Singer demonstrate in their book on drug ethnography (2010). They also make a strong argument that the study of drugs has done much for the wider development and promotion of ethnographic methods, in particular helping develop techniques for accessing hard-to-reach populations using illicit drugs. Often, ethnographic and quantitative methods are used together, producing a rich and nuanced mixed methods approach.

While nineteenth-century anthropologists often relied on information of other societies gathered by the likes of missionaries and explorers – a practice that became pejoratively known as 'armchair anthropology' – the twentieth century saw anthropological research became almost synonymous with long-term fieldwork among communities different from the anthropologist's own. This fieldwork under the influence of the likes of Bronislaw Malinowski ideally involved learning the local language, living among the community for a sustained period and getting to know the people, their culture and social structure through participating in community life – the method of *participant observation*. Geertz famously described this immersive methodology as 'deep hanging out' (1998) resulting in 'thick description' (Geertz 1973). This captures much of the experience of ethnography, which can indeed involve much sitting around and waiting for things to happen, as well as witnessing social action and conducting interviews and surveys. While, in this way, ethnography can be an open-ended method where much of the material collected can relate more to serendipity (e.g. random encounters with people that lead the research in interesting directions), the ethnographic method as drawn up by Malinowski and others involved much rigour too. The anthropologist was to constantly write up detailed fieldnotes, draw detailed diagrams relating to kin relations, write out glossaries of key local terms and so forth – the material that would then be written up later on in the ethnographic monograph, the book about a community that ideally resulted from this fieldwork.

Regarding drugs, the application of ethnographic methods had the great benefit of bringing out the actual lived realities of drug users – and more recently traders and producers – and foregrounding their voices, rather than allowing stereotypes to define them. This is critical where drug users are often stigmatised. As discussed in Chapter 1, twentieth-century drug ethnography developed through research by social scientists (many sociologists) in urban centres in the US, although anthropologists became involved too, such as Preble and Casey whose participant observation, life histories and interviews with heroin users in New York refuted stereotypes of heroin addicts as people trying to escape from real life: their lives are actually very busy as they try to secure their hit of heroin and avoid withdrawal (1969). They specifically evoked Malinowski in describing their methods of observing 'interpersonal events' among communities of users (ibid. 3).

Conducting research among drug producers, traders and consumers – especially where the substances are illegal or stigmatised and where they are being used by marginalised and hard-to-find populations – is clearly not straightforward, and there are risks both for the research participants and the researcher. In this regard, ethnography through its emphasis on getting to know a community over time can come into its own, as this time spent with a community can help build up rapport and trust between researcher and participants (Page and Singer 2010: 17–18), and through time, a wider network of participants can be established as the place of the ethnographer in the community becomes more familiar and accepted. The studies of Bourgois (1995) with drug traders in New York and Angela Garcia (2008) on heroin addiction in New Mexico that we will come back to in the book make clear how building up trust requires great care and sensitivity, and also how such research among people living extraordinarily hard lives can take its toll on the researcher too. Yet in contexts all over the world, sensitive ethnography has revealed much about the lives of people involved with drugs, and this book will include examples of such work throughout.

Much has of course changed in ethnographic research over the century or so in which its methods have been honed, although long-term engagement with research participants has remained key. One key change links to increasing anthropological focus from the 1990s onwards with themes of globalisation, transnational processes and migration (see earlier). While research in one particular place can reveal much about these processes (e.g. Carrier 2016), anthropologists have developed multi-sited research methods to deepen understanding (Marcus 1995): for example, Peggy Levitt conducted research in both the Dominican Republic and in Boston to understand how some people from the Dominican Republic live their lives transnationally, constantly crossing a recrossing international borders (Levitt 2001). Such multi-sited research features in recent work on the transnational flows of drugs, including khat (Carrier 2007, Anderson et al. 2007) where researchers have studied both in East Africa and the Horn of Africa, and in khat-using diaspora communities in the Global North.

Anthropologists have also explored their own positionality in regard to drugs, linking to contemporary issues in the field of auto-ethnography, a technique that can bring powerful insight through exploring how the researcher's own life links to the topic at hand (Reed-Danahay 2017). This links to an important question of the researcher's own drug use: how *sober* is ethnographic research? Given stigma surrounding drug use, use by anthropologists of intoxicants and stimulants might well get suppressed in how research is written up, even when those substances are legal such as alcohol, or khat in East Africa. Interesting work by Johannes Fabian (2000) looked at how various altered states mediated relations between nineteenth-century European explorers and Central African communities: these were not 'sober' Europeans who might represent the height of rationality. An interesting recent ethnography by Jason Pine (2019) focuses on methamphetamine production and use in the US, and he weaves his own use of an amphetamine – albeit a legal, prescribed one: Adderall – into the narrative, raising interesting questions about whether from some perspectives use of legal amphetamines is all that different from use of illegal ones.

There are many other methodological approaches being used in anthropology today, approaches that often respond to changes in the wider world. These include the increasing importance of digital technology in our lives, and research into online lives is now well advanced within the discipline (for a classic ethnography of an online world, see Boellstorff 2015). An example from the study of drugs is Hupli et al.'s (2019) 'netnographic' study of psychedelic microdosing by analysing YouTube videos. Other approaches include an expansion of visual methods, including integrating photography into research, something already pursued by Bourgois and Schonberg in their work on homeless drug users in San Francisco (2009). In short, while much of the impetus of ethnographic research remains the same – generating thick descriptions through immersive methodologies – there are ever more sophisticated techniques being developed, techniques that could well be applied to the study of drugs.

Ethical Considerations

The American Anthropological Association's Principles of Professional Responsibility guide anthropological studies of drugs.[2] These include the primary principle of doing no harm and also highlight the need to be open and honest with interlocutors about work and the need to obtain informed consent using necessary permissions. To receive funding and publish their research, scholars must have their protocols reviewed by institutional boards to ensure that best practices are in place to protect people from harm. It is especially challenging to adhere to the policy of doing no harm in the study of illegal drugs, particularly among marginalised populations. As Page and Singer (2010) emphasise, drug users tend to be an especially vulnerable, often with mental health burdens, a history of involvement with the criminal justice system, and poverty. Another challenge comes from the personal relationships that ethnographers develop with their interlocutors, leading to the blurring of professional boundaries that make both researcher and researched vulnerable. Intimacies in the field can also lead to feelings of betrayal when study participants read research findings that they find objectionable (Benson 2018).

Postcolonial Perspectives

Ethnography – like anthropology more generally – is faced with additional critical challenges regarding the ethics of its practice. This links heavily to the changing context in which anthropologists work, especially in classic regions of anthropological research such as in Africa and among indigenous populations around the world where anthropologists had much access in the colonial era. Scholars like Talal Asad (1973) and Michael Taussig (1987) challenged anthropology to consider the role of anthropologists in upholding colonialist and imperialist agendas both through direct action (working for colonial governments to further colonialist agendas) or indirectly through theories and perspectives that speak *for* colonised peoples, establishing dominant narratives that have the potential to disempower and further subjugate (Chakrabarty 1992, Coronil 1996).

Parallel with postcolonial critiques have been critiques of the overall epistemological and ethical bases of the ethnographic method often associated with postmodernism. The 1980s were a watershed decade for ethnography, as important texts such as *Writing Culture* (Clifford and Marcus 1986) drew close attention to how ethnography was written in such a way as to reinforce the perceived ability of the ethnographer to speak authoritatively of a people and showed instead how ethnographic truths – based as they are on limited engagement in terms of sample sizes and on fieldwork conducted at a particular moment of time – are inevitably *partial*, so pulling apart claims of anthropologists to be able to speak for particular groups of people.

The colonial past of the discipline still looms large, even as the colonial period recedes into the past. While anthropologists now work in all regions of the world, and while anthropologists hail from every part of the world and there are growing numbers of anthropology departments and anthropologists in the Global South, the discipline is still dominated by Euro-American scholars conducting research in poorer parts of the world. Scholars in places like Africa are often structurally disadvantaged in global academia through lack of access to journals, and less time to publish, so scholars from the Global North remain dominant (Mama 2007). Related to this, the movement to decolonise curricula and to include scholars of varied backgrounds is gaining increasing strength in universities across the world.

Decolonising movements often focus on curricula, and the anthropological canon as conventionally taught is distinctly white (Harrison 1991), and so is much of the anthropology of drugs. There certainly is a need for more diverse voices in the anthropology of drugs.

Methodologies also need decolonising to include and recognise the voices of collaborators in the process of creating knowledge. As Linda Tuhiwai Smith wrote some time ago (1999), the 'pursuit of knowledge is deeply embedded in the multiple layers of imperial and colonial practices' (1999: 2), and to counter this, it is beneficial when research participants – especially those from indigenous communities – take more of a lead. More collaborative approaches are being developed where research is done in partnership, not only with academics from the countries in which anthropologists are working but also with the research participants themselves. Beyond this, anthropology – especially in collaboration with communities among whom it works – can play a critical role in reimagining our world and pushing towards more hopeful futures, as Anand Pandian (2019) has powerfully argued.

Many ethnographers and anthropologists of drugs have worked hard to apply their work in the real world – to have *impact* in the jargon of British academia – and as we will discuss in Chapter 8, they have contributed much to harm reduction initiatives in particular. But there is much more that anthropology can do in this regard, and by embracing decolonial initiatives, and through collaborative projects built on mutual respect and care with communities involved with drugs, we are confident that more hopeful and more just futures can be imagined, a first step in a longer process of bringing these futures into reality.

We will return to these themes and approaches throughout the book, as they frame many aspects of the anthropological discussion of drugs.

Notes

1 This revised statement is available online: www.americananthro.org/Partici pateAndAdvocate/AdvocacyDetail.aspx?ItemNumber=25769#:~:text=Backgro und%3A%20Human%20Rights%20and%20the%20AAA&text=The%20fi rst%20statement%20was%20written,Rights%2C%20chaired%20by%20Elea nor%20Roosevelt (accessed November 2022).
2 Available online on the American Anthropological Association's website: https://eth ics.americananthro.org/category/statement/ (accessed November 2022).

Works Cited

Allen, Catherine J. 1988. *The Hold Life Has: Coca and Cultural Identity in an Andean Community*. Washington, DC: Smithsonian Institution Press.
Anderson, David M., Susan Beckerleg, Degol Hailu, and Axel Klein. 2007. *The Khat Controversy: Stimulating the Drugs Debate*. Oxford: Routledge.
Appadurai, Arjun. 1986. *The Social Life of Things: Commodities in Cultural Perspective*. New York, NY: Cambridge University Press.

Asad, Talal. 1973. *Anthropology and the Colonial Encounter*. Ithaca, NY: Ithaca Press.

Avena, Nicole M., Pedro Rada, and Bartley G. Hoebel. 2008. "Evidence for Sugar Addiction: Behavioral and Neurochemical Effects of Intermittent, Excessive Sugar Intake." *Neuroscience and Biobehavioral Reviews* 32 (1): 20–39.

Beauvais, Fred. 1998. "American Indians and Alcohol." *Alcohol Health & Research World* 22 (4): 253.

Benedict, Ruth. 1934. *Patterns of Culture*. Boston, MA: Houghton Mifflin Company.

Benson, Peter. 2018. "Tobacco Capitalism, an Afterword: Open Letters and Open Wounds in Anthropology." *Journal for the Anthropology of North America* 21 (1): 21–34.

Bergschmidt, Viktoria B. 2004. "Pleasure, Power and Dangerous Substances: Applying Foucault to the Study of 'Heroin Dependence' in Germany." *Anthropology & Medicine* 11 (1): 59–73.

Boellstorff, Tom. 2015. *Coming of Age in Second Life: An Anthropologist Explores the Virtually Human*. Princeton, NJ: Princeton University Press.

Bourgois, Philippe I. 1995. *In Search of Respect: Selling Crack in El Barrio*. Cambridge: Cambridge University Press.

———. 2018. "Decolonising Drug Studies in an Era of Predatory Accumulation." *Third World Quarterly* 39 (2): 385–398.

Bourgois, Philippe, and Jeffrey Schonberg. 2009. *Righteous Dopefiend*. Berkeley, CA: University of California Press.

Brown, Michael. 2008. "Cultural Relativism 2.0." *Current Anthropology* 49 (3): 363–383.

Bunzel, Ruth. 1940. "The Role of Alcoholism in Two Central American Cultures." *Psychiatry* 3 (3): 361–387.

Campbell, Howard. 2009. *Drug War Zone: Frontline Dispatches From the Streets of El Paso and Juárez*. Austin: University of Texas Press.

Carrier, Neil. 2005. "Under Any Other Name: The Trade and Use of Khat in the UK." *Drugs and Alcohol Today* 5 (3): 14–16.

———. 2007. *Kenyan Khat: The Social Life of a Stimulant*. Leiden: Brill.

———. 2021. "Sub-Saharan Africa, Cannabis and Contemporary Drug Policy." In *Cannabis: Global Histories*. Cambridge, MA: The MIT Press.

Carrier, Neil, and Gernot Klantschnig. 2016. "Illicit Livelihoods: Drug Crops and Development in Africa." *Review of African Political Economy* 43 (148): 174–189.

———. 2018. "Quasilegality: Khat, Cannabis and Africa's Drug Laws." *Third World Quarterly* 39 (2): 350–365.

Chakrabarty, Dipesh. 1992. "Postcoloniality and the Artifice of History: Who Speaks for 'Indian' Pasts?" *Representations* 37: 1–26.

Clifford, James and George E. Marcus, eds. 1986. *Writing Culture: The Poetics and Politics of Ethnography*. Berkeley, CA: University of California Press.

Commager, Steele. 1957. "The Function of Wine in Horace's Odes." *Transactions and Proceedings of the American Philological Association* 88: 68–80.

Coronil, Fernando. 1996. "Beyond Occidentalism: Toward Nonimperial Geohistorical Categories." *Cultural Anthropology* 11 (1): 51–87.

Courtwright, David T. 2001. *Forces of Habit: Drugs and the Making of the Modern World*. Boston, MA: Harvard University Press.

Crenshaw, Kimberlé. 1989. "Demarginalizing the Intersection of Race and Sex: A Black Feminist Critique of Antidiscrimination Doctrine, Feminist Theory and Antiracist Politics." *University of Chicago Legal Forum* 1989 (1): 139–167, Article 8.

Deleuze, Gilles, and Felix Guattari. 1987. *A Thousand Plateaus: Capitalism and Schizophrenia.* Minneapolis, MN: University of Minnesota Press.

Douglas, Mary. 1987. *Constructive Drinking Perspectives on Drink from Anthropology.* London: Routledge.

Duranti, Alessandro. 1997. *Linguistic Anthropology.* Cambridge: Cambridge University Press.

Escobar, Arturo. 1995. *Encountering Development: The Making and Unmaking of the Third World.* Princeton, NJ: Princeton University Press.

Fabian, Johannes. 2000. *Out of Our Minds: Reason and Madness in the Exploration of Central Africa.* Berkeley, CA: University of California Press.

Farmer, Paul. 2004. *Pathologies of Power: Health, Human Rights, and the New War on the Poor.* Berkeley, CA: University of California Press.

Fortes, Meyers. 1949. *Social Structure: Studies Presented to A.R. Radcliffe-Brown.* Oxford: Clarendon Press.

Fox, Nick J., and Pam Alldred. 2019. "New Materialism." In *SAGE Research Methods Foundations*, edited by P.A. Atkinson, S. Delamont, A. Cernat, J.W. Sakshaug, and M. Williams. London: Sage.

Garcia, Angela. 2008. "The Elegiac Addict: History, Chronicity, and the Melancholic Subject." *Cultural Anthropology* 24 (4): 718–746.

Geertz, Clifford. 1973. *Thick Description: Toward an Interpretive Theory of Culture.* New York, NY: Basic Books.

———. 1984. "Distinguished Lecture: Anti Anti-Relativism." *American Anthropologist* 86 (2): 263–278.

———. 1998. "Deep Hanging Out." *The New York Review.* 22 October 1998.

Gell, Alfred. 1998. *Art and Agency: An Anthropological Theory.* Oxford: Oxford University Press.

Gezon, Lisa L. 2012. "Drug Crops and Food Security: The Effects of Khat on Lives and Livelihoods in Northern Madagascar." *Culture, Agriculture, Food and Environment* 34 (2): 124–135.

Ghiabi, Maziyar. 2022. "The Everyday Lives of Drugs." *Third World Quarterly* 43 (11): 2545–2556.

Hardon, Anita, and Emilia Sanabria. 2017. "Fluid Drugs: Revisiting the Anthropology of Pharmaceuticals." *Annual Review of Anthropology* 46 (1): 117–132.

Harrison, Faye V (ed.). 1991. *Decolonizing Anthropology: Moving Further toward an Anthropology for Liberation.* Washington DC: American Anthropological Association.

Holden, William. 2021. *President Rodrigo Duterte and the War on Drugs: Fear and Loathing in the Philippines.* Lanham, MD: Lexington Books.

Horton, Donald. 1943. "The Functions of Alcohol in Primitive Societies: A Cross-Cultural Study." *Quarterly Journal of Studies on Alcohol* 4 (2): 199–320.

Hunt, Geoffrey, and Judith Barker. 2001. "Socio-cultural Anthropology and Alcohol and Drug Research: Towards a Unified Theory." *Social Science and Medicine* 53: 165–188.

Hupli, Aleksi, Moritz Berning, Ahnjili Zhuparris, and James Fadiman. 2019. "Descriptive Assemblage of Psychedelic Microdosing: Netnographic Study of

Youtube™ Videos and On-going Research Projects." *Performance Enhancement & Health* 6 (3–4): 129–138.

Latour, Bruno. 2007. *Reassembling the Social: An Introduction to Actor-Network-Theory*. Oxford: Oxford University Press.

Levitt, Peggy. 2001. *The Transnational Villagers*. Boston, MA: Boston University.

Mama, Amina. 2007. "Is It Ethical to Study Africa? Preliminary Thoughts on Scholarship and Freedom." *African Studies Review* 50 (1): 1–26.

Marcus, George E. 1995. "Ethnography in/of the World System: The Emergence of Multi-Sited Ethnography." *Annual Review of Anthropology* 24: 95–117.

Marshall, Mac. 2013. *Drinking Smoke: The Tobacco Syndemic in Oceania*. Honolulu: University of Hawai'i Press.

McDonald, Maryon (ed.). 1994. *Gender, Drink and Drugs*. London: Routledge.

Mead, Margaret. 1928. *Coming of Age in* Samoa. New York, NY: William Morrow and Company.

Miller, Daniel. 2005. "Materiality: An Introduction." In *Materiality*, edited by Daniel Miller, 1–50. Durham, NC: Duke University Press.

Mintz, Sidney. 1986. *Sweetness and Power: The Place of Sugar in Modern History*. New York, NY: Viking.

Muehlmann, Shaylih. 2018. "The Gender of the War on Drugs." *Annual Review of Anthropology* 47: 315–330.

Nader, Laura. 1972. *Up the Anthropologist: Perspectives Gaines from Studying Up*. Washington, DC: ERIC Clearinghouse.

Nutt, David J., Leslie A. King, and Lawrence D. Phillips. 2010. "Drug Harms in the UK: A Multicriteria Decision Analysis." *The Lancet* 376 (9752): 1558–1565.

Ortner, Sherry B. 1984. "Theory in Anthropology since the Sixties." *Comparative Studies in Society and History* 26 (1): 126–166.

———. 2016. "Dark Anthropology and its Others: Theory since the Eighties." *HAU: Journal of Ethnographic Theory* 6 (1): 47–73.

Page, J. Bryan, and Merrill Singer. 2010. *Comprehending Drug Use: Ethnographic Research at the Social Margins*. New Brunswick, NJ: Rutgers University Press.

Pandian, Anand. 2019. *A Possible Anthropology: Methods for Uneasy Times*. Durham, NC: Duke University Press.

Pine, Jason. 2019. *The Alchemy of Meth: A Decomposition*. Ann Arbor, MI: University of Michigan Press.

Preble, Edward, and John J. Casey. 1969. "Taking Care of Business – The Heroin User's Life on the Street." *International Journal of the Addictions* 4: 1–24.

Radcliffe-Brown, Alfred R. 1924. "The Mother's Brother in South Africa." In *Structure and Function in Primitive Society*, 15–31. London: Routledge & Kegan Paul.

———. 1952. *Structure and Function in Primitive Societies: Essays and Addresses*. London: Cohen and West.

Raikhel, Eugene, and William Garriott. 2013. *Addiction Trajectories*. Durham, NC: Duke University Press.

Reed-Danahay, Deborah. 2017. "Bourdieu and Critical Autoethnography: Implications for Research, Writing, and Teaching." *International Journal of Multicultural Education* 19 (1): 144–154.

Room, Robin. 1984. "Alcohol and Ethnography: A Case of Problem Deflation?" *Current Anthropology* 25 (2): 169–191.

Rosaldo, Michelle Z. and Louise Lamphere (eds.). 1974. *Woman, Culture, and Society*. Redwood City, CA: Stanford University Press.

Russell, Andrew. 2019. *Anthropology of Tobacco: Ethnographic Adventures in Non-Human Worlds*. London: Routledge.

Shipton, Parker MacDonald. 1989. *Bitter Money: Cultural Economy and Some African Meanings of Forbidden Commodities*. Washington DC: American Anthropological Association.

Singer, Merrill. 2008a. *Drugging the Poor: Legal and Illegal Drugs and Social Inequality*. Long Grove, IL: Waveland Press, Inc.

———. 2008b. *Drugs and Development: The Global Impact on Sustainable Growth and Human Rights*. Long Grove, IL: Waveland Press.

Singer, Merrill, and J. Bryan Page. 2014. *The Social Value of Drug Addicts: Uses of the Useless*. London: Routledge.

Smith, Linda Tuhiwai. 1999. *Decolonizing Methodologies*. London, England: Zed Books.

Taussig, Michael T. 1987. *Shamanism, Colonialism, and the Wild Man: A Study in Terror and Healing*. Chicago, IL: University of Chicago Press.

Tsing, Anna L. 2015. *The Mushroom at the End of the World: On the Possibility of Life in Capitalist Ruins*. Princeton, NJ: Princeton University Press.

Tyndall, Mark, and Zoe Dodd. 2020. "How Structural Violence, Prohibition, and Stigma Have Paralyzed North American Responses to Opioid Overdose." *AMA Journal of Ethics* 22 (1): 723–728.

van Schendel, Willem, and Itty Abraham. 2005. *Illicit Flows and Criminal Things: States, Borders, and the Other Side of Globalization*. Bloomington, IN: Indiana University Press.

Willis, Justin. 2002. *Potent Brews: A Social History of Alcohol in East Africa, 1850–1999*. Athens, OH: Ohio University Press.

Wilson, Monica. 1951. *Good Company: A Study of Nyakyusa Age-Villages*. London: Oxford University Press.

3 Drugs in Archaeological and Historical Perspective

Drugs permeate much of our contemporary society and culture, making them rich subjects for ethnographic research and anthropological theorisation. They also have rich histories and pre-histories in the human past, and these are the focus of this chapter. We take a tour of key research in archaeological and historical studies of drugs, as well as some evolutionary conjectures. Such research reveals that our relationship with psychoactive substances is millennia-old, and that this relationship could at times be extremely consequential for human society: indeed, drugs are implicated by some researchers in major transitions such as the shift in the Neolithic to sedentary settlement and agriculture, and to the expansion of global trade in the early modern period.

However, while evidence does point to the importance of these substances in our past, there are dangers of exaggerating their significance, and we will argue that much evidence needs to be treated with caution. There is also a danger of what is termed *presentism*: interpreting the past through our contemporary eyes. This is very much an issue in interpreting drug use: given how powerfully controversial and sensationalised these substances are today, it is hard to look back at past cultures of drug consumption and not see them through our present concerns. As we argue in the book, drugs are ascribed much potency in contemporary discourse, and this might well lead us to see their role in the past as equally potent. This is not to deny their significance in certain cases, but to argue that we need to be cautious in assessing this significance, and not assume that drugs everywhere and throughout time have always been key drivers of history.

Drugs and Human Transformation

There is little doubt that various species of plants with potential for psychoactive use have been found in close proximity to humanity for millennia. It is very likely that many of these species were made use of by our ancestors, although to what extent and why will remain hazy, especially the further back in time we go. This has led to speculation about when humans began

DOI: 10.4324/9781003109549-3

using them, and some speculation ascribes to them a transformational role in our evolutionary past. However, it is also possible that there was never a start point of human use of these substances, as usage might stretch back to before *Homo sapiens* evolved as a species. Given that use of intoxicants and stimulants is not just a human pastime, it is also very possible that earlier hominid species used such substances too. Indeed, other animals frequently experience intoxication – think of how cats are drawn to catnip, or how a range of animals from insects to large mammals such as elephants regularly get drunk (although some research questions this in relation to elephants [Morris et al. 2006]).

There is a broad popular fascination with the idea that hallucinogens in particular (the subject of Chapter 4) have been critical in human evolution and in the evolution of spirituality and organised religion. A preeminent scholar of religion, Huston Smith (1919–2016), affirmed the idea of the possible role of psychedelics in bringing about ideas of the afterlife and the origin of religions in a footnote in his review of R. Gordon Wasson's book, *Soma, Divine Mushroom of Immortality* (Wasson 1968). Wasson was an amateur ethnomycologist and professional banker who was obsessed with hallucinogenic mushrooms. Smith supports this idea by quoting the poet Mary Barnard, who conjectures that an idea of the afterlife was likely to have been induced by 'the accidental discovery of hallucinogenic plants that give a sense of euphoria, dislocate the center of consciousness, and distort time and space … causing [people] to think of things they had never thought of before' (Smith 1972: 481). He adds to that a similar conjecture by Wasson, wherein the discovery of hallucinogenic experiences was 'a veritable detonator to his soul, arousing in him sentiments of awe and reverence' (Mary Bernard, quoted in Smith 1972: 481). He further mentions that some Algonquin indigenous people from Quebec believe that they eat mushrooms in heaven.

On a related note, the ethnobotanist Terence McKenna is known for is his *Stoned Ape* theory, presented in *Food of the Gods* (1992). He proposed that the use of psilocybin mushrooms was evolutionarily adaptive and helped propel early human ancestors to develop full human consciousness. He argued that at first, low doses of psilocybin increased hunting abilities by strengthening visual recognition. Later, the mushrooms were at the forefront of spirituality and community bonding. He argued that psilocybin mushrooms influenced the development of complex religious ritual after the domestication of cattle (since mushrooms are found in cattle dung). While an engaging idea, other researchers have pointed out that attributing human consciousness to a single factor is unrealistic, and ultimately impossible to prove (Tattersall 2004, Graziano 2018). Nevertheless, the suggestion that drug-induced altered states of consciousness played an adaptive role in human evolution has drawn attention.

Another theory is that of the 'drunken monkey' (Dudley 2014). Dudley points to a plethora of anecdotal and entertaining stories of animals inebriated from consuming the ethanol/alcohol of fermented fruit. Experimental studies of fruit flies and humans suggest positive effects of consuming low levels of alcohol. The 'drunken monkey' hypothesis proposes that 'alcohol can be used by fruit-eating animals as a reliable long-distance indicator of the presence of sugars' (Dudley 2014: 6). The evolutionary value of the alcohol, then, would not be in causing an altered state of consciousness but rather in indicating the presence of ripe fruit.

Drugs in Deep Time

These ideas about the impact of drugs on our evolutionary past rely much on speculation. However, archaeological research has provided us with firmer evidence for an association of people and drugs millennia ago, and Elisa Guerra-Doce has written good overviews of this research (2015, 2022) for Eurasia, while Schwartzkopf (2022) has written on the evidence for the Americas, and Scott Fitzpatrick's volume *Ancient Psychoactive Substances* offers interesting case studies from both regions (2018). Archaeology is of course closely related as a discipline to anthropology, and in the North American tradition, it is one of the four fields that constitute anthropology (alongside cultural anthropology, linguistic anthropology and biological anthropology). There is also close dialogue between socio-cultural anthropologists and archaeologists in relation to theory: while usually working with different methods and types of evidence, how the evidence is interpreted often draws on the same theoretical currents. For an overview of the relationship between archaeology and anthropology, Chris Gosden's book on this theme is worth reading (Gosden 1999).

Archaeological evidence relating to drugs comes in a number of forms. Firstly, plant drugs can leave their mark in archaeological sites, as traces of pollen and seeds can occasionally be well-preserved, sometimes in fossilised forms. Secondly, material culture of the past – for example pottery sherds, amphoras and pipes – can form evidence of usage of such substances, either through inference of what they contained or through scientific residue analysis for molecular traces. Finally, iconography can give clues to earlier drug use, as the shape of material objects, or early forms of art often appear to depict drugs or drug experiences. There are other methods used to piece together the earlier cultural worlds of drugs, however, including linguistic analysis – for example, Du Toit tracks the spread of cannabis in Africa through analysis of terms used for the substance (Du Toit 1980) – as well as molecular and genetic analysis (in relation to cannabis, see McPartland et al. 2019 on using archaeobotany and molecular archaeology to explore early origins of cannabis cultivation in Asia).

In terms of botanical traces, the oldest potential evidence for the use of psychoactive plants comes from a Neanderthal burial site in northern Iraq (Shanidar Cave), which contained pollen of *Ephedra altissima* alongside several other plant species. *Ephedra altissima* is part of the Ephedra family of shrubs that have stimulant properties through their alkaloids ephedrine and pseudoephedrine. This pollen has been dated to 50,000 years ago (Merlin 2003: 300). It is supposed that the Neanderthal person was buried 'on a bed of woody branches and flowers sometime between May and July' (ibid.), and some argue that the presence of the psychoactive *Ephedra* plant in the burial assemblage suggests that it may have had some cultural importance, perhaps even as 'an entheogen for ritualistic, spiritual purposes, and/or medicinal' (ibid.). However, there are other potential explanations for its presence, including that it contaminated the site through the activity of burrowing rodents. Ephedra species have been found in much later sites associated with *Homo sapiens*, and they have long been documented as medicines in East Asia in particular. Therefore, the Neanderthal burial site may indeed have had some deeper significance, although this is lost to the mists of time.

Other wild plants found in the archaeological record include *Hyoscyamus niger* – black henbane – a member of the nightshade family with known intoxicating effects that has been associated with European witchcraft (Guerra-Doce 2022: 39). Seeds of this plant have been found in Neolithic sites from around 8,000 years ago, including on pots from a Scottish burial site of the Late Neolithic. Charred seed pods of another psychoactive night-shade family plant – *Datura stramonium* – thornapple – have also been found in Spanish sites from around 4,000 years ago. Plant remains such as seeds of *Papaver somniferum* – the poppy species native to the eastern Mediterranean from which opium is derived – are found in European sites from the early Neolithic period around 8,000 years ago, and opium seems to have quickly become an important cultivated plant throughout Europe, including in Neolithic Britain, seeds being found in a Northamptonshire site dated to 6,000 years ago (ibid. 42). Botanical remains of cannabis have also been found in many sites from Eurasia, and it is suggested that the plant was first domesticated in the steppe regions of Central Asia, before spreading east- and westwards (ibid. 44); there are also finds of seeds associated with pottery from Japan around 10,000 years ago (Ren et al. 2021), as well as numerous other more recent sites including seeds found in tombs in Ukraine and Russia from around 4,000 years ago (Guerra-Doce 2022: 44). Cannabis pollen has also been found in Madagascar dating from around 2,000 years ago, suggesting that early settlers of the island may have brought the plant and potentially its use with them (Duvall 2019).

In the Americas, there are some archaeobotanical remains of various drug plants, including the hallucinogenic cacti San Pedro and peyote. In the case of the former, there are some fossilised traces in occupied cave sites in Peru from around 8,000 years ago (Guerra-Doce 2015: 98), and of the latter, there are traces of 5,000-year-old peyote in cave sites in Texas (Rafferty 2018). Also in Peru, ancient coca leaves and calcite (a mineral commonly used in combination with coca leaves as it activates the cocaine alkaloids) were found in remains of houses from around 8,000 years ago (Guerra-Doce 2015 99). Archaeobotanical traces of tobacco have also been found from around

2500–1800 BC in Peru, and tobacco seeds have been found in the American Southwest dated to around 1000 BC (Rafferty 2018).

Material culture remains that suggest associations with early drug production and use have also been found widely. This is especially the case with alcoholic beverages, and several sites in different parts of the world show evidence of alcohol production, including sites of the Natufian culture of the Levant region from around 15,000 to 11,000 years ago (Hayden et al. 2013), a culture area where agriculture is reckoned to have developed, including the domestication of grains. Indeed, some evidence of fermentation from stone mortars in Israel from around 13,000 years ago forms the earliest possible evidence for brewing (Liu et al. 2018). The site of Jerf el Ahmer in Syria – dated to around 9500 BC – has stone equipment that some suggest was used in grain processing for brewing, while a fully fledged winery with wine press, fermentation vats and other equipment was found at the Areni-1 cave complex in Armenia and dated to around 6,000 years ago (Barnard et al. 2011). Chemical analysis of this latter material culture has detected traces of red wine. Chemical analysis has also suggested that fermented brews might have not just relied on alcohol for their psychoactive properties. In analysis of a drinking vessel found at a burial site in Spain of the Bell Beaker culture dated to around 5,000 years ago revealed traces of hyoscyamine, an active compound of the likes of henbane and Datura species, alongside traces of barley beer (Guerra-Doce 2015: 100). Just as drugs like Ayahuasca are mixtures of different ingredients whose compounds act synergistically, so some ancient drugs are likely to have been similarly composed of different ingredients. More recently, archaeological finds of pipes can give important clues for the earlier use of substances such as tobacco and cannabis. In the case of cannabis in Africa, some of the earliest evidence for its use comes from molecular analysis of ceramic pipe bowls found in Ethiopia and dated to around 1320 AD (Van der Merwe 1975). Pipes are commonly found items of more recent material culture in Europe too, and pipes from three centuries ago or so commonly appear at low tide in mud on the River Thames. They were recently found by colleagues of one of the authors (Carrier) at an archaeological dig at Royal Fort gardens at the University of Bristol. Archaeological finds of Neolithic Chinese pottery are decorated with patterns likely based on hemp textiles that are suggestive of the ancient importance of cannabis products for ancient Chinese cultures (Li 1974).

Human remains have also provided evidence of early drug use. This includes teeth stained red by betel-nut chewing (betel nut is known for turning saliva red) found in the Philippines and dated to around 2680 BC (Guerra-Doce 2015: 98). Mummified bodies from South America have also revealed the antiquity of coca chewing as a practice, including from mummies found in Chile and dated to around 3,000 years ago (Rivera et al. 2005), while mummies from Peru dating to 2,000 years ago were discovered with small bags of coca (Stolberg 2011: 128). Also, traces of the fungus ergot – which contains LSD compounds – were found in the stomach of the preserved body of a man found in Denmark (Guerra-Doce 2022: 39). Furthermore, two male adult skeletons found in Spain and dated to around 6,000 years ago revealed traces of opiates, likely ingested for pain relief given there was evidence they underwent surgical procedures (ibid. 43).

Material objects have also given clues to earlier use and exchange of drugs through iconography (the representation of drugs or drug experiences through how objects are shaped), or through pictorial art. Some intriguing speculation suggests that cave art from Europe and Africa represents visual phenomena seen during altered states of consciousness, possibly caused by ingestion of drugs. This idea owes much to the work of archaeologist David Lewis-Williams (2002), who argued that geometric abstract forms found in Palaeolithic cave art both in European and southern African sites were cultural representations of *entoptic phenomena*, visual shapes produced by the brain during altered states. In the Americas too, researchers have argued that complex cave arts found in Texas were made by shamans depicting what they experienced in hallucinogen-inspired trances (Newcomb 1967: 65–80). Regarding psilocybin fungi – 'magic mushrooms' – their ancient importance to Mayan cultures has been supported by stones sculpted into the shape of mushrooms found in Guatamala (Lowy 1971) and dated to 1000 BC onwards (see also Chapter 4). Previously viewed as phallic objects, their distinctive shape – combined with known use of psilocybe mushrooms in Central America – struck mid-twentieth-century researchers as instead being objects from an ancient cult built around the consumption of such fungi. On the other side of the world, the Minoan 'poppy goddess' found in Crete and dated to around 1400–1100 BC seems a clear example of a representation of the opium poppy (Julyan and Dircksen 2011): the figure is wearing a diadem on top of which are three representations of poppy seed capsules, perhaps a reference to the goddess as a bringer of sleep, opium poppies having that resonance in the ancient world (see later).

It is important to remember that caution is required in interpreting all this iconography. Certainly, iconographic evidence can be rather tenuous. For example, there is speculation that 6,000-year-old art from the Selva Pascuala cave in Spain depicts some hallucinogenic fungi. The Selva Pascuala mural features a bull, alongside some figures that could feasibly represent mushrooms given their stalks and conical heads, and some researchers (Akers et al. 2011) have made the case that they are *Psilocybe hispanica*, a Spanish hallucinogenic fungi. In addition to the suggestive shapes that could be mushroom-like, the researchers support their theory by linking to ethnographic evidence from elsewhere in the world for shamanic use of such fungi, and the work of the likes of Lewis-Williams. While intriguing, this of course relies heavily on many what-ifs, especially as the 'fungal' shapes are not all mushroom-like. Another example of this need for caution is recent analysis of Cypriot juglets thought previously to have contained opium due to their shape resembling a poppy seed capsule. These are late Bronze Age containers likely used for liquid commodities, and the notion that they were for transporting opium has long been promoted, first by R.S. Merrillees (1962). It is certainly conceivable that the shape of the juglets was to advertise what they contained. However, more recent molecular analysis suggests that there may have been some poppy-related oils in some of the juglets, although many actually contained aromatic oils (Chovanec et al. 2015, Smith et al. 2018).

That the Cypriot juglets may have contained other products of the poppy rather than opium latex connects to a key limitation in all this: while many of the finds of psychoactive species at human-occupied sites may well suggest they were being used for their psychoactive effects, it is very hard to verify this. This is especially the case for multi-use species of plants such as cannabis and the opium poppy. Both are also valuable sources of nutrition through their seeds and oils, while cannabis – in the form of hemp – is also a source of valuable fibres for textiles and rope. Thus, even if the presence of these plants signifies that they were meaningfully used, quite what they were used *for* may remain unclear. Furthermore, there is great danger here that we can project our own ideas of drug consumption back in time, whereas ancient cultures of their consumption might have been radically different.

Similarly, that many of the earlier finds were made in the context of burials can lead us to see ancient drug consumption as being highly ritualised and religious in nature. Of course, contemporary drug use is often sacred in nature – think of the Catholic sacrament of wine, or Rastafarian spiritual use of cannabis, as well as shamanic use of hallucinogens – and so there is no reason to doubt that ancient use in some cases linked to spirituality and religiosity. However, as we also know from our own age, drug use is often highly secular and even frivolous at times. It can also be something people indulge in for *fun*. The association of ancient drug use with burials can in this way obscure the frivolous and the fun, things we need to take seriously in the study of drugs, even though catching something as ephemeral as fun in the archaeological record is not easy.

Such caution is not to downplay the importance of archaeological research into drugs. Research clearly shows an age-old association of humanity with psychoactive substances, even if it cannot let us enter fully into the cultures of consumption (and trade and production) in which they were embedded, nor allow us to speculate that drug use was a human universal (and many people today, of course, shun the consumption of these substances). Furthermore, molecular analysis of pottery residues and other forms of molecular archaeology – and genetic analysis of drug species – are likely to shine further light on drug use of the past.

Drugs, Domestication and the Coming of Inequality

The earlier survey of evidence for ancient drug use certainly gives a sense of how widespread they were, and some argue that their importance for humans led to them – alcoholic beverages in particular – playing a key role in the process of 'neolithicization' (Wadley and Hayden 2015), that is to say, in the Neolithic transitions whereby bands of nomadic hunter-gatherers switched to livelihoods based around settled agriculture and larger communities following the domestication of plant and animal species. This process occurred at different times in different places, and may not have been a linear process, with some societies oscillating between periods of settlement in larger communities, and periods of mobility in smaller groups (Graeber and Wengrow 2021).

The earliest such transition is thought to have taken place in the Fertile Crescent of the Middle East around 10,000 years ago. As well as being a process of domestication and settlement, the Neolithic transition is also commonly seen as being a moment in time where social inequality and stratification emerged, as agricultural surpluses and higher population density allowed some to gain forms of political power. While this account of profound changes to human society through Neolithic transitions is one usually associated with agriculture, the typical focus of this has revolved around subsistence agriculture, that is to say, the production of wheat and other cereal crops for bread and other foods. However, Greg Wadley and Brian Hayden (2015) argue strongly that the production of alcoholic beverages – alongside the production of other psychoactive crops such as tobacco and coca in the Americas – was a primary driver of the transition to agriculture and stratified, settled societies.

Hunter-gatherer societies in his view also used psychoactive substances in the past, but these were primarily hallucinogens used for shamanic, spiritual purposes (substances we will focus on in Chapter 4), whereas in the Neolithic transition, there was a switch to 'mood-altering' drugs such as alcohol and coca. Demand grew for such drugs with their capacity to encourage 'pro-social' behaviour, and to cope with the stresses of living in socially dense communities, and so the ability to control the supply of them through agriculture became a source of power. Wadley and Hayden (2015) put much emphasis on the role of feasting in such ancient societies, and on the ethnographic record that shows how feasting – often competitive in nature – has been a crucial aspect of life in many societies. Indeed, from Melanesia and competitive feasts where 'Big Men' try and outdo each other in generosity (see, e.g., Young 1971), to the classic ethnographic case of the potlatch of the Kwakwaka'wakw people of the Pacific Northwest that has been frequently analysed within anthropology as a reciprocal institution where people compete for political influence and status through feasts and gift giving, feasting features strongly as a social institution.

Building on such ideas, Wadley and Hayden's work argues that drugs were a key part of such feasts, and that providing large amounts of alcoholic beverages in particular at feasts was a driver of cereal crop domestication, and thus a factor in the emergence of social stratification, for 'successful organizers [of feasts] can and do obtain political power and reproductive success' (Wadley and Hayden 2015: 568). In the Americas, Stacey Schwartzkopf (2022) analyses the role drugs played in Mayan, Aztec and Incan societies, arguing similarly that control of the production, exchange and consumption of mood-altering drugs – and in some cases, hallucinogens – was an essential part of political power, creating reciprocal ties and forming visible signs of wealth and prestige. Again, while we should be cautious in assessing such theories, that drugs played a key role in earlier societies appears likely.

Ancient Literature

> Then Helen, daughter of Zeus, took other counsel. Straightway she cast into the wine of which they were drinking a drug to quiet all pain and strife, and bring forgetfulness of every ill. Whoso should drink this down, when it is mingled in the bowl, would not in the course of that day let a tear fall down over his cheeks, no, not though his mother and father should lie there dead, or though before his face men should slay with the sword his brother or dear son, and his own eyes beheld it. Such cunning drugs had the daughter of Zeus, drugs of healing, which Polydamna, the wife of Thon, had given her, a woman of Egypt, for there the earth, the giver of grain, bears greatest store of drugs, many that are healing when mixed, and many that are baneful ... .
>
> (Homer, Odyssey, Book 4 219–230 [translated by A.T. Murray 1919])

While archaeological research continues to expand our knowledge of ancient drug production, trade and use, analysis of ancient texts can also provide insight into older cultures of consumption, insight that can be triangulated – that is to say, used alongside other forms of evidence such as the archaeological – to put our knowledge of drugs in antiquity on a surer footing. Indeed, a number of ancient texts provide clues about drug pharmacopoeias and cultures of consumption, not just texts from the ancient Greek and Roman world but also from the wider Mediterranean world and from ancient China. In some cases, mentions of possible psychoactive substance use in ancient texts have led to detective work attempting to identify plants or fungi that might fit the descriptions given in the texts. For example, in Book 4 of Homer's Odyssey, written around the eighth century BCE, we learn of *nepenthe*, a substance added to wine and said 'to quiet all pain and strife' whose name means something like 'anti-sorrow'. There is much speculation that this refers to opium, or a concoction containing opium among other ingredients (Carod-Artal 2013: 31). The earlier translation of the passage demonstrates well the ambivalence that still revolves around drugs such as opiates, drugs that can bring not only much therapeutic benefit but also much potential harm. Nepenthe is qualified in the ancient Greek by the term *pharmakon*, a term analysed heavily for its ambivalence and ambiguity, referring to this potential for healing and harm (Derrida 1981). While *nepenthe* need not necessarily refer to a real drug, it is not inconceivable that it might refer to something containing opiates given the description of its effects, and given what we know from other texts of the importance of opium in the Ancient world. Later Greek texts reveal that it was used much in medicine for a wide range of ailments, being mentioned by the 'father of medicine' Hippocrates (Carod-Artal 2013: 31–32). Its toxicity at high doses was also known, and it was reported to have been used for euthanasia, while Theophrastus in the second century BC gives a clear description of the process of extracting opium latex from the poppy heads.

Identifying a plant found in Asia known as *soma* mentioned in the 3000-year-old or so texts of the Rig Veda has also intrigued many historians. The Rig Veda is one of four Vedas, sacred texts for Hindus that 'are regarded as the original revelation ... heard by the seven sages or inspired poets, the Rishis, and then transmitted orally generation after generation' (Torri 2022: 97). The Rig Veda contains over a thousand hymns, some of which focus on Soma, 'at the same time a god, plant and intoxicant juice' (ibid.). There are clues as to the identity of the plant in the texts, as it is said to come from a mountainous region, its stalks were pressed to extract juice, and its effects are said to give immortality and inspiration (ibid. 98). While scholars have proposed a range of plants for Soma, including Ephedra and *bhang* (a drink made from cannabis), one of the most famous hypotheses for its identity was made by R. Gordon Wasson, the amateur mycologist mentioned earlier. His hypothesis was that Soma was actually a mushroom, *Amanita muscaria*, the famous red and white mushrooms known for being used as intoxicants in Siberia and elsewhere. He published his hypothesis in the book *Soma: Divine Mushroom of Immortality* (1968). While the mystery of Soma remains, exploring the possible candidates for Soma brought focus to the role of drugs in ancient Asia, showing the wide range of use and how closely linked drug use can be with religiosity, as Torri emphasises (2022).

Another book, this time co-written by Wasson alongside Albert Hofmann (who first synthesised LSD in 1938), and Carl Ruck (coiner of the term *entheogen*), *The Road to Eleusis* (2008) focuses on the Eleusinian mysteries, a long-standing rite of renewal in ancient Greece focused on the Goddess of agriculture and fertility, Demeter. The Mysteries involved initiation into the cult of Demeter and were held every year. Initiates had to drink *kykeon*, a brew made from cereals such as barley, said to inspire revelation. And the authors of the book argue that the brew might have derived its divine properties from the parasitic fungus ergot that can cause hallucinations (ergot contains LSD-like compounds), and which often contaminated bread supplies through attacking cereals. Of course, this is once again a very speculative hypothesis.

More recently, the amateur scholar Brian Muraresku wrote *The Immortality Key* (2020), where he continues in Wasson's and Hofmann's footsteps in trying to solve the riddle of the role of hallucinogens in the ancient Greek Eleusinian Mysteries. He provides support for Wasson and Hofmann's assertions that the psychedelic substance in a drink they took was the ergot fungus. He goes further than that in proposing a controversial claim that the original Christianity Eucharist contained wine with hallucinogens in it, inspired by ancient Greek religious practice. While Muraresku's work has garnered high praise from the ethnobotanist Mark Plotkin (2021), other responses have been more reserved, at least about the claims about the Christian Eucharist. Historian Dan Williams wrote that

> the documentary evidence that we have from the Pauline epistle of 1 Corinthians (mid-1st century) and the three Synoptic gospels suggest the Christian Eucharist's origins in the Jewish rite of Passover ... . The documentary evidence that we have from the mid-2nd century writer Justin Martyr's description of the Eucharist as it was celebrated in his own time also gives no hint of anything psychedelic.
>
> (Williams 2021, pers. comm.)

Scholars have also sought to identify drugs that might have been used in the famous Delphic oracle at the Temple of Apollo where a priestess known as Pythia would utter prophecies to those who came to consult the oracle, an institution some date back as far as 1400 BC. Anthropologist Scott Littleton wrote an article (1986) about such 'shamanic' practices in Ancient Greece, reporting how ancient writers spoke of the priestess being surrounded by fragrant fumes – *pneuma enthusiastikon* (inspirational exhalation) – that would inspire her prophecies. While this is described as emitting from the ground in ancient texts, Scott Littleton and others reckon that rather than some sort of gas coming from the earth, the fumes may have been the smoke of hallucinogenic herbs such as henbane or Datura. Recent research, however, has suggested that the geology at the oracle may have generated a heady mix of carbon dioxide, methane and benzene that could have generated the priestess' altered state (Etiope 2015).

The identity of other drugs and their use in ancient texts is more certain, including cannabis. The ancient Greek historian Herodotus (also sometimes thought of as an early anthropologist for his focus on different cultures) wrote about the Scythians, a nomadic people of Eurasia, inhaling the fumes of cannabis seeds at funerary rites. The passage in question (Herodotus' *Histories* Book IV, Section 75) is translated thus by G.C. Macaulay:

> The Scythians then take the seed of this hemp and creep under the felt coverings, and then they throw the seed upon the stones which have been heated red-hot: and it burns like incense and produces a vapour so thick that no vapour-bath in Hellas would surpass it: and the Scythians being delighted with the vapour-bath howl like wolves.

This is a famous passage in cannabis history, and it is cited as an early reference to psychoactive use of cannabis. However, Herodotus goes on to say that this process is like 'washing' for the Scythians; this, combined with the fact that Herodotus talks of seeds which are not in themselves psychoactive, and that he talks about cannabis for hemp production (which usually lack potency), would suggest that intoxication was not the primary purpose of this Scythian use of the plant. Chris Duvall has studied cannabis history and spread in detail and urges caution in reading psychoactivity into this passage from Herodotus (who was also known for sensationalising his accounts), suggesting that it is a case of *presentism*, reading the past through the interests of the present (Duvall 2015: 51).

Yet it is clear from ancient literature that the cannabis plant was well known and used, even if it seems more for textiles and food. In China too, cannabis has long been known for these uses, and for use as medicine. There is textual evidence of awareness of cannabis psychoactivity millennia ago – for example the herbal Pen-ts'ao Ching (compiled in the early first millennium AD) states that 'ma-fên (fruits of hemp) ... if taken in excess will produce hallucinations (literally "seeing devils"). If taken over a long term, it makes one communicate with spirits and lightens one's body' (translation in Li 1974: 446). However, Duvall suggests these effects were not sought out deliberately in Ancient China, instead the worth of the plant being in its fibre and seeds (2014: chapter 2).

As is still the case, alcoholic drinks were the most prevalent drugs used in the ancient world. References to it are everywhere in ancient literature and history: for example, David Courtwright reports that the Bible refers to wine around 165 times (Courtwright 2001: 10). Drunken revelry was also celebrated (or lamented) in the form of the Greek God Dionysus, and Roman God Bacchus – divine personifications of wine and the ecstasy (and sometimes agony) that wine could bring. And we mentioned in Chapter 2 Horace's famous poem (Ode 3.21, published in 23 BC) addressed to a wine jar that gives a clear impression of the ambiguity and ambivalence with which wine was viewed in Ancient Rome. Wine formed a key commodity of ancient Europe, and viticulture spread widely through the Roman Empire (e.g. vineyards in Switzerland owe their origins to Roman occupation [Mencarelli and Tonutti 2013]), and frescos throughout the ancient Roman and Greek world depicted wine and the social occasions where it was consumed.

While, just as today, many shunned consumption of wine and similar beverages, for others wine's intoxicating effects were highly valued. These contrasting perceptions of intoxication are analysed in a recent book by Michael Rinella (2010) called *Pharmakon* (the word which, as mentioned earlier, encapsulates much ambivalence to drugs). He argues that states of intoxication often derived from wine mixed with other intoxicants, and that these intoxicated states of ecstasy were highly valued in Greek society until the influence of the philosopher Plato in the fourth century BC and his emphasis on the need for rationality and contemplation of the eternal. Plato set the scene, according to Rinella, for later views on intoxication as not suitable for rational, worthy individuals, a thread that still runs through our contemporary views of intoxicants and altered states as things that can stop us working hard in the pursuit of supposedly rational goals. In Chapter 5 we will discuss how the industrial age and attempts to keep the workforce disciplined reinforced this sense of intoxication and altered states as things themselves to be disciplined.

Early Modern and Modern History

Historians have investigated various aspects of intoxicant and stimulant use in the Europe of the Middle Ages, though alcohol features heavily, as, for example, in Richard Unger's book on beer in the Middle Ages and Renaissance (2004). However, expanding trade networks and expanding European Empires from the eleventh century AD onwards, and especially from the early modern period onwards (beginning roughly in 1400 AD), reveal the role of drugs as commodities that have helped shape the modern world. The centrality of the last 600 or so years for historians of drugs is evident in the dominance of the theme of the 'global' in their writing and research. Indeed, a major new resource is a handbook entitled *The Oxford Handbook of Global Drug History* (Gootenberg 2022). David Courtwright summarised well why drug historians have focused so heavily on drug commerce and commodities in that era:

> The expansion of oceangoing commerce is the single most important fact about the early modern world … . The globalization of wine, spirits, tobacco, caffeine-bearing plants, opiates, cannabis, coca and other drugs … would transform the everyday consciousness of billions of people and, eventually, the environment itself.
>
> (2001: 9)

As Gootenberg writes too, historians became interested in drugs in the 1990s, a time when globalisation and transnationalism were quickly expanding themes in the social sciences, anthropology included. This provides the intellectual context in which interest in the likes of tobacco as 'global commodities' grew among historians (2022: 8).

This interest in the relationships between globalisation and consumption connects to research into the spice trade and the global connections that these spurred. Schivelbusch in his book (1992) that draws spices and drugs into a similar category of 'articles of pleasure', traces how demand for 'exotic' spices became a craze as growing wealth divisions between the feudal lords and their subjects became increasingly marked by consumption patterns, and luxury goods from the 'Orient' especially grew in demand. This did not just entail spices but also fabrics and textiles. For Schivelbusch, this was an important part of world history, as 'hunger for spices' created dependence on trade routes to the East, transforming not only consumption and class distinctions in Europe but also the world economy as these connections were forged and consolidated (1992: 8–9). This demand for spices kept on growing as 'nouveau-riche urban middle classes imitated the nobility in their ostentatious display of luxury' (ibid. 10). Spices we now see as ordinary and everyday – for example pepper – were then luxury items sold at great expense, and control over their trade could bring great wealth. The demand for spices can even be linked to the arrival of Europeans in the Americas, as the quest for a quick sea route to India drove the likes of Christopher Columbus.

As these global interconnections were being forged by the early modern period, Europe began to get a taste for exotic drugs too, and the likes of tobacco, tea, coffee and even sugar – which some see as a drug food – spurred yet more production, trade and consumption. The story of how sugar became a key commodity and consumer item in Europe, and how this rising demand connected to Caribbean plantations and the slave trade is one told by anthropologist Sidney Mintz in a famous book entitled *Sweetness and Power* (1985), a classic political economy analysis of global trade. While a historical book in the main, it does draw too on Mintz's fieldwork in Puerto Rico and elsewhere in the Caribbean on peasant workers. Sugar first came to Europe from the East alongside other spices, at first used sparingly as a condiment by the wealthy, and for preserving food. As European colonialism expanded, sugar cane production began in earnest in colonies in the Americas and Caribbean, forming part of the infamous Atlantic triangle whereby European commodities such as textiles and rum were exchanged for slaves on the west coast of Africa, who were then transported across the Atlantic as labour on sugar cane and tobacco plantations, their products then being shipped to Europe. Mintz also highlights how sugar's meaning shifted within European societies such as early modern and modern England, where it became far more commonplace a substance, its consumption playing a role in fuelling the capitalist and industrial transformation of the country at that time, not only by its value as a commodity but also by the cheap energy it could give to factory workers and others. Like many spices such as pepper, sugar switched from being a luxury good to an abundant commodity that helped transform societies and economies far and wide through its production and consumption.

Tobacco has also featured strongly as a subject of historical and anthropological research. Its history in the Americas goes back millennia as a substance used much in indigenous healing and social life. However, following European arrival in the Americas in the late fifteenth century, tobacco would rapidly spread around the world, accelerating sharply in the seventeenth century. Tobacco has been ascribed much agency historically (see, e.g., Russell 2019 for an anthropological account that treats the substance as a social actor in its own right). Some have attributed its power to its addictive qualities, and others to its ability to sustain workers similarly to sugar in the context of a capitalist ethos (Norton 2022: 135). Like sugar too, it spurred the development of plantations in the colonies, as well as different cultures of consumption in Europe, although it did face a hostile reaction too. For example, King James VI and I of Great Britain wrote in 1604 an anti-tobacco tract called *A Counterblaste to Tobacco*.

Marcy Norton (2022) emphasises that influence on tobacco's global spread emerged from its indigenous contexts of use, and through moments of encounter between Europeans and indigenous Americans. Indeed, the ways tobacco was consumed in the Americas followed it around the world, for Europeans and people of African descent (who also played a role in the spread of tobacco beyond the Americas) developed their knowledge and practices related to tobacco in interaction with indigenous peoples of the Americas. Similarly, in relation to cannabis, geographer Chris Duvall (2019) also highlights the agency of Africans in its history as African farming knowledge and practices, as well as cultural innovations such as the invention of the water pipe, were significant in the further spread of the substance. Pulling out people and places overlooked in previous accounts of drug histories is a key strand of current historical research into drugs.

Analyses of how 'exotic' drugs like tea, coffee and tobacco were integrated into European cultures often revolve around the theme of class as well as forms of sociality. The institution of the coffee shop in early modern and later Europe features strongly, and has been the subject of research (e.g. Markman 2004). People have been drinking coffee for centuries in parts of the Middle East and East Africa, where it originated in Ethiopia. Europeans first became familiar with coffee in the 1500s, after they learned about its social consumption in Ottoman culture. Early travel writers likened the coffee houses they encountered to English alehouses. Coffee was first consumed in Europe in Venice, and coffee houses became important in part of British life in the 1600s. Cowan (2005: 82) argues that the coffeehouses of the 1600s and 1700s in England became venues for the introduction of new consumption habits, such as tobacco, tea and hot chocolate. They were patterned after norms of social drinking in the inns and taverns, but they were novel institutions that formed in concert with values of the English intelligentsia, or virtuosi, who first experimented with these novel substances. The impact of these coffee shops on European towns and cities was profound, being predominantly male spaces critical in the creation of a number of aspects of our contemporary capitalist economies: in England, coffee shops were places where business was conducted, and they became prototype stock exchanges and insurance markets. They were also places regarded with much suspicion in their early days as places of potential sedition, so associated were they with lively debate. An anonymous seventeenth-century political pamphlet entitled *The Women's Petition against Coffee* (Anonymous 1674) conveys humorously much of the way coffee shops and coffee drinkers were seen by some in England at that time, ridiculing coffee consumers as effete and emasculated, lamenting that men were turning to coffee away from good old-fashioned English ale.

Respectability also has much resonance in historical studies of stimulant and intoxicant use. 'Respectability' became soaked in its usage in Europe and North America from the eighteenth century with ideas of morally upstanding middle-class lifestyles which eschewed excess. As Woodruff Smith has it, respectability very much emerged in European class structures, and someone 'who claimed to be respectable was in essence demanding deference from social inferiors and respect from equals and superiors' (2014: 144). However, it differed from earlier values of gentility which linked to 'descent', that is to say, being born into high status. Instead, becoming 'respectable' was something all could theoretically embrace through behaving in ways regarded as moral. Items of consumption became important markers of this respectability, and social stimulants such as tea and coffee became crucial components of this, as the stereotypical image of the middle-class British high tea with all its porcelain and manners makes clear. Ideas of self-control also became important in some forms of respectability (Smith 1992). These meshed with the temperance movement, as excessive alcohol consumption came to be seen as distinctly *not* respectable. Certain types of respectability very much demanded sobriety.

Histories of Prohibition

As Singer (2008) points out, drugs that are illegal today were, until the early 1900s, internationally legal and traded – although there were exceptions, as some substances were subject to legal restrictions in individual countries. However, the twentieth century would see the coming of increasing international moves to restrict and outright prohibit certain substances. Histories of legality are important for any consideration of drugs, as prohibition and its countercurrents have affected how we not only treat drugs and drug users but also how we *see* them (see Chapter 8). Historians have focused in detail on the processes that led to prohibition and the late twentieth-century militarisation of drug policy in the form of the 'war on drugs'. A key process in all this is the development of new ways of seeing certain drugs as especially dangerous: rather than being forms of habit, drug use came to be seen as something more sinister, *addiction* (Hickman 2022). How the concept of addiction was constructed historically is a fascinating one to which we turn in Chapter 6 where we focus more directly on the concept in exploring ideas of power and agency in relation to drugs. However, it is worth noting here that in this kind of analysis, historical and anthropological research mesh together well, as both explore how such ideas are not only straightforward reflections of a reality of people's relationships with drugs but also are very much mediated both historically and culturally.

A key part of history greatly significant for the development of prohibition were the 'Opium Wars' of the nineteenth century that revolved around attempts by British traders and others to control the opium trade and promote British economic interests. In the late 1700s, one of Britain's main crops in India was opium that was destined for China (Singer 2008, Courtwright 2002). The standard story of the Opium Wars runs as follows: the British wanted Chinese exports such as silk and tea, but China did not want their products as much, giving China a trade advantage. Although the Chinese banned the opium trade in 1729, the British and the Americans illegally sold opium from India to China. This fuelled an epidemic of addiction in certain Chinese provinces. The addictions disrupted the Chinese economy and social life and caused tension with the British. The tensions led to two Opium Wars in the mid-1800s: China lost both, and one of the consequences was that they had to stand by while Britain increased their opium sales in China (Courtwright 2002).

This very broad outline of these wars developed in twentieth-century historical writings, and the idea of the Chinese becoming addicts at the hands of evil drug pushers – even prepared to go to war to defend their lucrative trade – had an impact on the development of drug prohibition, spurring anti-drug campaigners throughout the world to develop international systems to control and regulate drugs. However, new sources available to historians of the twenty-first century have led to revisionist writing about Chinese opium consumption and the Opium Wars (Mills 2022). Work by Yangwen Zheng (2005) showed how Chinese opium consumption was far more complicated a story than one of simple addiction, one that linked to ideas of elite leisure as well as the medicinal power of the substance. While some Chinese undoubtedly did become dependent on the substance, Chinese consumption was driven by many other factors than addiction. Furthermore, Mills (2022) shows how British interests were also very mixed, with different factions pushing in different directions in terms of policy. The simple narrative of evil pushers and passive addicts of the usual rendering of the Opium Wars comes apart in such revisionist accounts – as usual, history is far more complicated than such simple narratives can capture.

Opium cultivation has been tied up with war and imperialism from the 1700s, and with crime and war since it has been regulated and prohibited for non-medical uses from the early 1900s. In the first attempt to attain global consensus for prohibiting the non-medical use of opium, the US convened the International Opium Commission (IOC) in Shanghai in 1909. Its nonbinding resolutions were aimed at opium smoking and at smuggling opium into countries where they were illegal. The Hague Opium Convention of 1912 followed and established the control of opium as an international treaty and legally binding under the United Nations.[1] After that, individual countries made their own laws prohibiting narcotics. The push to regulate opium, especially the smoking of it, has been tied to the targeting of Chinese migrants. In the UK, Virginia Berridge has highlighted how concern with opium also linked strongly to fears of Chinese immigration (Berridge 1999a). The US banned only opium prepared for smoking in 1909, again, targeting the Chinese community. This pattern has been common for other drugs as well, and in different parts of the world, as moves towards prohibition have coincided with fears of ethnic and racial others. Gillogly (2008), for example, observed that, in Thailand, the politically and economically dominant lowland peoples consider the 'hill tribe' people (living in the opium Golden Triangle) uncivilised and dangerous, partly because of their association with opium production. In the US, for example, heroin was publicly associated with African American men at the beginning of Nixon's drug war. Cannabis was outlawed in the early 1900s because of its association with immigrant labourers from Mexico (Singer 2008). Many European nations took part in the IOC, as well as China, Persia (now Iran), Russia and Siam (now Thailand).

Not just the likes of opium, cocaine and cannabis came under scrutiny by law-makers in the US: so did alcohol, leading to the 18th amendment of the US Constitution that banned alcohol on a Federal level between 1920 and 1933. The history of alcohol prohibition is one much told (see, e.g., McGirr 2015), and one that emerged out of the Temperance movement of the nineteenth century that considered many societal ills to derive from drunkenness, and that garnered increasing support from mainly Protestant Americans. State-level prohibitions were experimented with in the nineteenth century, but campaigners pushed hard for a utopian vision of a future 'dry' America and overcame pushback from the drinks industry. Like all such utopian visions, cracks soon appeared as reality bit: tax revenue plummeted while bootleggers such as Al Capone ensured supply could meet the continuing demand for alcoholic drinks. This history is often used as proof that prohibiting drugs can never work, although some argue that there is evidence that prohibitions can sometimes – albeit partially – be effective in reducing harms to public health and society (Hall 2010).

Despite the apparent failure of alcohol prohibition, national and international laws continued to tighten restrictions on other drugs over the twentieth century. Figures like Harry Anslinger of the Federal Bureau of Narcotics in the US pushed hard in the 1930s for strong penalties for those trading or using cannabis at a time where sensationalised portrayals of cannabis were common in popular media. Elsewhere in the world, the push to prohibit was felt strongly too, including in relation to khat which the British colonial state tried to ban, albeit unsuccessfully (Anderson and Carrier 2009). Ideas of drugs as dangerous and in need of restriction had very much gone global by the early to mid-twentieth century. Later, the Single Convention on Narcotic Drugs was signed in 1961 by the UN Economic and Social Council to standardise drug designations and control globally. It established the International Narcotics Control Board (INCB) for monitoring the implementation of the treaties by signatory parties, and was revised in 1971 and 1988. It established categories of likelihood for abuse and medical use called Schedules. Schedule I drugs were held to the most restrictive control. In the revised Convention in 1971, Schedule I drugs were deemed to be the most susceptible to abuse and without medical, or therapeutic, usefulness. Examples of Schedule I drugs under the 1988 Convention include MDMA, LSD, khat and cannabis. Because of its medical usefulness, opioids are considered Schedule II drugs. Cocaine is also considered a Schedule II drug because of its history of use as an anaesthetic, even though it is rarely used as such anymore. Many have noted the ironies of the scheduling, considering that pharmacological risks do not always coincide with the severity of the scheduling.

This ever-expanding restrictive approach to drugs was driven by a range of political interests, though often the US has appeared as the lead force in all this, including in the increasing militarisation of the so-called drug war under the Nixon and Reagan administrations. This saw harsher penalties for those found with drugs in the US, penalties which often had a racialised dimension, including in how from the 1980s onwards penalties for convictions involving crack cocaine (most associated with use in black communities) were much harsher than for powder cocaine (more associated with whites). It also saw increasing export of the 'war on drugs' as US security agencies gave military assistance to countries like Colombia in striving to control the production and export of cocaine. We will return to the theme of the 'war on drugs' and its vast impact on societies around the world in Chapter 8.

However, it is important to note that such a policy is not just an imposition on the rest of the world by the US. Such policies have very much suited other governments and government agencies, for whom repressive drug policies can serve wider vested interests, as described by Gernot Klantschnig in relation to Nigeria and its National Drug Law Enforcement Agency (2013). Going back in time, Isaac Campos (2012) also describes well how Mexican policy towards cannabis was not simply driven by US interests but also grew out of more local experiences with the substance and anxieties about its use that well predate the 'war on drugs'. In such ways, historical research continues to nuance our understanding of how drug policy developed in recent centuries, not just in relation to policies of prohibition but also counter-initiatives such as harm reduction measures (like needle exchange) which emerged in the 1980s due to concern with the spread of blood-borne diseases such as HIV-AIDS through needle-sharing (e.g. see Berridge 1999b).

History and Anthropology

Ideas about the past of drugs are socially relevant in the present, and, even if not historically accurate, such ideas can be potent. Conceptions about the use of drugs in our early human ancestors, for example, shape ideas about their acceptability today. This chapter's survey only gives a taste of the full range of historical research regarding drugs, research that is ever-expanding in scope, especially as new resources (archival and archaeological) become available, and oral histories are collected of more recent patterns of drug production, trade and use. It is also worth mentioning important research of recent decades into aspects of drug pasts previously neglected. For example, the history of alcohol and drugs in African countries is being studied in-depth, and we urge readers to explore pioneering work by Emmanuel Akyeampong on alcohol and its relation to power in Ghana since the nineteenth century (1996), as well as Justin Willis on alcohol and power in East Africa (2002). All this focus on the past of these substances is crucial for anthropology too, giving vital historical context for the use of drugs in contemporary human society, and also encouraging interdisciplinary collaboration that can truly enhance methodological and theoretical approaches to drugs within anthropology itself. It can also encourage anthropologists themselves to incorporate historical methods and make themselves at home in the archives as well as in the field.

Note

1 The treaty can be read online here: www.unodc.org/unodc/en/data-and-analysis/bulletin/bulletin_1959-01-01_1_page006.html (accessed November 2022).

Works Cited

Akers, Brian P., Juan Francisco Ruiz, Alan Piper, and Carl A. P. Ruck. 2011. "A Prehistoric Mural in Spain Depicting Neurotropic Psilocybe Mushrooms." *Economic Botany* 65 (2): 121–128.

Akyeampong, Emmanuel. 1996. *Drink, Power, and Cultural Change: A Social History of Alcohol in Ghana, c. 1800 to Recent Times*. Portsmouth, NH: Heinemann.

Anderson, David, and Neil Carrier. 2009. "Khat in Colonial Kenya: A History of Prohibition and Control." *The Journal of African History* 50 (3): 377–397.

Anonymous. 1674. *Women's Petition Against Coffee*. Printed in London.

Barnard, Hans, Alek N. Dooley, Gregory Areshian, Boris Gasparyan, and Kym F. Faull. 2011. "Chemical Evidence for Wine Production around 4000 BCE in the Late Chalcolithic Near Eastern Highlands." *Journal of Archaeological Science* 38 (5): 977–984.

Berridge, Virginia. 1999a. *Opium and the People: Opiate Use and Drug Control Policy in Nineteenth and Early Twentieth Century England*. New York, NY: Free Association Books Limited.

———. 1999b. "Histories of Harm Reduction: Illicit Drugs, Tobacco, and Nicotine." *Substance Use and Misuse* 34 (1): 35–47.

Campos, Isaac. 2012. *Home Grown: Marijuana and the Origins of Mexico's War on Drugs*. Chapel Hill, NC: University of North Carolina Press.

Carod-Artal, Francisco J. 2013. "Psychoactive Plants in Ancient Greece." *Neurosciences and History* 1 (1): 28–38.

Chovanec, Zuzana, Shlomo Bunimovitz, and Zvi Lederman. 2015. "Is There Opium Here? Analysis of Cypriote Base Ring Juglets from Tel Beth-Shemesh, Israel." *Mediterranean Archaeology and Archaeometry* 15: 175–189.

Courtwright, David T. 2001. *Forces of Habit: Drugs and the Making of the Modern World*. Boston, MA: Harvard University Press.

Cowan, Brian. 2005. *The Social Life of Coffee: The Emergence of the British Coffeehouse*. New Haven, CT: Yale University Press.

Derrida, Jacques. 1981. *Dissemination*. Translated by Barbara Johnson. Chicago, IL: University of Chicago Press.

Dudley, Robert. 2014. *The Drunken Monkey: Why We Drink and Abuse Alcohol*. 1 ed. Berkeley, CA: University of California Press.

DuToit, Brian Murray. 1980. *Cannabis in Africa: A Survey of Its Distribution in Africa and a Study of Cannabis Use and Users in Multi-Ethnic South Africa*. Rotterdam: Balkema.

Duvall, Chris. 2015. *Cannabis*. Chicago, IL: University of Chicago Press.

———. 2019. *The African Roots of Marijuana*. Durham, NC: Duke University Press.

Etiope, Giuseppe. 2015. "Seeps in the Ancient World: Myths, Religions, and Social Development." *Natural Gas Seepage* edited by Giuseppe Etiope, 183–193. Switzerland: Springer International Publishing.

Fitzpatrick, Scott M. 2018. *Ancient Psychoactive Substances*. Gainesville, FL: University Press of Florida.

Gillogly, Kathleen A. 2008. "Opium, Power, People: Anthropological Understandings of an Opium Interdiction Project in Thailand." *Contemporary Drug Problems* 35: 679–715.

Gootenberg, Paul. 2022. *The Oxford Handbook of Global History*. New York: Oxford University Press.

Gosden, Chris. 1999. *Anthropology and Archaeology: A Changing Relationship*. London: Routledge.

Graeber, David, and David Wengrow. 2021. *The Dawn of Everything: A New History of Humanity*. London: Penguin Books.

Graziano, Michael S.A. 2018. *The Spaces between Us: A Story of Neuroscience Evolution and Human Nature*. New York, NY: Oxford University Press.

Guerra-Doce, Elisa. 2015. "Psychoactive Substances in Prehistoric Times: Examining the Archaeological Evidence." *Time & Mind: The Journal of Archaeology, Consciousness & Culture* 8 (1): 91–112.

———. 2022. "Psychoactive Drugs in European Prehistory." In *The Oxford Handbook of Global Drug History*, edited by Paul Gootenberg, 35–55. New York: Oxford University Press.

Hall, Wayne. 2010. "What Are the Policy Lessons of National Alcohol Prohibition in the United States, 1920–1933?" *Addiction* 105 (7): 1164–1173.

Hayden, Brian, Neil Canuel, and Jennifer Shanse. 2013. "What Was Brewing in the Natufian? An Archaeological Assessment of Brewing Technology in the Epipaleolithic." *Journal of Archaeological Method and Theory* 20 (1): 102–150.

Herodotus. 1890. *Herodotus' Histories* Book IV, Section 75. Translated by George C. Macaulay. London: MacMillan and Co.

Hickman, Timothy. 2022. "Dangerous Drugs from Habit to Addiction." In *The Oxford Handbook of Global Drug History*, edited by Paul Gootenberg, 213–229. New York: Oxford University Press.

Julyan, Marlene and Marianne Dircksen. 2011. "The Ancient Drug Opium." *Akroterion* 56: 75+.

King James VI and I. 1604. *A Counterblaste to Tobacco*. London: R.B.

Klantschnig, G. 2013. *Crime, Drugs and the State in Africa: The Nigerian Connection*. Leiden: Brill.

Kohrman, Matthew, Quan Gan, Wennan Liu, and N. Proctor Robert. 2018. *Poisonous Pandas: Chinese Cigarette Manufacturing in Critical Historical Perspectives*. Stanford, CA: Stanford University Press.

Lewis-Williams, David. 2002. "Three-Dimensional Puzzles: Southern African and Upper Palaeolithic Rock Art." *Ethnos* 67 (2): 245–264.

Li, Hui-Lin. 1974. "An Archeological and Historical Account of Cannabis in China." *Economic Botany* 28 (4): 437–448.

Littleton, C. Scott. 1986. "The Pneuma Enthusiastikon: On the Possibility of Hallucinogenic "Vapors" at Delphi and Dodona." *Ethos* 14 (1): 76–91.

Lowy, B. 1971. "New Records of Mushroom Stones from Guatemala." *Mycologia* 63 (5): 983–993.

Markman, Ellis. 2004. *The Coffee House: A Cultural History.* London: Orion Publishing.

McGirr, Lisa. 2015. *The War on Alcohol: Prohibition and the Rise of the American State.* New York, NY: W.W. Norton & Company.

McKenna, Terence K. 1992. *Food of the Gods: The Search for the Original Tree of Knowledge: A Radical History of Plants, Drugs, and Human Evolution.* New York, NY: Bantam Books.

McPartland, John M., William Hegman, and Tengwen Long. 2019. "Cannabis in Asia: Its Center of Origin and Early Cultivation, Based on a Synthesis of Subfossil Pollen and Archaeobotanical Studies." *Vegetation History and Archaeobotany* 28 (6): 691–702.

Mencarelli, Fabio, and Pietro Tonutti. 2013. *Sweet, Reinforced and Fortified Wines: Grape Biochemistry, Technology and Vinification* Chichester: Wiley-Blackwell.

Merlin, Mark D. 2003. "Archaeological Evidence for the Tradition of Psychoactive Plant Use in the Old World." *Economic Botany* 57 (3): 295–323.

Merrillees, Robert S. 1962. "*Opium Trade in the Bronze Age Levant.*" *Antiquity* 36: 287–292.

Mills, James H. 2022. "Colonialism, Consumption, Control: Drugs in Modern Asia." In *The Oxford Handbook of Global Drug History*, edited by Paul Gootenberg, 95–110. New York: Oxford University Press.

Mintz, Sidney. 1985. *Sweetness and Power: The Place of Sugar in Modern History.* London: Penguin.

Morris, Steve, David Humphreys, and Dan Reynolds. 2006. "Myth, Marula, and Elephant: An Assessment of Voluntary Ethanol Intoxication of the African Elephant (Loxodonta africana) Following Feeding on the Fruit of the Marula Tree (Sclerocarya birrea)." *Physiological and Biochemical Zoology* 79 (2): 363–369.

Murareshu, Brian. 2020. *The Immortality Key.* New York, NY: St. Martin's Press.

Newcomb, William. 1967. *The Rock Art of Texas Indians.* Austin, TX: University of Texas Press.

Norton, Mary. 2022. "Tobacco's Cultural Shifts as an Early Atlantic Drug." In *The Oxford Handbook of Global Drug History*, edited by Paul Gootenberg, 95–110. Oxford: Oxford University Press.

Plotkin, Mark. 2021. "The Immortality Key: The Secret History of the Religion with No Name." *HerbalGram* (131): 67–69.

Rafferty, Sean. 2018. "Prehistoric intoxicants of North America." In *Ancient Psychoactive Substances* edited by Scott C. Fitzpatrick, 112–127. Gainesville, FL: University Press of Florida.

Ren, Guangpeng, Xu Zhang, Ying Li, Kate Ridout, Martha L. Serrano-Serrano, Yongzhi Yang, Ai Liu, Gudasalamani Ravikanth, Muhammad A. Nawaz, Abdul S. Mumtaz, Nicolas Salamin, and Luca Fumagalli. 2021. "Large-Scale Whole-Genome Resequencing Unravels the Domestication History of Cannabis sativa." *Science Advances* 7 (29).

Rinella, Michael. 2010. *Pharmakon.* Blue Ridge Summit, PA: Lexington Books.

Rivera, Mario A., Arthur C. Aufderheide, Larry W. Cartmell, Constantino M. Torres, and Odin Langsjoen. 2005. "Antiquity of Coca-Leaf Chewing in the South Central Andes: A 3,000 Year Archaeological Record of Coca-Leaf Chewing from Northern Chile." *Journal of Psychoactive Drugs* 37 (4): 455–458.

Russell, Andrew. 2019. *Anthropology of Tobacco: Ethnographic Adventures in Non-Human Worlds*. London: Routledge.

Schivelbusch, Wolfgang. 1992. *Tastes of Paradise: A Social History of Spices, Stimulants, and Intoxicants*. Translated by David Jacobson. New York, NY: Pantheon.

Schwartzkopf, Stacey. 2022. "Ancient American Civilizations, States and Drugs." In *The Oxford Handbook of Global Drug Histories*, edited by Paul Gootenberg, 73–94. New York: Oxford University Press.

Singer, Merrill. 2008. *Drugs and Development: The Global Impact on Sustainable Growth and Human Rights*. Long Grove, IL: Waveland Press.

Smith, Huston. 1972. "Wasson's 'Soma': A Review Article." Review of SOMA, Divine Mushroom of Immortality, R. Gordon Wasson, W. D. O'Flaherty. *Journal of the American Academy of Religion* 40 (4): 480–499.

Smith, Rachel K., Rebecca J. Stacey, Ed Bergström, and Jane Thomas-Oates. 2018. "Detection of Opium Alkaloids in a Cypriot Base-Ring Juglet." *Analyst* 143 (21): 5127–5136.

Smith, Woodruff D. 1992. "Complications of the Commonplace: Tea, Sugar, and Imperialism." *The Journal of Interdisciplinary History* 23 (2): 259–278.

Smith, Woodruff. 2014. *Consumption and the Making of Respectability, 1600–1800*. London: Routledge.

Stolberg, Victor B. 2011. "The Use of Coca: Prehistory, History, and Ethnography." *Journal of Ethnicity in Substance Abuse* 10 (2): 126–146.

Taber, Augustus. 1919. *The Odyssey with an English Translation*. Translated by Augustus Taber Murray. London, New York, NY: William Heinemann.

Tattersall, Ian. 2004. "What Happened in the Origin of Human Consciousness?" *The Anatomical Record Part B: The New Anatomist* 276B (1): 19–26.

Torri, Davide. 2022. "Soma and Drug History in Ancient Asia." In *The Oxford Handbook of Global Drug History*, edited by Paul Gootenberg, 95–110. New York: Oxford University Press.

Unger, Richard W. 2004. *Beer in the Middle Ages and the Renaissance*. Philadelphia, PA: University of Pennsylvania Press.

ven der Merwe, Nikolaas J. 1975. "Cannabis Smoking in 13–14th Century Ethiopia." In *Cannabis and Culture*, edited by Vera Rubin, 77–80. The Hague: Mouton.

Wadley, Greg, and Brian Hayden. 2015. "Pharmacological Influences on the Neolithic Transition." *Journal of Ethnobiology* 35 (3): 566–584.

Wasson, R. Gordon. 1968. New York, NY: Harcourt, Brace & World.

Wasson, R. Gordon, Carl A. Ruck, Huston Smith, and Peter Webster. 2008. *The Road to Eleusis: Unveiling the Secret of the Mysteries*. Berkeley, CA: North Atlantic Books.

Willis, Justin. 2002. *Potent Brews: A Social History of Alcohol in East Africa, 1850–1999*. Athens, OH: Ohio University Press.

Yangwen, Zheng. 2005. *The Social Life of Opium in China*. Cambridge: Cambridge University Press.

Young, Michael W. 1971. *Fighting with Food: Leadership, Values and Social Control in a Massim Society*. London: Cambridge University Press.

4 Food of the Gods?

Psychedelics, Spirits and Healing

Hallucinogens, also known as psychedelics or entheogens, may be the class of drugs most associated with anthropology, as these drugs are sometimes used in indigenous religious and ritual practices, especially those connected with shamanism and healing. The study of hallucinogens captured the wider public imagination of the twentieth century, with its romantic views of anthropologists and ethnobotanists off in jungles 'tripping' with tribes. In contemporary studies of hallucinogens, anthropologists are careful not to project an impression of timeless, 'traditional', indigenous practices but rather of a fluid and constantly changing landscape of hallucinogen use globally, whether it be in places traditionally associated with its use or within Western practices that have adopted their use. In all this, anthropology has engaged with other academic disciplines, such as ethnobotany, as well as with wider publics in various forms, including in psychotherapy and the New Age movement. Today, many people use the term 'hallucinogen' to refer to a broad category of substances that include dissociative anesthetics, deliriants, and classic psychedelics (Nichols et al. 2023).

Hallucinogens, Psychedelics and Entheogens

Definitions

There are several near synonyms for this class of drugs. Hallucinogen comes from 'hallucinate', which dates to the 1600s at least, meaning 'to be deceived [or] have illusions', with Latin and Greek roots meaning 'gone astray in thought' (*hallucinari* Latin) and 'to be uneasy or distraught' (*alussein*, Greek).[1] A current definition of hallucinate is 'to see or hear things that are not really there because of illness or drugs'. The term 'hallucinogen' was coined in 1954 to refer to substances that cause hallucinations. Some found the term 'hallucinogen' to be objectionable because of the negative connotation of assuming that the drug's effects are deceptive. The psychiatrist Humphrey Osmond (1957) introduced what he considered a more appropriate term: 'psychedelic'. It comes from Greek words meaning 'to reveal the mind or soul'. He

DOI: 10.4324/9781003109549-4

formally introduced it at the meeting of the New York Academy of Sciences in 1957, and the term has continued to be used. Entheogen is yet another, more recent term for substances taken in the context of shamanic rituals or similar contexts to alter states of consciousness. This term, from the Greek words for 'inspired by god' and 'coming into being', refers to the capacity of the drugs that cause one to become inspired, or 'to become the divine from within'.

Pharmacology

Pharmacologically, hallucinogens are compounds, natural and synthetic that mimic neurochemicals and alter neurofunctioning. Effects include perceptual distortions and intensifications and 'sensory experiences that originate without external stimuli' (Waters 2021: S100). Emotional effects include euphoria and a heightened sense of consciousness on the positive side and fear, paranoia and feelings of loss of control on the negative side. There are rare long-term cases of people suffering psychosis after taking a hallucinogen as well as 'flashbacks' that replay the experiences of the 'trip', both positive and negative (Waters 2021: S100). It is important to note that the intensity of the experience, and in fact whether one will experience hallucinations at all, is dependent on the particular compound, the dose, what it is mixed with (admixtures), the frame of mind and expectations of the consumer, and the context of use – *drug*, *set* and *setting*. Substances referred to as classic hallucinogens include psilocybin (the active compound in mushrooms), N,N-dimethyltryptamine (DMT) (the active compound in ayahuasca), mescaline (the active compound in the peyote cactus) and LSD. Other substances that are sometimes associated with hallucinogenic effects, including MDMA, tobacco and ketamine, are associated with different neurological receptor systems.

Ethnobotany and Anthropological Connections

Scholarly awareness of hallucinogens owes much to the growth of ethnobotany in the US and Europe. Some of the earliest scientific accounts of their use were recorded by botanists, who also observed the cultural contexts in which they were consumed. These studies have been popularised through the writings of ethnobotanists Wade Davis (1985, 1996), Mark Plotkin (1993 and Terence McKenna (1992). In *The Serpent and the Rainbow* (1985), Wade Davis realised that the ritual contexts led by priests within Vodun/Voodoo secret societies are what made people culturally recognisable as 'zombies', as opposed to being simply victims of poisoning from Datura and tetrodotoxin (a powerful poison found in a kind of fish).

Connections between ethnobotany and anthropology have been strong, especially in studies of the Americas. Anthropologists Gerardo Reichel-Dolmatoff and Weston La Barre were close associates of Richard Evans Schultes (see Chapter 1), and the anthropologist Peter Furst (1922–2015) consulted extensively with Schultes in writing his book *Hallucinogens and Culture* (1976).

A Note on Shamanism

Early anthropological and ethnobotanical work with psychedelics revealed their use in contexts of healing and *shamanism*. Shamans are leaders who mediate between this world and the spirit world for various purposes, including healing, divining, ensuring success in hunting and even attacking enemies (Narby and Huxley 2001). The term shaman comes from the Tungus language of Siberia but has become generalised to refer to any religious practice involving a practitioner going into an altered state of consciousness (not always using drugs) and contacting the spirits on behalf of the community. Shamans often go through an intense apprenticeship, where they learn specialised healing techniques. They are generally recognised as knowing the world differently from other people, even within their own society (Narby and Huxley 2001). It has traditionally been associated with religion among hunter-gatherers or forest-based horticulturalists, often in the Americas.

Shamanism is often linked to the ritualised use of hallucinogens, including ayahuasca, the fly-agaric and psilocybin mushroom, peyote and San Pedro cacti, and tobacco. Dobkin de Rios wrote of the shaman as the manager of the hallucinogenic experience: 'The shaman ... is the stage manager, and through music, chants, whistling or percussion strokes, he [or she] evokes patterned visions that have specific cultural significance' (1993: 2). Ingesting hallucinogens is not the only way for shamans to go into an altered state of consciousness. Other ways include music, dance rhythmic movement, ascetic rites, fasting and other sensory deprivation, and meditation by themselves can also generate such states. Many societies in sub-Saharan Africa have possession states that are not induced by drugs. In these states of possession, they are not shamans communicating with the spirit world; instead, they are mediums in contact with ancestors.

It is tempting to see shamanistic practice as static and unchanging over time. Historical and cultural changes, however, reveal the dynamic nature of shamanism, and any cultural-religious practice. For one, the cultural setting in which shamanism is practiced has shifted and expanded as colonial capitalism changed the global landscape. The practice of shamanism is no longer concentrated in hunter-gatherer and forest-based horticulturalist societies. American anthropologist, Michael Brown (2001) studied among people with shamanistic practices living in the Peruvian Amazon who now grow cash crops. Many shamans in South America are urban-based mestizos (Labate and Cavnar 2014). In the context of his studies of shamanism among the Sora of India and the Sakha of Siberia the British anthropologist, Piers Vitebsky (2001) identified very different relationships with shamanism: whereas the Sora were abandoning it, it was the subject of ethnic revitalisation among the Sakha in the wake of communist repression. Shamanism has also taken on a global component, as New Age Westerners adopt their practices. Even in indigenous contexts traditionally associated with shamanism, it has not everywhere been an ancient practice.

Old and New World Hallucinogen Use: 'A Statistical Question'

Natural hallucinogens are found in many different kinds of plants, including mushrooms, cacti and other flowering plants (angiosperms) (Furst 1976: 33). One of the questions that has perplexed scholars is why there seems to be more extensive use of hallucinogens in the Americas as compared with the rest of the world ('Old World'). Schultes first posed this question, noting that 'the New World boasts at least 40 species of hallucinogenic or phantastica narcotics ... as opposed to half a dozen species native to the Old World' (Schultes quoted in La Barre 1970: 73). In a piece entitled 'Old and New World Narcotics: A Statistical Question and an Ethnological Reply', La Barre (1970) proposed, and Furst (1976) later concurred, that the reason for greater use of hallucinogens in the Americas is because indigenous peoples of that region descended from the shamanistic, mushroom-using, hunting peoples of Siberia and so were 'culturally programmed' to explore their natural environment, find plants with psychotropic properties and identify supernatural power in them. Carneiro (2022: 62) proposed that an important factor that encouraged them to retain psychedelic use was the survival of indigenous hunter-gatherer knowledge in the Americas. In the Old World, farming and pastoralism mostly replaced hunter-gatherer societies. Hierarchical, agriculture-based societies often find the supernatural in cosmic gods tended to by priests, rather than in forces of nature tended to by shamans. In the Americas, however, Furst (1976) and La Barre (1970) noted that the state-level societies never fully eliminated shamanism. The Aztec, Maya and Inca all used a variety of psychedelic plants in their rites (La Barre 1970: 78, Davis 1996). This may be because, as Furst (1976) hypothesised,

> prior to European colonization the New World as a whole never knew the intolerant fanaticism that is the hallmark of some of the major Old World religions, particularly Christianity and Islam, both of which massively transformed the areas in which they took hold.
>
> (p. 6)

Note that there is much left unexplained by this theory, namely the lack of systematic hallucinogen use in areas without extensive hierarchical political control, as in much of Africa, parts of Asia and Australia. It is also possible that Old World hallucinogens are simply not as well-studied by Western scholars, a consideration La Barre points out as well.

Psychedelics in Cultural Contexts

We focus on several drugs to exemplify anthropological approaches to their study. The section is not comprehensive, and we do not include some important substances, such as plants of the nightshade family like *Datura stramonium*.

Iboga(aine)

Tabernanthe iboga is a West African shrub collected in the wild or cultivated with powerful hallucinogenic effects. Ibogaine is an alkaloid that is both a hallucinogen and a stimulant depending on dose and context. It is most concentrated in the root bark, which people take either ground up as a powder or soaked in water as an infusion (Furst 1976: 40). Iboga(aine) is most well known in anthropology in its place in the Bwiti religion of the Fang people of Gabon, studied first by James Fernandez in the 1960s (2019[1982]). More recently, in the West, iboga(aine) has been used as a way to counter drug addiction (Fernandez and Fernandez 2001) and by people taking it to seek personal growth.

Despite the probable pre-colonial use of iboga, Bwiti is a religion squarely situated within a colonial context. Bwiti came about in response to colonial hardships, as a reaction to the pathologies and oppressions of colonisation. Those include a generally paternalistic attitude, focused on moulding the Fang to French cultural ways. On a material basis, it included forced labour and taxation with heavy penalties for non-payment. It left people feeling detached, cut off in both time and space: removed in time from ancestors and tradition, and cut off in space from their sense of place in their traditional ways of livelihood. The Bwiti religion sought to reconnect Fang people with their ancestors, a connection disrupted by missionaries and colonial authorities. James and Renate Fernandez wrote that 'The promise is that Bwiti, through iboga(aine), would restore directionality to the lost and wandering, and, to their desultory lives, would restore the purposefulness of a ritual project' (Fernandez and Fernandez 2001: 239). They argued that the Bwiti and related iboga-taking religious groups they studied saw iboga as 'a sacred substance that powerfully facilitated access to a greater reality than the reality of everyday life in this workaday world – a reality that bound together past, present, and future and life and death' (Fernandez and Fernandez 2001: 245). This case reveals how a postcolonial lens illuminates contexts of use in adapting to world-changing imperialistic disruptions.

Mushrooms

The use of hallucinogenic fungi – mostly of the genus *Psilocybe* – is historically associated with Central America, though used nowadays throughout the world. Pharmacologically, psychoactive mushrooms are less potent than

LSD, though there are similarities in their chemical structure. The active properties in *Psilocybe* fungi, psilocybin and psilocin were first identified and synthesised in a laboratory by Albert Hofmann (famous for synthesising LSD) at the Sandoz laboratory in Switzerland in 1958. There are species of the *Psilocybe* genus on all continents. In Britain is found *Psilocybe semilanceata*, otherwise known as liberty caps or magic mushrooms. It is much speculated in the popular arena that they were used ritually by ancient Celtic druids and that both *Psilocybe* and the fly-agaric mushrooms were used by Irish people throughout history, though there is no direct material evidence. Anthropologists and missionaries have reported the eating of hallucinogenic mushrooms by New Guinea highlanders (Thomas 2002: 321–323). Evidence of ancient use of outside of the Americas is mainly based on iconography, with little to no direct evidence in the archaeological record to this point. There are, for example, murals on Tassili n'Ajjer cave walls in the Sahara Desert that show people seeming to carry mushrooms (Froese et al. 2016). Mushroom shapes also appear 'on the wall of a rock shelter in the prehistoric archeological site Selva Pascuala in Spain, 6000–4000 BCE' (Froese et al. 2016: 109), though caution is required in arguing these represent hallucinogenic fungi as we argued in Chapter 3.

Early colonists in the Americas reported the use of psychoactive mushrooms in Mexico in ritual, including among the Aztec, who called them *teonanácatl*, translated as 'flesh of the gods'. Many sources from the 1500s mention it, including a document written by the grandson of the Aztec ruler Moctezuma, who said that it was taken in crowning ritual of Moctezuma in 1502, as it had been for other leaders. The Catholic friar, Bernardino de Sahagún, who spent more than 50 years studying and writing about Aztec customs, described the mushrooms and how they were taken, saying that 'they could have either pleasant or frightening effects' (Furst 1976: 83). Illustrations of Aztec gods depict mushrooms, suggesting their sacred nature. Catholic priests condemned it as devil worship (Davis 95–96). Use of psilocybin mushrooms in ritual and healing has been documented in Mexico. It first came to the attention of the public when R. Gordon Wasson (1898–1986) published his account of 'magic mushrooms' in 1957 in *Life* magazine. In the article, Wasson told the story of his experience participating in 'age-old rituals of Indians who chew strange growths that produce visions' (Wasson in *Life* 1957: 101).

As for mushrooms further south, in Mayan areas of Central America, ancient use of hallucinogenic mushrooms is primarily available indirectly, in iconographic form, such as in stone sculptures that were often between 1 and 2 feet tall. They have mushroom caps, with carvings of people or animals below. Guerra-Doce describes these as 'small stone sculptures crowned with an umbrella-shaped top, found at a number of pre-Hispanic sites in Guatemala, Mexico, Honduras, and El Salvador, which have been dated between 500 BC and AD 900' (2015: 101). Many believe these to be evidence of the sacred standing of the mushrooms, though it is based on speculation.

Furst (1976: 77–79) documented evidence of other mushroom effigies found in western Mexico, dating about 2,000 years old, and in the art of the Moche of Peru (400 BC–AD 500).

Another prominent hallucinogenic mushroom, which does not contain psilocybin, is the fly-agaric, or *Amanita muscaria*, most associated with its use in Siberia and in shamanistic practices throughout the northern forests of Eurasia. It is found throughout the northern hemisphere in cool climates and at higher elevations in warmer areas (Furst 1976: 90). We discussed in Chapter 3 Wasson's hypothesis that the intoxicating *Soma* of the Rig Veda was this mushroom.

Mescaline

The two main sources of natural mescaline are the peyote cactus (*Lophophora williamsii)* and the San Pedro cactus (*Trichocereus pachanoi*). The San Pedro cactus is native to the Andes: Ecuador and Peru in particular, at high altitudes. Its column-like stalks can get up to 20 feet tall. The stalks are traditionally boiled and the infusion is consumed as a tea. Archaeological evidence suggests it has been used for at least 8,000 years in Peru (Guerra-Doce 2015). The peyote cactus is native to the Chihuahuan desert of northeastern Mexico and parts of Texas along the Rio Grande River. During the colonial period, Catholic missionaries observed peyote use and interpreted it as of the devil. One Jesuit missionary described it in 1653 as 'the plant with which the Devil deceived the Indians of Peru in their paganism' (quoted in Jay 2019: 25). Like several other hallucinogens, it is also used currently by Westerners in search of drug experiences.

Peyote has been studied more extensively by anthropologists than San Pedro. Weston La Barre is best known for his book the *Peyote Cult* (1989[1938]). In it he provides a comprehensive review of peyote ethnobotany and comparative cultural practices in Mexico (especially among the Huichol and Tarahumara), the Mescalero Apache, and the Plains Native American groups. La Barre wrote that ritual use of peyote began before European contact in Mexico, probably in northeastern Mexico, where it grew abundantly (110). In the Plains of the US, on the other hand, it was adopted in the late 1800s when indigenous peoples learned of it from the Mescalero Apache, who had adopted it around 1870 (Boyer et al. 1973). Peyote use did not take off everywhere it was introduced to Native American groups. However, La Barre wrote that 'once it reached the individualistic vision-valuing Plains, it fairly ran riot' (1989 [1938]: 40). It was less popular in places with more integrated and hierarchical politico-religious organisation. The Mescalero Apache, in fact, abandoned its use by all but a few shamans in the early 1900s (Boyer et al. 1973, Jay 2019).

In ritual, La Barre explained that the primary uses were different in Mexico than in the Plains of the US. The Huichol of Mexico used it only seasonally and primarily for healing. For the people of the Plains, the primary function was to gain individual power and instruction in tipi-based all-night cere-monies. In Mexico, there was not any mixture with Christianity, whereas among some of the Plains groups there was some mixture with Christianity, in conjunction with the Native American Church. In Mexico, women could participate, but women's participation was variable among the Plains peoples. Despite the differences, there are some common elements, including a ceremonial trip to acquire it, rituals at night, feathers, fire, birds, incense, abstinence from salt, a ritual breakfast, singing, tobacco ceremonials, public confession and Morning Star symbolism.

Barbara Myerhoff (1974) wrote about her experience on a peyote hunt with an apprentice shaman and a small group of Huichol people in nor-thern Mexico. It was on this yearly pilgrimage that they collected peyote for consumption by the group throughout the year. The hunt was laden with ritual, symbolism connected with a deer-maize-peyote complex and mytho-logical ties. It included food and drink restrictions, confessions and mutual forgiveness. The goal of the pilgrimage was to return to 'birthplace of the gods, where all will be a unity' (240). During the hunt, they went into a godly state, returning to a paradise like that which existed before time and the creation of the world. The shaman played the role of mediator between the worlds. During the pilgrimage, there was a breakdown of social divisions that is typical of liminal spaces. It was only the shaman who had visions that had meaning. The others were 'for beauty' (164).

Tobacco

It might seem surprising to see tobacco listed as a hallucinogen, given that it is often thought of as a stimulant and it is not a classic hallucinogen. Pharmacologists identify it as having a biphasic in effect – a stimulant in small doses, but a depressant in larger doses. We know from the ethno-graphic and historical literature that in the right cultural setting, it can even be trance-inducing. In fact, tobacco is one of the most widespread and oldest plants used in shamanism in the Americas. It has been used in many forms, including as snuff, tobacco paste that is licked, as an enema, mixed with water to make a juice that is either drunk or snorted, chewed, rolled in leaves and smoked as cigars, or smoked in a pipe (von Gernet 2007). Sometimes it is taken by itself, and sometimes in combination with other hallucinogenic plants. Different routes of administration are more potent than others, with chewing being less potent than drinking, snuffing and smoking it.

It is hard to tell how long people have been using tobacco. Direct archaeobotanical evidence consists of a pipe with nicotine in 300 BC, but evi-dence of pipe smoking (not necessarily tobacco) goes back to about 2000 BC. There are many ways to consume tobacco that the archaeological record has not been able to capture. It is likely that tobacco was native to South America and then spread rather quickly throughout the Americas and the Caribbean through human dispersion (Wilbert 1980). Ancient Maya people integrated it into their ritual and cosmology. The Popol Vuh (the sacred book of Maya in Guatemala written in the 1550s) told the story of a challenge by the rulers of the Underworld to the Hero Twins from the Upperworld to keep two cigars lit all night long. Many Maya people today still believe in the power of tobacco to protect them from evil from the Underworld.

European explorers learned of tobacco's effects almost immediately, and there are accounts of European smoking from the early 1500s. The British took particularly quickly to tobacco consumption and had started manufacturing pipes by the late 1500s (smoking was a new concept at that time). They began carrying tobacco as a trade item that was useful particularly in the fur trade because tobacco was highly sought out by the indigenous hunters. By the early 1600s, tobacco was grown by colonists in both Spanish and English colonies. Tobacco consumption quickly took off in England and other parts of Europe in part because of its perceived medical benefits (von Gernet 2007). Even though pre-Colombia tobacco use is restricted to the Americas, when the Europeans started trading it, its use spread quickly.

Ritual use of tobacco has continued to be widely reported in the Americas. Furst (1976) reported that Huichol shamans of north central Mexico used tobacco alongside peyote. Wilbert (1980) described the use of tobacco in paste and liquid form among the Jivaro people, who live in the Montaña area east of the Andes in a tropical forest environment. He found gendered differences in the way it is consumed (Wilbert 1980: 18). There were times when young men consumed it heavily to learn about 'their fortune in warfare and life in general' (Wilbert 1980: 19), in isolation from the rest of the villagers for several days. Young women, on the other hand, drank it during a fertility rite of initiation, when the tobacco water invites a spirit to enter her body and give her power.

With commercial cigarettes came more casual use of tobacco in Amerindian societies. Applied anthropologists have studied the relationship between commercial cigarettes and ritual use of tobacco in order to design more effective smoking cessation programs. Alderete et al. (2010) found different cultural frameworks based on age in the Andes. While ritual use was associated with reciprocity, solidarity, respect and honouring Mother Earth (*Pachamama*) for indigenous elders, smoking commercial cigarettes was associated with individualistic recreational use among youth. The authors recommended that smoking cessation projects tap into those cultural models to increase the ability of youth to resist the pressures to smoke (Alderete et al. 2010). Likewise, Daley et al. (2006) formed a team along with the Oklahoma Area Indian Health Service to enhance recreational tobacco cessation programs for native people of North America with strong histories of spiritual tobacco use. They found that it was important to respect and even promote sacred tobacco use in moving towards a reduction of recreational uses and of nicotine addiction.

Ayahuasca

Ayahuasca is perhaps the most studied hallucinogen in anthropology. It is a brew made from the vine *Banisteriopsis caapi* combined with various other plants. It is native to the Amazon and Orinoco River basins in South America. Its name, meaning 'vine of the soul' or 'vine of the dead', comes from Quechua, the language of the Inca Empire and a lingua franca for the areas it ruled over. It is also called variously *yagé or yajé* (Colombia), *caapi* (Brazil), and there are dozens more local names for it. Ayahuasca refers to either the vine itself or to the tea that is made from the vine, often with the addition of other plants that may also have psychotropic effects. Pharmacologically, ayahuasca's active compound is DMT. The admixture plants (often *Psychotria viridis)* increase its psychoactivity and may contain nicotine, caffeine or cocaine (Morales-García et al. 2017).

In indigenous contexts, as with other shamanic hallucinogens, ayahuasca is used to enhance communication between humans and other beings, including spirits. Some common experiences include the sensation of flight and of the soul going on a trip outside of the body, visions of snakes and jaguars (elaborated by Reichel-Dolmatoff [1975]) and hallucinations that they interpret as being visions of demons or deities (Harner 1973). Among the Runa people of Ecuador, Kohn noted that people have given ayahuasca to dogs to facilitate interspecies communication (Kohn 2007).

Once again, we encourage an analysis of drug use as always historically situated, even among indigenous people and often within the context of the spread of global capitalism. Ayahuasca shamanism is often portrayed as a timeless tradition of the Amazon that has spread from indigenous groups to wider society including mestizos and whites. But the work of several scholars shows that pattern of its use has changed over time, even in indigenous contexts. Peter Gow (2015) hypothesised that extensive use of ayahuasca by indigenous Amazonian communities is actually relatively recent and corresponds with responses to the rubber boom of the late 1800s. Pantoja (2014) wrote about a new form of ethnic self-identification, which includes the use of ayahuasca, among a group who were previously known as mestizo rubber tappers.

In the period of early colonial incursion, in the 1600s while the Spanish were extracting gold from rivers, shamanism grew as a form of resistance from intrusion by the Franciscan friars. During that time, friars tried to convert the people and force them to work for them. Michael Taussig, who wrote about the role of terror in subjugating the people of the Amazon, told how the Catholic Church in the Putumayo region justified the use of force and imprisonment against the people to get them to comply. This ties in with the friars' belief that the indigenous people had been conquered by the devil, who lived within them and manifested through sorcery and idolatry (Taussig 1987: 143). During that time, shamans became instrumental in leading revolts. Missionaries reported that the shamans were the main obs-tacle to converting the locals, and that they were responsible for inspiring rebellions against the Spanish. Eventually, the Franciscans left at the end of the 1700s. After that, there was about a century with little white presence in the Putumayo region. Oral histories continue to tell stories of this resistance, however. Langdon documented some of these narratives, indicating 'how shamanic practices based on *yajé* became the primary mode of resistance to external control' (Langdon 2016: 185).

The next phase of extraction was first quinine and rubber at the end of the 1800s, and then oil in the mid-1900s. The Capuchin friars were given authority over the Putumayo region of the Amazon basin in 1900, ushering in the downward trajectory for shamanic control and the overall demise of indigenous peoples. Factors contributing to the complete breakdown of the role of the shaman and their use of *yajé* included the introduction of cash crops, missionary activities that included forced education of children in mission schools (Capuchin missionaries forced children to go to boarding school among other things), loss of territory, epidemics that took many lives, the discovery of oil and building of roads in the 1950s, and Western ways of being (food, dress, language) brought to the area by outsiders moving in who discriminated against and marginalised them. Langdon explained that the last Siona shaman of that period of decline died in the early 1960s, and no one locally felt competent to replace him: *Yajé* experiences can bring 'bad visions' and be frightening, which deterred some. Throughout the 1970s, after the death of the last shaman, the Siona were still taking *yajé* but with shamans from neighbouring Amazonian groups. Despite this, they still held to their core cosmology about relationships between the spirit world, nature and humans. Revitalisation began slowly the emergence of new Siona sha-manic leaders in the late 1970s but did not really take shape until the 1990s, when larger shamanic networks and centres (called *molacas*) had been established locally and in urban centres, and a global network of shamanic practice came to be recognised.

Langdon reported that in her observations, in the new shamanistic networks that the Siona participate in, there were no longer references to sorcery, nor did shamans, known as *taitas*, transform into animals during their rituals. There has been some homogenisation of a generic Amazonian shamanism and syncretic inclusion of Christian elements, 'including prayers, blessings, music' (Langdon 2016: 198). Langdon emphasises, however, that the case of the Siona experience with the revitalisation of the use of *yajé* presented here must be seen as a 'strategy of survival that has emerged from their autochthonous shamanic practices and knowledge, and not one that is merely an appropriation of external forms and demands' (Langdon 2016: 199). The Siona no longer survive through their traditional subsist-ence strategies but are dependent for their living on their participation in the global capitalist economy. *Yajé* performances are an important way for them to express 'identity in a post-colonial violent setting' (Langdon 2016: 198).

Synthetic Hallucinogens

In addition to occurring naturally in plants, scientists have been replicating the chemical structures of hallucinogens in laboratories since the early twentieth century. LSD is the first to have been synthesised, in 1938, by Albert Hofmann, a chemist working for a research laboratory in Switzerland, when he was developing drugs to combat circulatory and respiratory ailments. Psychiatrists became interested in it because its psychological effects mimicked psychosis and schizophrenia. It was also used to treat such ailments as depression and anxiety. At one point in the 1940s and 1950s, the secretive US Central Intelligence Agency investigated its potential, especially as a truth serum (Waters 2021: S103). Other synthetic compounds with psychedelic effects (even if not all are classic psychedelics) include psilocybin, MDMA (known by multiple street names including 'ecstasy' and 'molly'), PCP and ketamine.

It is important to remember that the effects of hallucinogens are as much cultural as pharmacological. In each context of use, there are individual expectations and cultural models that shape one's experience and that pattern experiences among people with similar cultural frameworks. Recall the terms *drug* (chemical structure), *set* (individual orientation) and *setting* (sociocultural framework) that guide us in interpreting a drug's effects. Also recall the 'new materialism' perspective that coaxes us to recognise the potency of all three facets.

Psychedelics and Social Movements

Counterculture and New Age Contexts

Public enthusiasm for hallucinogens grew markedly in the 1950s and 1960s, influenced by writers like Aldous Huxley in his book *The Doors of Perception* (1954) and the wider counterculture of the time. Mescaline was the first drug to hit the psychedelic scene, and several names are important in tracing its place in Western popular culture. As described in Mike Jay's (2019) *Mescaline: a global history of the first psychedelic*, mescaline first caught the attention of scientists because of its use in Native American communities. Pharmacologists isolated its active compound in 1897 and synthesised it in a laboratory in 1919. While mescaline brought the West to awareness of psychedelics, it was LSD that led in popular consumption by the 1960s, in large part because of its increased potency. Several people were prominent in bringing LSD to popular awareness, including Timothy Leary, who was fired from Harvard University for violating ethical principles in his clinical studies of psychedelics (including giving them to undergraduate students). After he left Harvard, Leary became a vocal proponent of psychedelics for spiritual discovery and mind expansion. He was associated with such phrases as: 'Turn on, tune in, drop out'. Ken Kesey also popularised the use of LSD in a well-publicised cross-country bus ride. These adventures were the focus of Tom Wolfe's novel, *The Electric Kool-Aid Acid Test* (1968)

The use of psychedelics in countercultures was not restricted to Western countries. There were cultural similarities, including music, protests against the status quo and the use of hallucinogens, in counterculture movements in many parts of the world, including eastern Europe (Soviet Union [Czechoslovakia, Russia]) and Latin America (Mexico, Chile, Argentina). Barr-Melej (2017) wrote about counterculture in Chile that was both distinct from and linked to that in the US in its embracing of the use of cannabis and LSD. Just as US counterculture was rooted in post-WWII anxiety and protests against the war in Vietnam, '*hippismo*' existed in Allende's Chile within its own political and class struggles.

Anthropology Meets Counterculture: Carlos Castaneda

Along similar lines as Aldous Huxley's *The Doors of Perception*, Carlos Castaneda's writings about Don Juan have inspired those interested in psychedelic experiences for decades. Carlos Castaneda was a doctoral student in anthropology at UCLA in the 1960s. He wrote his first book, *The Teachings of Don Juan: A Yaqui Way of Knowledge* (1968), supposedly based on an apprenticeship with Don Juan, a shaman originally from the Sonoran Desert, Mexico, who was living in Arizona during the time Castaneda knew him. With Don Juan, Castaneda experienced the hallucinogenic effects of Datura (Jimson Weed), peyote and psilocybe mushrooms. The book was originally his PhD thesis and included an anthropological structural analysis in the last part. The book soon became a bestseller. He went on to publish nine more books based on his meetings with Don Juan, making many millions of dollars. Castaneda became one of the world's most famous anthropologists and a prominent influencer in the consumption of hallucinogens. He even appeared on the cover of *Time* Magazine in 1973.

But despite lavish praise by some, doubt was cast early on about the rigour of Castaneda's contributions to ethnography and later to the existence of even Don Juan himself. Indeed, his works were accused of being a hoax and works of fiction, not reports of actual encounters with real people. Early criticism came from anthropologist Edward H. Spicer (1969), who had spent his career studying Yaqui indigenous culture. While Spicer gave him high marks for describing his personal experiences, he rejected any suggestion that Castaneda contributed to Yaqui ethnography. Weston La Barre, who had written the *Peyote Cult* in 1938 about the use of Peyote in central Mexico, gave Castaneda's second book an even more scathing review. He agreed with Spicer that it bore no relation to Yaqui ethnography and added that it contributed nothing to ethnographic knowledge of the use of peyote. He panned it as narcissistic generic mysticism (Noel 1976: 41). Despite the criticisms, Castaneda's books have remained popular and have continued to sell well.

Anthropologists have tended to consider his work as a breach of professional ethics both for the falsity of his ethnographic descriptions and because of the harm he brought to the indigenous people in Mexico, as drug-adventure seekers, looking to replicate Castaneda's experiences, brought disruption first to the Yaqui, before realising that they do not take peyote, and then the Huichol, who do use peyote (Fikes 1993). Ethical issues aside, we can note that anthropologists contributed to popular interest in psychedelics and mysticism in the 1970s and beyond. Anthropology stepped in in response to disillusioned Westerners looking to indigenous society for alternative ways of living, especially those linked to altered states.

Globalisation and Change: New Religious Contexts

Religious change accompanies political and economic upheaval. In his opus, *The Ghost Dance*, Weston La Barre (1970) chronicles revitalisation religious movements globally, led by prophets with ideologies that promise the dawning of a new day when sickness and troubles would be dispelled. These movements include the Ghost Dance, which is the precursor to the Native American Church. Sometimes, syncretic religious movements arise that blend more than one religious or spiritual tradition. Psychedelics have been incorporated into some of these.

Native American Church

Similar to iboga in the Bwiti religion of the Fang people of Gabon in Africa (see earlier), use of peyote for the Native American Church is not an age-old tradition, but one with a dynamic history of use in different contexts. La Barre noted the diversity within the branches of the Native American Church. Although there were forerunners of the church in the late 1800s and early 1900s, it was first incorporated in 1914 as the First-born Church of Christ, revealing its syncretic nature, and in 1918, it incorporated as the Native American Church, which underscored the pan-tribal nature of it. An important motive to incorporate the church was to secure legal permission to use peyote despite criticisms coming from legislatures, religions groups and certain people within the Native American community at the time (La Barre 1970: 167). La Barre explained that they sought a blend with Christianity 'to use the White man's weapons in their own defense' (La Barre 167).

Weston La Barre and other anthropologists defended the use of peyote by the Native American Church when the Church faced prosecution for use of peyote in the 1960s (see Chapter 1). Despite his support for the ritual use of peyote by Native Americans, he was more critical in his views of avowedly religious use of peyote by Anglo Americans of the 'Neo-American Church' formed in the 1960s as part of the psychedelic movement. La Barre's reaction to their use of hallucinogens demonstrates how anthropologists of that era saw a difference between 'authentic' indigenous use and inauthentic use by others, revealing suspicion by such ethnographers of non-indigenous drug culture (see later for a discussion of authenticity).

Santo Daime

In the case of ayahuasca, we see the global spread with the Santo Daime and similar churches, now with branches around the world (Labate and Cavnar 2014). Santo Daime developed in the outskirts of Rio Branco, a frontier town surround by forest and the capital of the Acre state at the southwest corner of the Brazilian Amazon. The Santo Daime church was first developed in the 1920s by a migrant to Amazonia of African descent (Raimundo Irineu Serra) who took part in local indigenous ayahuasca ceremonies while stationed as a border guard. He had a vision of a female figure who gave him instructions for healing, a new religious doctrine that combined Christian with other spiritual elements and a set of new rituals that included ayahuasca as a sacrament (MacRae 2004). During one ritual, Irineu had a vision that instructed him to form the Santo Daime path.

Some of the first Daime followers were rubber tappers who moved to cities after the rubber boom collapsed, finding themselves marginalised within these urban environments (MacRae 2004). The movement grew, and by the 1980s, Daime communities were formed in many major Brazilian cities and included not only marginalised poor people but also middle-class adherents. Alex Polari de Alverga, a Daime leader, expressed the need for new paths in order to meet the new era. As one of these paths, 'Santo Daime combines the inheritance of the Christian esoteric tradition with the spiritual legacy and indigenous force of the pre-Colombian people' (Polari de Alverga 1999: 2–3).

Edward MacRae (2004) argued that Santo Daime and other new ayahuasca religions have been important aids to social integration amid upheaval. While it originally helped poor migrants adapt to urban environments, in Brazil it now speaks to people facing rapid changes in economic and family structures. This highly structured path has also helped people overcome alcohol and other drug addictions. Santo Daime has spread globally and it has become an established practice in some European countries. Because of the tightly organised and regulated set of practices, MacRae (2004) argued that it is a 'non-drug' in the sense that it is purposeful, ritualised consumption, where access to the substance is controlled.

Drug Tourism and Recreational Contexts

Westerners in search of drug adventures began following highly publicised accounts, such as that by Wasson in *Life* magazine (1957) and other magazines and by Castaneda's books. The effects of this tourism were sometimes devastating. Stephen Siff (2018) tells of the effects on the healer, María Sabina, who conducted the rituals Wasson participated in that led to the story in *Life* magazine. Sabina suffered backlash from other villagers for bringing commercial exploitation to the area. Her home was burned and she was briefly jailed. In 1970, she was reported to be living in poverty.

Castaneda was similarly accused of bringing harm to the people claimed to be representing. The anthropologist Jay Courtney Fikes and others accused him of making it harder for indigenous people to use peyote both because of the over-exploitation of the cactus and disrupting their lives because of the pressure the drug-adventure seekers put on local people. Furthermore, on a political level, because of his depiction of them as spiritual and mystical people, Castaneda is accused of oversimplifying them in a way that detracts from the hardships they have experienced as indigenous people. A review of the one of his books by Paul Boyer (1994), the editor of *Tribal College: Journal of American Indian Higher Education*, shared these concerns about the depiction of indigenous peoples. Boyer warned of people falling prey to 'plastic shaman' who 'make a mockery of sacred ceremonies and perpetuate simplistic images of the mystical native'.

The international search for hallucinogenic experiences continues. Westerners have been going to South America for guided shamanic experiences, and ayahuasca rituals have spread globally. The Brazilian anthropologist Beatriz Labate (2014) writes about the internationalisation of what she calls Peruvian '*vegetalismo*', which refers to a wide variety of ayahuasca practices, including the blurry categories of mestizo, gringo and indigenous practices. Labate identifies the 'psychologization' of ayahuasca, in international contexts, meaning that the taker's intent is often centred on increasing self-knowledge. This contrasts with the focus in many indigenous contexts on social relationships, including even ones that include negative intents (i.e. so-called 'witchcraft' or 'sorcery') as well as rites of passage (Dobkin de Rios 1993). Labate and Cavnar (2014) juxtapose this psychologisation (a move towards Western interpretations) with a simultaneous 're-traditionalisation', or even 'hyper-traditionalisation', as some foreign converts and experimenters cling to the myth of ayahuasca rituals as ancient and unchanged even while pursing Western psychological experiences.

This lends itself to the fraught concept of 'authenticity' (as we saw earlier in La Barre's reaction to 'neo-American Church'), leading critics to condemn some practices as more 'authentic' than others and some practitioners as 'pseudo-shamans' or hoaxers. What Labate and her co-authors emphasise, however, is that appropriation of cultural traditions goes both ways. They use the term 'transculturation' to refer to 'a concept that emphasizes the often-ignored impact of the peripheral culture on the one that assumes dominance' (Labate and Cavnar 2014: 5). In the case of internationalised ayahuasca ceremonies, we find practitioners who have incorporated not only Christianity into their practice (like with the Santo Daime) but also elements of New Age, Eastern spiritual practices and a generic transnational shamanism into their mix (Labate and Cavnar 2014: 188).

Ayahuasca tourism has been heavily criticised for multiple reasons, including that it commoditises traditional culture, that it exacerbates inequalities among native peoples and that it exploits tourists when opportunistic 'shamans' take advantage of people economically and sexually. Finally, there are concerns that inadequate supervision threatens the consumers' mental and physical health (Dobkin de Rios 1993). Fotiou (2014) cites a gender-based criticism of ayahuasca shamanism as sexist and male-dominated, since most of the shamans are males. On the other side, it is common to see the ayahuasca vine as embodying feminine energy and there are some movements honouring female shamanism and the 'divine feminine' (see also Hewitt 2019 on 'psychedelic feminism').

In addition to intentionally seeking transcendent experiences, many people take hallucinogens in recreational contexts and for self-actualisation. Fotiou (2014) differentiates shamanic tourism from drug tourism, since some tourists seek drug experiences simply for recreational purposes. One recreational context is at raves and parties. In the tourism context, some, whom d'Andrea (2007) has described as 'global nomads', travel around the world to such places as San Pedro La Laguna on Lake Atitlán (Gezon 2017) (Goa [India]), and Ibiza (Spain) (d'Andrea 2007), often to participate in electronic dance music raves while on psychedelics. The line between spiritual seeking and pleasure seeking is blurry; however, since some who simply seek a good time end up having spiritual experiences.

In another study, Briggs and Turner (2011) have written about the motivations of British youth in traveling to the holiday destination of Ibiza, which is known for its '"wild" party scene and easy access to illegal substances' (Briggs and Turner 2011: 81). Written from a criminology perspective, the authors found that motivations include the creation of memorable experiences in a place where their identities are anonymous, and it feels like there are few constraints on acceptable behaviour. These youth are engaged in identity formation in an environment where the behaviour is risky to their health but in a highly scripted environment, where such behaviour is 'expected and typical' (Briggs and Turner 2011: 88). Outside the context of tourism, there has been little written about Westerners taking psychedelics recreationally and for self-actualisation from an anthropological perspective, perhaps reflecting how recreation is not taken as seriously in scholarship as weighty themes such as 'ritual'. Indeed, 'fun', as experienced in culturally constructed social contexts, has been neglected in studies of drug consumption, perhaps mistakenly.

Drug Studies and Psychedelic Psychotherapy

There is growing evidence that psychedelics can help in depression and other mental health conditions in Western clinical settings. Indeed, there are clinical trials testing the effectiveness of several psychedelics ongoing in several countries. Such usage of psychedelics may differ in various ways from shamanic use, but it appears to have similar healing potential in both settings. This is due in part to the properties of the substances, and in part to the healthcare setting that frames expectations. Scientific study of hallucinogenic effects and the use of psychedelics in psychotherapy have been of interest since the early 1900s, when Western scientists were first identifying and synthesising hallucinogenic compounds. Research on the therapeutic uses of psychedelics stopped by 1971 in the US, because the substances were outlawed by the Controlled Substances Act. The next studies to be approved for research into the potential therapeutic use of psilocybin in the US were in 2003.

In addition to clinical trials, there is growing tendency for people to self-administer LSD and other hallucinogens in what is called microdosing. James Fadiman (2011), a psychologist who studied with Richard Alpert (Ram Dass) as an undergraduate at Harvard, introduced the term 'microdose' to the public in 2011 in his book *The Psychedelic Explorer's Guide: Safe, Therapeutic, and Sacred Journeys*. Microdosing has been defined as 'the ingestion of sub-perceptual dosages of "classical psychedelics" every few days for an extended period of time to improve cognitive and affective processes' (Hupli et al. 2019: 130). Some people microdose to self-treat anxiety and other obstacles to mental health. One study of microdosing had insignificant results: there were no significant improvements in cognition and unclear results regarding mood (Yanakieva et al. 2019). On the other hand, a study of subjective reports of LSD microdosing revealed positive effects on mood, anxiety reduction and an increased feeling of success (Bershad et al. 2019).

As for the cultural context, it is valuable to recognise that therapeutic psychedelic research is a historically situated cultural phenomenon. From the promise of the drugs in the 1950s and earlier, when the compounds were first being discovered by Western scientists, to the fear of psychotropic drugs in the late 1960s (encouraged in part by reactions against the counterculture tied up with fear of rebellion and part in the political economic spirit of pharmaceutical control), to the current fascination of the potential for these substances to heal many kinds of mental and physical suffering, there are cultural assemblages that shape discourses and (potential) outcomes. Symbolic distinctions are important in distinguishing 'safe' versus 'dangerous', legal versus illegal, recreation versus therapy, pharmaceutical versus drug. For example, Hendy (2019) found that pharmaceutical scientists intentionally chose to refer to a substance as MDMA instead of the more culturally charged but more common term, 'ecstasy'. They did that in order to underscore its safety and eligibility to move out of Schedule I drugs, defined as ones that are prone to abuse with no therapeutic application.

Studies of cultural contexts also trace the formalisation and sometimes institutionalisation of new cultural assemblages as drug use patterns change and become culturally engrained. Several studies investigate the emergence of cultural assemblages consisting of new knowledge, moral codes and practical wisdom about how to use drugs safely and ethically. Boothroyd and Lewis (2016), in exploring techniques of harm reduction (see Chapter 5), point out that regimes of knowledge about drug use emerge from within user groups, and the online world is important here. Barratt et al. (2014) explored how, despite dominant discourses condemning drug use, online forums generate alternative moral conceptions – ones that resist seeing drug use as pathological and instead acknowledge the possibility of drug use being pleasurable and a rational and informed choice for some. They describe the internet as 'a technology of resistance' (ibid. 988) in reconceptualising the moral space of substance use.

As for understanding potential efficacy of psychedelics in therapeutic settings, medical anthropologists have underscored the importance of the total healthcare system for understanding how healing works. This system includes beliefs (cognitive aspect), emotions and experiences (phenomenological), practices (including rituals), practitioners and other parts of a social network. Together, these are components in cultures of drug consumption, ripe with social connections and cultural meanings. Studies of placebos show that it is the total context of healing that is important to a health outcome (Moerman 2002, Miller and Kaptchuk 2008). Healthcare systems help to establish the *set* and *setting* in which the drug is used for therapy. Fotiou (2020), in writing about ayahuasca tourism in Peru, identifies ritual elements of effectiveness for the Western tourists who attend. It is a syncretic form of ayahuasca shamanism where 'local shamanic practices converge with western ideas of spirituality and healing and create a highly dynamic practice' (Fotiou 2020: 224). This is accomplished through a ritual framing that includes Western narratives of selfhood, mind/body relationships and the Western psychotherapeutic narrative of the importance of emotional release and self-love – tropes familiar to Westerners that prepare participants for personal transformation. Ritual, both secular and religious, is an important way to reinforce all aspects of the healthcare system, from belief to experience.

The formalisation and ritualisation of cultural practices provides an opportunity to examine how they intersect with social determinants of health (SDH): are there categories of people who are negatively impacted by these cultural practices? Are there some who have greater access to these than others? How and why, if so? The following questions are important too: how accessible are these practices? Do the practices maximise well-being of some while putting others at risk? Barratt et al. (2014) identify dangers of framing well-being, or harm to it, as existing within a neoliberal discourse touting individual responsibility, or, we could add, individual pursuit of opportunity. Assuming that people are capable of making decisions fails 'to adequately acknowledge the constraints of the socio-cultural context within which they are embedded' (Barratt et al. 2014: 993). For example, Fotiou (2014) identified criticisms of certain practices of ayahuasca shamanism as sexist and potentially harmful to women. As the use of hallucinogens for psychotherapy, their illegal status puts everyone involved at risk, and some more than others due to various kinds of profiling. Legal forms that exist are often costly and hard to access for common people. This attention to social and structural factors echoes Singer et al.'s (2019) emphasis on a Critical Health/ Medical Anthropology approach that recognises structural barriers to health, which include such factors as poverty, racism and sexism. Indeed, attention to SDH has become central to public health measures globally.

In sum, anthropologists have a large role to play in contributing to ongoing studies of psychedelics in medical, legal and cultural contexts.

Anthropology and Psychedelics

Hallucinogens are the kinds of drugs most associated with anthropology. Anthropologists have also been influential in encouraging their use by Westerners, sometimes knowingly and other times not. In so doing, they have contributed to broad and pervasive social movements that shape our world today. Their indigenous use is often portrayed as timeless, but anthropologists now emphasise their historicity and the politics of their use.

As anthropologists, we engage with discourses of new materialism to ask whether the substances themselves have power, and what the role is of cultural constructions of experiences of active chemical substances. Marlene Dobkin de Rios (1939–2012), one of the first anthropologists to write extensively about hallucinogens (ayahuasca and the San Pedro cactus for healing in an urban slum in Peru), noted that hallucinogens often are found within spiritual traditions for common reasons: 'because of their perceived ability to access spiritual realms' (p. 2). She goes on to note the interaction of chemicals with the mind: 'That is to say, if we change our body chemistry, we can ascertain realms of being that are not ordinarily available to most human beings' (p. 2). That same chemical power of altered perception, however, is interpreted differently in a cultural context that does not recognise spirit realms, as in much of Western science. There, the explanation for hallucinogenic effects has traditionally been about 'faulty wiring', where, Dobkin de Rios argues, the plant chemicals deceive and trick (recall the definition of 'hallucinate'). In a Euro-American rational world, there is no spirit realm to access, so we are merely left with 'tricks of the mind'. Dobkin de Rios leads us to consider that chemicals have power, but that power is defined and interpreted within historical and cultural contexts.

Chapter 5 considers psychoactive substances in contexts where they are part of people's everyday lives, to the extent that people sometimes forget that they even have drug effects: these substances include tobacco, tea, coffee – and even sugar. These substances are often stimulants, helping fuel people's wakefulness and productivity. As you transition to Chapter 5, think about how and why some substances are presented as more 'normal' or 'dangerous' than others.

Note

1 Definitions from the Oxford Learners Dictionaries online, available here: (www. oxfordlearnersdictionaries.com/us/definition/english/hallucinate (accessed November 2022).

Works Cited

Alderete, Ethel, Pamela I. Erickson, Celia P. Kaplan, and Eliseo J. Pérez-Stable. 2010. "Ceremonial Tobacco Use in the Andes: Implications for Smoking Prevention Among Indigenous Youth." *Anthropology & Medicine* 17 (1): 27–39.

Barratt, Monica J., Allen, Matthew, and Lenton, Simon. 2014. "PMA Sounds Fun": Negotiating Drug Discourses Online. *Substance Use & Misuse* 49 (8): 987–998.

Bershad, Anya K., Scott T. Schepers, Michael P. Bremmer, Royce Lee, and Harriet de Wit. 2019. "Acute Subjective and Behavioral Effects of Microdoses of Lysergic Acid Diethylamide in Healthy Human Volunteers." *Biological Psychiatry* 86 (10): 792–800.

Boothroyd, Dave, and Sarah Lewis. 2016. "Online Drug Scenes and Harm Reduction from Below as Phronesis." *Contemporary Drug Problems* 43 (3): 293–308.

Boyer, L. Bryce, Ruth MacDonald Boyer, and Harry W. Basehart. 1973. "Shamanism and Peyote Use among the Apaches of the Mescalero Indian Reservation." In *Hallucinogens and Shamanism*, edited by Michael J. Harner 53–66. London, Oxford, New York, NY: Oxford University Press.

Boyer, Paul. 1994. "Carlos Castaneda, Academic Opportunism and the Psychedelic Sixties." *Tribal College: Journal of American Indian Higher Education* 5 (4). https://tribalcollegejournal.org/carlos-castaneda-academic-opportunism-psychedelic-sixties/

Briggs, Daniel, and Tim Turner. 2011. "Risk, Transgression and Substance Use: An Ethnography of Young British Tourists in Ibiza." *Studies of Transition States and Societies* 3 (2): 14–25.

Brown, Michael. 2001. Dark Side of the Shaman. In *Shamans Through Time: 500 Years on the Path to Knowledge*, edited by Jeremy Narby and Francis Huxley, 251–256. New York: Tarcher.

Carneiro, Henrique S. 2022. Plant Drugs and Shamanism in the Americas. In *The Oxford Handbook of Global Drug History*, edited by Paul Gootenberg, 56–72. Oxford University Press.

Castaneda, Carlos. 1968. *The Teachings of Don Juan: A Yaqui Way of Knowledge*. Oakland, CA: University of California Press.

D'Andrea, Anthony. 2007. *Global Nomads: Techno and New Age as Transnational Countercultures in Ibiza and Goa*. New York, NY: Routledge.

Daley, Christine Makosky, Aimee S. James, Randall S. Barnoskie, Marcia Segraves, Ryan Schupbach, and Won S. Choi. 2006. "Tobacco Has a Purpose, Not Just a Past: Feasibility of Developing a Culturally Appropriate Smoking Cessation Program for a Pan-Tribal Native Population." *Medical Anthropology Quarterly* 20 (4): 421–440.

Davis, Wade. 1985. *The Serpent and the Rainbow*. New York: Simon and Schuster.

———. 1996. *One River: Explorations and Discoveries in the Amazon Rain Forest*. New York, NY: Simon & Schuster.

de Alverga, Alex Polari. 1999. *Forest of Visions: Ayahuasca, Amazonian Spirituality, and the Santo Daime Tradition*. South Paris, ME: Park Street Press.

Dobkin de Rios, Marlene. 1993. "Twenty-Five Years of Hallucinogenic Studies in Cross-Cultural Perspective." *Anthropology of Consciousness* 4 (1): 1–8.

Fadiman, James. 2011. *The Psychedelic Explorer's Guide: Safe, Therapeutic, and Sacred Journeys*. South Paris, ME: Park Street Press.

Fernandez, James W. 2019. *Bwiti: An Ethnography of the Religious Imagination in Africa*. Princeton: Princeton University Press.

Fernandez, James W., and Renate L. Fernandez. 2001. "Chapter 13 'Returning to the Path': The Use of Iboga[ine] in an Equatorial African Ritual Context and the Binding of Time, Space, and Social Relationships." *The Alkaloids* 56: 235–247.

Fikes, Jay C. 1993. *Carlos Castaneda, Academic Opportunism and the Psychedelic Sixties*. Victoria (Canada): Millennia Press.

Fotiou, Evgenia. 2014. On the Uneasiness of Tourism: Considerations on Shamanic Tourism in Western Amazonia. In *Ayahuasca Shamanism in the Amazon and Beyond*, edited by Beatriz Labate and Clancy Cavnar, 159–181. Oxford University Press.

———. 2020. "The Importance of Ritual Discourse in Framing Ayahuasca Experiences in the Context of Shamanic Tourism." *Anthropology of Consciousness* 31 (2): 223–244.

Froese, Tom, Gaston Guzman, and Laura Guzman-Davalos. 2016. "On the Origin of the Genus Psilocybe and Its Potential Ritual Use in Ancient Africa and Europe." *Economic Botany* 70 (2): 103–114.

Furst, Peter T. 1976. *Hallucinogens and Culture*. Novato, CA: Chandler & Sharp.

Gezon, Lisa L. 2017. "Global Scouts: Youth Engagement with Spirituality and Wellness Through Travel, Lake Atitlán, Guatemala." *Journal of Tourism & Cultural Change* 16 (4): 365–378.

Gow, Peter. 2015. "Methods of Tobacco Use among Two Arawakan-Speaking Peoples in Southwestern Amazonia: A Case Study of Structural Diffusion." In *The Master Plant*. New York: Routledge.

Guerra-Doce, Elisa. 2015. "Psychoactive Substances in Prehistoric Times: Examining the Archaeological Evidence." *Time & Mind: The Journal of Archaeology, Consciousness & Culture* 8 (1): 91–112.

Harner, Michael J. 1973. *Hallucinogens and Shamanism*. Oxford: Oxford University Press.

Hendy, Katherine. 2019. "MDMA Is Not Ecstasy: The Production of Pharmaceutical Safety through Documents in Clinical Trials." *Medical Anthropology Quarterly* 35 (1): 5–24.

Hewitt, Kim. 2019. "Psychedelic Feminism: A Radical Interpretation of Psychedelic Consciousness?" *Journal for the Study of Radicalism* 13 (1): 75–120.

Hupli, Aleksi, Moritz Berning, Ahnjili Zhuparris, and James Fadiman. 2019. "Descriptive Assemblage of Psychedelic Microdosing: Netnographic Study of Youtube™ Videos and On-going Research Projects." *Performance Enhancement & Health* 6 (3–4): 129–138.

Huxley, Aldous. 1954. *The Doors of Perception*. New York: Harper & Row.

Jay, Mike. 2019. *Mescaline: A Global History of the First Psychedelic*. New Haven, NJ: Yale University Press.

Kohn, Eduardo. 2007. "How Dogs Dream: Amazonian Natures and the Politics of Transspecies Engagement." *American Ethnologist* 34 (1): 3–24.

La Barre, Weston. 1970. *The Ghost Dance: Origins of Religion*. New York: Doubleday.

Labate, Beatriz. 2014. The Internationalization of Peruvian Vegetalismo. In *Ayahuasca Shamanism in the Amazon and Beyond*, edited by Beatriz Labate and Clancy Cavnar, 182–205. Oxford University Press.

Labate, Beatriz Caiuby, and Clancy Cavnar. 2014. *Ayahuasca Shamanism in the Amazon and Beyond*. Oxford: Oxford University Press.

Langdon, Esther Jean. 2016. "The Revitalization of Yajé Shamanism among the Siona: Strategies of Survival in Historical Context." *Anthropology of Consciousness* 27 (2): 180–203.

MacRae, Edward. 2004. "The Ritual Use of Ayahuasca by Three Brazilian Religions." In *Drug Use and Cultural Context 'Beyond the West': Tradition, Change and Post-Colonialism*, edited by Ross Coomber and Nigel South, 27–45. London: Free Association Press.

McKenna, Terence K. 1992. *Food of the Gods: The Search for the Original Tree of Knowledge: A Radical History of Plants, Drugs, and Human Evolution*. New York: Bantam Books.

Miller, Franklin G., and Ted J. Kaptchuk. 2008. "The Power of Context: Reconceptualizing the Placebo Effect." *Journal of the Royal Society of Medicine* 101: 222–225.

Moerman, Daniel E. 2002. *Meaning, Medicine and the 'Placebo Effect' (Cambridge Studies in Medical Anthropology, Series Number 9)*. Cambridge: Cambridge University Press.

Morales-García, Jose A., Mario de la Fuente Revenga, Sandra Alonso-Gil, María Isabel Rodríguez-Franco, Amanda Feilding, Ana Perez-Castillo, and Jordi Riba. 2017. "The Alkaloids of Banisteriopsis Caapi, the Plant Source of the Amazonian Hallucinogen Ayahuasca, Stimulate Adult Neurogenesis in Vitro." *Scientific Reports* 7 (1): 1–13.

Myerhoff, Barbara G. 1974. *Peyote Hunt: The Sacred Journey of the Huichol Indians*. Ithaca: Cornell University Press.

Narby, Jeremy, and Francis Huxley. 2001. *Shamans Through Time: 500 Years on the Path to Knowledge*. New York: Tarcher.

Nichols, David E. Charles D. Nichols, and Peter S. Hendricks. 2023. Proposed Consensus Statement on Defining Psychedelic Drugs. *Psychedelic Medicine* 1 (1): 1–2.

Noel, Daniel C. 1976. *Seeing Castenada: Reactions to the 'Don Juan' Writings of Carlos Castaneda*. New York, NY: Putnam.

Osmond, Humphry. 1957. "A Review of the Clinical Effects of Psychotomimetic Agents." *Annals of the New York Academy of Sciences* 66 (3): 418–434.

Pantoja, Mariana Ciavatta. 2014. "Kuntanawa: Ayahuasca, Ethnicity, and Culture." In *Ayahuasca Shamanism in the Amazon and Beyond*, edited by Beatriz Labate, 40–58. Oxford: Oxford University Press.

Patrick, Barr-Melej. 2017. *Psychedelic Chile: Youth, Counterculture, and Politics on the Road to Socialism and Dictatorship*. Chapel Hill, NC: The University of North Carolina Press.

Plotkin, Mark J. 1993. *Tales of a Shaman's Apprentice: An Ethnobotanist Searches for New Medicines in the Amazon Rain Forest*. New York, NY: Viking.

Reichel-Dolmatoff, Gerardo. 1975. *The Shaman and the Jaguar: A Study of Narcotic Drugs among the Indians of Colombia*. Philadelphia: Temple University Press.

Siff, Stephen. 2018. "R. Gordon Wasson and the Publicity Campaign to Introduce Magic Mushrooms to Mid-Century America." *Revue Francaise d'Etudes Americaines* 156 (3): 91–104.

Singer, Merrill, Hans Baer, Debbi Long, and Alex Pavloski. 2019. *Introducing Medical Anthropology: A Discipline in Action* (3rd ed.) Washington D.C.; Washington D.C.: Rowman and Littlefield.

Spicer, Edward H. 1969. "Review: The Teaching of Don Juan: A Yaqui Way of Knowledge." *American Anthropologist* 71 (2): 320–322.

Taussig, Michael T. 1987. *Shamanism, Colonialism, and the Wild Man: A Study in Terror and Healing*. Chicago: University of Chicago Press.

Thomas, Benjamin, 2002. '"Mushroom Madness" in the Papua New Guinea Highlands: A Case of Nicotine Poisoning?'. *Journal of Psychoactive Drugs*, 34 (3): 321–323.

Vitebsky, Piers. 2001. *Shamanism*. Norman, OK: University of Oklahoma Press.

von Gernet, Alexander. 2007. "Nicotian Dreams: The Prehistory and Early History of Tobacco in Eastern North America." In *Consuming Habits*, 64–85. London: Routledge.

Wasson, Robert Gordon. 1957. "Seeking the Magic Mushroom." *Life* 49 (19): 100–102, 109–120.

Waters, Kristin. 2021. "Pharmacologic Similarities and Differences among Hallucinogens." *Journal of Clinical Pharmacology* 61: 100–113.

Wilbert, Johannes. 1980. "Magico-Religious Use of Tobacco Among South American Indians." In *Spirits, Shamans, and Stars: Perspectives from South America*, edited by David L. Browman and Ronald A. Schwarz, 13–38. The Hague (Netherlands): De Gruyter Mouton.

Wolfe, Tom. 1968. *The Electric Kool-Aid Acid Test*. New York: Bantam Books.

Yanakieva, Steliana, Naya Polychroni, Neiloufar Family, Luke T. J. Williams, David P. Luke, and Devin B. Terhune. 2019. "The Effects of Microdose LSD on Time Perception: A Randomised, Double-Blind, Placebo-Controlled Trial." *Psychopharmacology* 236 (4): 1159–1170.

5 Stimulating Sociality

While the previous chapter explored types of drugs and patterns of use associated with altered states of consciousness and the extraordinary, this chapter turns to substances used more for their mood-altering properties whose status as a drug sometimes goes unnoticed, and whose use can be seen as more ordinary and *everyday*. Many are legal in some or most places, including caffeine, alcohol and cannabis. Some are consumed as stimulants, that is to say, for their ability to help keep us awake, alert and focused, and others to relax and relieve stress. By focusing in this chapter on often socially acceptable, often unremarkable consumption of drugs, as well as less socially accepted use, we encourage the reader to think broadly about drugs, recognising how pervasive they are in most cultural contexts. It is important to recognise that what is deemed socially acceptable varies widely across time and space. For example, whereas the consumption of alcohol may be unremarkable in some contexts, it may be prohibited even subject to penalty of death in others. Likewise, some drugs have many different contexts and perceptions of use within given cultural contexts: tobacco, for example, may be used both ceremonially and as an everyday practice of consumption by the same people in different contexts (Alderete et al. 2010). We must keep in mind that chemical effects of drugs are always culturally and socially co-constructed (Hardon and Sanabria 2017).

We look first at stimulants and later at alcohol to work towards a greater understanding of the place of those substances in various cultural contexts. Meanings associated with such drugs reveal and reinforce normative versus stigmatised behaviours. They also point to gendered, ethnic/racial, socio-economic class and other distinctions between people. As we will discuss, drug use is also deeply embedded within social inequalities, often perpetuating them.

Pharmacology and Toxicology

Many everyday drugs are stimulants. Stimulants are a category of drugs that act on our nervous systems to increase wakefulness, often also reducing

DOI: 10.4324/9781003109549-5

appetite and increasing stamina, though it should be noted that all such categories are artificial and ambiguous with some substances crossing categories, as we also saw with regard to tobacco in Chapter 4. However, stimulant compounds work as they mimic naturally occurring neural compounds that regulate our moods. Dopamine has been the focus of much pharmacological research, as compounds like cathinone, cocaine and amphetamine can increase its presence in the brain (Volkow et al. 2007). Dopamine is often described as a 'feel-good' compound that stimulates the reward area of the brain when people are feeling content, when eating, during sex etc. People taking stimulants often experience increased productivity, as their pharmacological action can help the consumer feel more focused and at ease in doing tasks. While all stimulants tend to keep people awake, caffeine has an additional mechanism, which is that it blocks receptors that bind with adenosine, a neurochemical that makes people feel sleepy. Consuming too much of a stimulant can induce anxiety, nausea, loss of appetite and increased heart rate and body temperature. It can even lead to seizures and death in extreme cases.

Not all stimulants are alike, and some are more toxic than others. What is socially acceptable is not necessarily the least toxic. In fact, tobacco, the drug with the highest associated mortality rate globally, is legal for adults in most places (note that mortality associated with tobacco is not just due to nicotine, whose lethal dose is 50 times higher than the effective dose [similar to caffeine], but also because of other poisons associated with its consumption, including tar and carbon monoxide, which cause cancer, cardiovascular problems and lung disease). Alcohol, one of the most toxic drugs (Nutt et al. 2010), is legal for adults everywhere except a handful of countries where Islam is the dominant religion, alcoholic drinks being seen as *haram* (forbidden) for Muslims. On the other hand, cannabis is illegal in most countries even though it is one of the safest drugs in terms of risk of overdose. This disconnect between toxicity and cultural acceptance gives much space for anthropologists and cultural epidemiologists to enquire into and shed light on socio-cultural contexts of use and how to confront social suffering associated with substance use.

Everyday Highs: Stimulants in Context

In this section, we focus on consumption as mundane, socially acceptable occurrences. Perhaps because their use is often considered ordinary, stimulants have not been nearly so conspicuous in the anthropology of drugs as hallucinogens. Nevertheless, because they are common and often socially acceptable, stimulants are a great example of how different theoretical approaches – ones that focus on individual behaviours, social relationships, cultural systems of meaning, social and structural determinants of health and the global capitalist economy – come together to explain from multiple points of view. We might call this blending of multiple ways of understanding a 'magpie' approach, which connotes an opportunistic blend of elements that work together to explain a particular phenomenon and that rejects simplistic mono-causal explanations.

Stimulating Culture

Of course, stimulants are often used for functional or instrumental purposes, especially in a capitalist context where people are expected to demand ever-increasing productivity from their minds and bodies, something which we will return to later in this chapter. Despite their often-functional use, stimulants are as caught up in sociality and webs of cultural meanings as other substances. Depending on the context, stimulants have varied cultures of consumption, from ceremonial or ritualised consumption to therapeutic consumption to unremarkable daily consumption. All uses of drugs take on cultural meanings and mark users with particular identities. Stimulants and their sharing also reinforce social bonds formed by reciprocity. This links to classic work in anthropology on exchange and consumption of material goods and services. Indeed, the exchange of objects and services has long been a focus of socio-cultural anthropology, partly spurred by the classic work on exchange by French sociologist and anthropologist Marcel Mauss, who published *The Gift* in 1925, drawing on work such as Malinowski's on the ceremonial exchange of the Kula Ring, a circular trade route in the Melanesian islands to the east of Papua New Guinea. Mauss proposed that all services and objects that change human hands are enmeshed in webs of meaningful exchange. Each transference of an object or service creates a social bond with an obligation that is either overt (in the case of a contract, a ritual or verbal promise) or unspoken and implicit, deeply embedded in taken-for-granted social norms. Even while we consume for practical reasons (to get nutrition, sleep, etc.), we are always doing so in social relationship with other people within systems of meaning that shape our choices.

Mary Douglas and Baron Isherwood (1996 [1979]) also emphasised the social importance of material objects. They argued that material objects, which take on cultural and symbolic meanings, mediate and help us navigate social relationships – they are part of the very fabric of sociality. They wrote that 'goods are part of a live information system' (1996: xiv) and are 'coded for communication' (xxi). They reinforce distinctions between social groups, often marking rank or some other socially meaningful difference. Ideas of moral conduct permeate material codes, signalling, for example, a relationship with money (frugality) or respect. Pierre Bourdieu (1979) argued that material codes separate socioeconomic classes and that certain consumption preferences become associated with people of different statuses, of more or less refined 'taste'. Consumption norms are both *prescriptive* (focusing on what is or what is not allowed) and *normative* (what we expect people to do, whether it is considered 'right' or 'wrong' – though it is always judged and evaluated). This recalls Clifford Geertz's approach to the concept of culture, when he stated that 'man is an animal suspended in webs of significance he himself has spun, I take culture to be those webs' (Geertz 1973:5).

How do we put this in the context of drugs? There are certainly laws as well as social norms about who should and does consume what. From legal prohibition of alcohol in the US, to laws against the consumptions of certain drugs today, to religious condemnation of the use of certain substances, we see drug use socially regulated. Many Christian churches forbid drinking alcohol, and The Church of Jesus Christ of Latter-day Saints (also known as Mormonism) prohibits the drinking of coffee as well as alcohol. Coffee was the source of fierce debate and occasional prohibition in the Islamic world in the 1500s, and in Europe upon its introduction, as discussed in Chapter 3. American colonists switched from drinking tea to coffee in protest of British rule in the late 1700s. In what may be the first written law regarding drugs, the Locrian code in ancient Greece in the seventh century BC forbade people from drinking undiluted wine for non-medical reasons.

Beyond laws, we can identify many unwritten norms about who should take what substance and what it means to consume something in a particular manner, in a particular place, with particular people. Douglas (1987) wrote about the symbolic meanings – the webs of significance – of drinking. She wrote that the act of drinking marks various aspects of meaning, including the differences between work and leisure, day and night, week and weekend. Drinking highlights and brings to life cultural notions of spontaneity, (dis)order, freedom, discipline, routine, order. To drink in a particular context evokes a myriad of cultural associations. Readers will certainly be able to think of a tradition of drug consumption they are familiar with – say, drinking cultures, or cultural norms around coffee, tea or cannabis – where there are laws, norms and expectations for consumption that are often different based on gender, ethnicity, age and abilities. Sometimes those expectations lead to discrimination and exacerbate social inequalities. White people have often undergone less scrutiny for consuming drugs illegally (Lowry 2017). In the US, for example, people have associated the consumption of powder cocaine with wealthy white people, and crack cocaine (which is less expensive) with poor people and minorities. Not surprisingly, crack cocaine use is more highly stigmatised (disapproved of), and offenders have received stricter sentencing. Furthermore, people of colour have been more likely to get heavier penalties than whites for the use of crack cocaine. After the 1986 federal law, mandating minimum sentencing for crack cocaine offenses, 'the average federal drug sentence for African Americans [for crack cocaine use] was 49% higher' than for whites (Vagins and Mccurdy 2006:3).

Stimulants from Ritual to Everyday Practice

Tea drinking provides an example of ritual consumption cross-culturally. We note, for example, the incredibly intricate Japanese tea ceremony, Chanoyu, the often highly ritualised teatime of the British middle classes, and lengthy tea preparation in various parts of West Africa (Masquelier 2013). In China, where tea was domesticated about 3,000 years ago, there is a long history of tea connoisseurship associated with deeply engrained cultural practices of consuming tea. A ritual way of preparing tea, *cha dao*, is linked with and a physical manifestation of Taoist philosophies of balance and harmony and goes back centuries – far earlier than tea drinking in the West (Towler 2010). A search through the Human Relations Area Files for 'tea' and 'ceremony' reveals that tea is a part of rituals around the world, both throughout East Asia and in places where it has been introduced more recently through imperialistic global movements.

Other stimulants have also been used as items of ritual exchange, ritual symbolism or in ritual consumption. Marshall (2013) describes how tobacco and betel (prepared by combining areca palm nut, slaked lime and betel leaves) have been used in ritual exchange in marriage, initiation and death rituals throughout the Pacific. Hirsch (2007) describes how betel fits in with ritual and cosmology, in addition to everyday secular consumption, in contemporary Papua New Guinea. Khat (leaves of the khat tree or bush) has been used as part of marriage exchange for the Meru people of Kenya (Carrier 2007): in this context, a special bundle of khat called *ncoolo* is prepared that separates this more ceremonial use from more mundane khat consumption.

Drucker-Brown (1995) writes about the role of the kola nut in chiefship in northern Ghana, where the use of this powerful stimulant permeates ritual and social life in chiefly mediated marriage exchanges, chiefly distributions, divination, greetings and other contexts. She writes that chewing kola with someone signals love, trust and social equality between chewers. Kola has been compared to coffee in the Sudan, where it has been chewed for at least 1,000 years and its trade extended throughout western Africa long before European explorers arrived in the 1400s (Lovejoy 2007). Europeans appropriated kola in the late 1800s at first for its perceived medicinal purposes. Even Coca-Cola, first invented in 1886, originally contained kola nut extract and was marketed as a 'brain tonic' (Lovejoy 2007:102).

Ritual use of coca leaves in the central Andes dates back centuries. In the early 1600s, for example, the missionary Bernabe Cobo observed Inca ritual invocations that involved tossing chewed coca onto graves and shrines in exchange for safe passage while traveling (Cobo 2010). Catherine Allen (1988) explains the many ways that the contemporary Andean community she studied used coca in their rituals to connect with the land and their livelihood. She wrote that 'Coca is the major vehicle for this ritual work' (Allen 1988: 32). She wrote that the line between ordinary, everyday behaviour and sacred ritual is blurry, describing that much of the ritual work is carried out throughout the day, without intentional reflection, in 'careful but habitual ceremony' (Allen 1988: 33).

Many cultural traditions involve everyday consumption, often with ritualised elements, that are not overtly connected with spirituality or religious practice. This includes coffee, tea, tobacco and even sugar. The contemporary art of making tea in the *gongfu* way in China provides an example of ritualised, secular consumption. It involves a small tea pot in which many small cups of tea are brewed and consumed in a session. d'Abbs (2019) explains that the history of *gongfu* is disputed, with some tracing it back to the Tang dynasty in the eighth century AD, while others trace it to the early 1700s. In any case, it has spread to Taiwan, Hong Kong and other parts of the mainland since the 1970s, where it has taken on new forms and meanings. d'Abbs (2019) observed this as an everyday practice in the Chaoshan region of China, the home of the contemporary *gongfu* way. He noted the use of specific utensils and a preparation process that involves attention to the strength and aroma of the tea, as well as the order in which it served. Tea drinkers associate it with values of relaxation and connection with friends and family, and with home and workplace life. While tea drinkers see it as an everyday activity, d'Abbs argues that it is also a refined art because of the attentiveness and creativity it requires.

Drugs as Identity

Drug consumption sends cultural messages about the social identity of the consumer. In early modern England, decorous tea rituals symbolised respectability and were originally promoted by women in explicit contrast with coffee drinking, since women were not allowed in coffee houses. That combined with economic reasons, since Britain lost out to the French and Dutch in the coffee trade. The British East India Company more than quadrupled its imports of tea to England in the 1700s. Teatime, initiated in the mid-1800s as a middle- and upper-class activity, took place in the home, where women were allowed to gather. It became highly regulated, associated with certain forms of fashion and even strict forms of etiquette that were codified in books that specified what could be discussed: Specifically, conversation was to be pleasant and not argumentative (Cusack 2014).

Drinking tea in certain forms has also been associated with national identity and political affiliation. In contemporary Hong Kong, anthropologist Veronica Sau-Wa Mak (2021) wrote that drinking milk tea in a particular way has come to symbolise heritage as postcolonial and urbane. There are, however, competing ways that Hong Kong citizens interpret the meaning of milk tea drinking: while government's official narrative promotes a vision of harmonious society, younger people take it to represent 'an alternate Hong Kong spirit of rebelliousness' (Mak 2021: 39). Mak shows how shifts in political awareness have become materially symbolised in the form of milk tea practices and new webs of meaning surrounding them.

Stimulants have also been used in state-making and heritage-building in the Middle East. Sachedina (2019) traces the history of the Omani coffee pot, whose associations have shifted from being an everyday utilitarian object to a political symbol of a particular kind of Omani national culture and civic virtues. Shryock (2004) describes how the hospitality, grace and refinement (*karam*) that surround greetings among the Bedouins in Jordan has been transformed into and marketed as an essential quality of the Jordanian people, confirming it as an attractive tourist destination. Coffee and its paraphernalia, as symbols of *karam*, fill marketplaces and public spaces as art in what Shryock refers to as a tourism-heritage alliance. It is not only stimulants that are associated with national heritage. Wang (2021) wrote about the creation of a wine heritage in Japan, looking to governmental tourism initiatives and redefinitions of local food traditions. Wang points out a similar practice establishing the prominence of Bordeaux wines in France.

It is common for drug consumption to mark ethnic or national identity. In Kenya, consumption of khat is a marker of Meru identity (Carrier 2007), while in Andean South America, consumption of coca leaves is a marker of indigenous identity. Cusicanqui (2005) explored, for example, how the consumption of coca leaves shifted from solely being associated with Bolivian indigeneity to being associated with modern, urban identity in northern Argentina. These new consumers embrace their identity as South American, and many are also involved in the revitalisation of Pachamama Mother Earth religious rituals. She writes that the coca-chewing habits of the low-status Bolivian labour migrants 'became incorporated into the cultural repertoires of contemporary Argentines who had no previous involvement in Andean culture, turning an "exotic" practice into an emblem of local identity' (Cusicanqui 2005:128). Such links to ethnicity and nationality can be powerfully symbolic, shaping political outcomes.

In addition to symbolising class and ethnic and national identity, consumption can mark gender and age status. Mimi Nichter (2015) wrote about cultures of tobacco smoking among young adults in college in the US – the age group with the highest prevalence of smoking. While quantitative studies suggest that there are no significant gender differences in the amount of smoking people do at that age, ethnographic studies reveal that there are very different beliefs about and patterns of smoking. Even though people considered it 'slutty' and 'trashy' for women to smoke, Nichter found that many college women did smoke. They smoked in ways that insulated them from negative stereotypes, since they often smoked in groups as a group activity, and even strategically used negative stereotypes to project an image of themselves as fun, out-going, just a little rebellious and mysterious. Nichter's study of gendered motivations and smoking behaviours suggests that ethnographic studies are critical for developing targeted tobacco cessation programmes.

In another study, Ting Liu (2017) wrote that smoking among minority women in Yunnan, China has decreased in the last 50 years. Liu explains that what contributed to high levels of smoking in the past was that it was culturally acceptable for women to smoke. Other factors contributing to women's smoking were religious rituals involving smoking, practical concerns about getting rid of mosquitoes and the use of tobacco to treat minor health problems. One factor that changed the acceptability of smoking, according to Liu, was the spread of majority Han Confucian cultural notions of male superiority that associate smoking with men. In addition to changes in gender ideology, people have stopped smoking because of public health campaigns against it and improved healthcare.

Statistics paint a picture of differences in gendered smoking patterns globally, with men being far more likely to smoke. The WHO reports that about 40% of men smoke globally but that only about 9% of women do.[1] Even when we know that men smoke more, ethnographic studies help understand what smoking means to people – where it fits into people's webs of significance. Much drug use is associated with gendered identities, with many tied to cultural ideals of masculinity, even if women also partake. In his study of smoking in Oceania on the Pacific Islands of Truk, for example, Mac Marshall (1979) found smoking and drinking to be important symbols of masculinity. Not only do more men smoke than women globally, but tobacco consumption is also associated with masculinity in many parts of the world (Kohrman 2004, Helme et al. 2021). Chewing of betel nut in Myanmar is linked with masculinity, sexual attractiveness and negotiating power vis-à-vis friends and family (Moe et al. 2017).

Stimulating Sociality: Community and Inequalities

Building Community

Cultural meanings and social relationships are intricately intertwined. The rituals described earlier, for example, clearly provide a context for social connections between participants. Likewise, ordinary use of stimulants has social as well as symbolic and ritualised elements. Drug use can be particularly effective at facilitating a feeling of collective effervescence and euphoria that connect people beyond the time of consumption. It facilitates a sense of *communitas*, a term Victor Turner uses to describe a transitory experience of collective belonging through shared experiences. There are many examples of drugs, such as alcohol, facilitating or being part of social relationships.

An important feature of collective stimulant use is that it provides a setting for people to share information. Stimulants are good for that, since they often make people talkative and generate conviviality. Collective stimulant use also becomes a setting where people pass the time amidst economic hardship. Masquelier describes this for the men drinking tea in Niger, who do so to relieve boredom, 'find refuge from formal social constraints', and create new, affirming ways of being amidst poverty (2013: 472). This is similar to khat-chewing in East Africa and Madagascar, where young men chew khat in the afternoons, either on street corners or in each other's homes, bonding over shared disappointments and visions of a better future (Gebissa 2010, Gezon 2012). Along with Niger, these countries share high unemployment rates, especially for people with degrees in higher education. Detractors of both tea and khat consumption in these contexts claim that such drug consumers are obstructing economic development through lazy idleness and that they are a threat to society by disrupting family life and spending money on drugs rather than food or other critical expenses (Gudata et al. 2019). The critics assume that the young men are choosing not to work, while ethnographic enquiry reveals a more complex situation, including a lack of jobs that pay enough to support a family. It is not only milder stimulants that the poor and hopeless turn to for respite and self-medication but also drugs such as alcohol, heroin, crack cocaine and methamphetamines (Bourgois 1995, Singer 2008).

Inequalities and Disintegration

The argument that drugs serve a function of reinforcing social bonds makes sense. However, we must be careful to avoid too functionalist an emphasis on social integration (Room 1984), as the use of stimulants can be socially divisive too: here we return to the theme of ambivalence mentioned in Chapter 2. While it strengthens some connections, it weakens or challenges others. Shryock (2004) describes the hospitality (*karam*) of greeting coffee rituals among the Balgwa Bedouin in Jordan, explaining that, while apparently convivial on the outside, they are also fraught with caution and even a kind of fear. Outsiders are brought into the privacy of the home and personal space, and the outsiders are at the mercy of their hosts. The host traditionally drinks the first cup of coffee to assure the guest of their safety, for example. Beyond physical safety, there is a sense that reputations are at stake. Drinking coffee together in greeting is a moment of precarity, and the outcome of increased solidarity is not to be taken as a given.

Any kind of social gathering whose apparent purpose is bringing people together (think about family holidays, or parties among friends) can end in discord, with some people feeling slighted or jealous of others, where alliances are made and broken. Human interactions are always complex and hold the potential for disharmony. In addition to interpersonal differences, there are always formal or informal structured inequalities within and between social groups. Furthermore, whether people are structural equals or not, there tend to be divisions in knowledge about processes and products (e.g. about drugs), with novices (or incompetents) and experts (or connoisseurs). The tea rituals of Japan and China, as well as of the men of Niger, are complicated and not readily available to the novice. Likewise, wine connoisseurs learn to identify complex nuances in taste and provenance. In all cases, there will be qualities associated with different varieties, preparations and sources that experienced people will be familiar with.

Another way that drugs can divide is in – and out-group membership, either between different groups of users or between users and non-users. Sometimes eligible users are culturally prescribed, as in the case of women not being allowed to drink in the early coffee houses of England or the men-only khat-chewing rooms (*mafrish*) in the UK that were popular among Somalis in the diaspora before khat was banned in the UK in 2014. Sometimes there are simply cultural norms discouraging some groups from using, as in the case of women being discouraged from using tobacco in many cultural contexts. Sometimes users are treated differently from non-users, as when smokers are only allowed to smoke in certain places. The other side of the conviviality in collective drug use is that it also creates and perpetuates divisions between people.

The barriers between groups of people intensify when dominant groups disapprove of (stigmatise) drug use because of the ability of the dominant groups to give negative sanctions to stigmatised users. Different consumption practices establish not just differences between groups but hierarchies between them. Khat, a drug with low potency when chewed, for example, has been made illegal in most high-income countries, marginalising immigrants from African and Arabian Gulf countries where it is chewed regularly (Gebissa 2012). For all illegal drugs, often uneven enforcement (targeting marginal people) leads to social hardships, including imprisonment, fines and marks on permanent records that can provide barriers to employment or housing. Consumption of some substances in some contexts can even be punishable by death. Amnesty International reported, for example, that a man in Iran was executed for drinking alcohol in 2020.[2]

The Need for Speed

The earlier sections examined drug consumption as a social and cultural practice. A related way to consider stimulant consumption is instrumental: What do they help people do? We will approach this from both emic and etic perspectives – in other words, from the perspective of what people themselves think in various cultural contexts, and what analysts have proposed.

Stimulating Labour: Disciplined Bodies

A dominant analytical (etic) position is that stimulants hold a unique role in history since the Enlightenment as drugs that are associated with rationality, in distinct contrast with alcohol, which had been a common, daily drink for many that left people feeling stupefied rather than encouraged to work hard. Stimulants have helped create a docile labour force due to their ability to suppress both hunger and sleepiness. Spanish conquerors in the 1500s recognised the energising function of coca and began issuing coca leaves to help 'improve the efficiency of the Incan workers at the mines located at 4,000 meters above sea level' (Kamienski 2016: 48). The Incas had used coca in many contexts, including ritual, healing, high altitude adaptation, combatting fatigue. Under the Spanish, Incan workers were given up to three breaks per day to chew the leaves. In order to multiply their profits, the Spanish colonists 'stripped coca of rite, religion, magic, and the social values that had previously accompanied its use' (48). The demand for tea, coffee, sugar and tobacco helped fuel early capital accumulation by Europeans who owned plantations in the tropics and used slave labour to produce it (see Chapter 3).

A functional analysis of stimulants links to a key aspect of our contemporary world – how it appears to be speeding up in an age where capitalism demands ever-increasing productivity. Anthropologist Thomas Hylland Eriksen has written a powerful book (Eriksen 2016) about our current era being one of *overheating*, not just in regard to climate change but also to the overheating of contemporary capitalism and consumerism (which of course link to the climate crisis). Understanding this socioeconomic context that shapes much of our lives can help us understand why we so often lean on drugs to help us cope with this context and its pressures, and how these pressures can lead to problematic – overheated – patterns of drug use. For example, high rates of methamphetamine use are linked to contexts of economic pressure from Thailand (Cohen 2014) to rural US (Garriott 2013). Cocaine use is also associated with high-pressure work in restaurants and in high finance. Furthermore, the coming of industrial capitalism led to different patterns of drug use that meshed with different ideas of the productive use of time, as weeks became divided between the working week and the weekend, a time for leisure. Typical patterns of drug use might involve much consumption of stimulants, such as caffeinated beverages in the working week, and alcoholic drinks at the weekend symbolising leisure time. We are expected to be productive global capitalist subjects in contexts where chemical impediments to productivity in the workplace reveal supposed idleness and immorality, but where they are permitted and even expected in other contexts.

It is easy to see how caffeine has become so ubiquitous in the contemporary economy of global capitalism. To this day, tea and coffee are the drugs of choice in the age of speed, suited to an ethic of sobriety and industry. The caffeinated worker embodies the neoliberal spirit of ever-growing productivity, and workers often feel a moral imperative to push themselves in achieving this in the form of the 'work ethic'. Stimulants help us adapt our bodies to these demands, calibrating our rhythms to the commoditisation of time. In this context, stimulants can also include substances not generally considered part of that category: for example, cannabis is associated in the West with recreational – or increasingly medicinal – contexts, yet in other parts of the world, including the Caribbean, ethnographic research has shown how it is often used in labour contexts, including working on farms (Schaeffer 1975). The work and efficiency imperative applies not only to labourers but also to students, who are using stimulants (from caffeine to amphetamines, such as the prescription drug Adderall) to do a different kind of labour, albeit one whose compensation is deferred.

Even in the global margins, outside of industrial and global capitalist elite zones, people use stimulants to get things done. Indeed, in northern Madagascar, Gezon (2012) found that taxi drivers, night guards and sex workers were the first to adopt khat-chewing in Madagascar. Before, the only people who chewed it were those of Yemeni descent whose ancestors brought khat with them to Madagascar when they worked for the French as dock workers in the early 1900s. Gradually, other people started chewing it to stay awake on their day jobs as labourers and office workers. The irony is that employers began banning khat-chewing on the job even while they continued to permit the consumption of other stimulants: cigarettes and coffee. Khat's association with a patently non-neoliberal way of passing time (during the afternoon with friends, when people were 'supposed' to be working) shaped dominant perceptions of the drug's effects. This reinforces the point that chemicals alone do not determine cultural perception of a drug's effects.

Stimulants and War

Perhaps the most extreme functional use of drugs is in warfare. Drugs have often been used cross-culturally to overcome fear and bolster courage in war, to reward behaviour, to enhance recruitment and to relax after stressful periods of combat. Kan (2009:49) identified four different sources of drug supplies in wartime use: those obtained and used in traditional contexts, often ritually; those present in transshipment areas – places like Guinea Bissau, where drugs like cocaine and heroin pass through on their way to Europe; drugs looted from pharmacies, clinics and hospitals; and finally, drugs administered through prescription or locally manufactured – for example, insurgents in Iraq and Myanmar have produced methamphetamines.

There are many examples of drugs being used in armed conflict cross-culturally. Kamienski (2016) documents ancient uses of hallucinogenic mushrooms in battle in conjunction with shamanic rituals in Siberia and among the Vikings. During colonial times, South American indigenous people in Bolivia used coca in their rebellion against the Spanish at La Paz, Bolivia in the late 1700s to help them survive the harsh conditions of cold and inadequate food supplies. Zulu warriors in southern Africa took cannabis in their conflict with the British in the late 1800s (Kan 2009). Alcohol has been used in military contexts cross-culturally and throughout history for multiple reasons, including bonding and building trust, building self-confidence and willingness to take risks, and providing health benefits of calories and in healing to anesthetise and prevent infections (Kamienski 2016).

The use of drugs continued during the wars of the twentieth century. In the late 1800s, European scientists experimented with coca and later with cocaine, an alkaloid that was first isolated from the coca leaf in a laboratory in 1859. Research showed that cocaine significantly improved physical endurance and reduced fatigue and appetite, recommending it for the military. During WWI, a Dutch company, officially neutral, sold cocaine to both the Central Powers and the Allies, producing about 14,000 kilograms of it per year (Kamienski: 96). Its price went from $280 per ounce in 1885 to $3 per ounce in 1914. Kamienski wrote that 'never before and never after did the military consume such large amounts of this drug as it did in 1914–18, not only for medical purposes but also for the enhancement of performance'.

During WWII, the preferred drugs were amphetamines, which had become common for treating medical ailments in the early 1900s. Norman Ohler (2017) extensively documents the use of amphetamines, including crystal methamphetamine in pill form (Pervitin), in the Third Reich. While the Nazis were the first to use amphetamines for their military, 'in the course of the Second World War the British, Americans, Japanese, and Finns followed suit in authorizing the distribution of speed to their military services' (Ohler 2017: 105). In the contemporary US American context, service members, particularly those involved in aerial operations (particularly pilots), have been issued both amphetamines (often Dexedrine) to keep them awake and sleeping pills to help them sleep.

In many non-European contemporary contexts, drugs (including amphetamines, crack cocaine and cannabis) have aided in war, sometimes, Kamienski describes, to induce child soldiers to fight. Kamienski quoted one former child soldier in Liberia as saying: 'You need the drugs to give you the strength to kill' (253). Non-state groups around the world, including terrorists, also strengthen their military resolve with the help of drugs. Combatants on both sides of the Syrian war, for example, have used an Amphetamine-Type Stimulant called Captagon, which not only energises but also significantly reduces inhibitions. In the Arabian Gulf countries, while the jihadists will not consume alcohol, stimulants are not prohibited. Additionally, khat-chewing has been associated with armed militia in Somalia.

Stimulants as Pleasure

Aside from their functional purposes, people often take drugs for the experience, often because it is pleasurable to do so. Some researchers have pointed out the value of recognising pleasure, not just to capture the human sensory experience with drugs but also, in applied work, to identify points of effective intervention. In the case of tobacco, some criticise studies focusing on the dire public health outcomes of smoking, saying that they ignore the pleasure people gain from it. Bell and Dennis (2013) wrote that tobacco users generally identify pleasure as a primary reason for consuming it, in addition to stress reduction and social connection. Pleasure was also an important part of the experiences of the college students who smoked in Nichter's (2015) study. Recognising the salience of pleasure as a factor helps in devising appropriate substitutions. Recognising pleasure need not take away from an analysis of its public health harms, however. Bevan (2016: 228) argued that recognising the pleasures of 'the small everyday pleasures and social relationships that unfold around smoking' is important in harm reduction strategies (see also Chapman [2020] on social drinking as therapeutic among Japanese immigrants to Hawai'i). Bevan argued for recognising that e-cigarette consumption, as a harm reduction strategy, can be a form of 'self-management of health' (Bevan 2016: 228). In research on HIV and drug use among gay men, Kane Race (2009) stated that openly acknowledging pleasure and developing 'respect for its importance in our lives is crucial if we want adequately to account for the social life and material effects of such drugs' (Race: 187). A critical medical anthropology approach would point out that not all people have equal access to pleasure: what is available and socially acceptable – or punishable – runs along lines of gender, ethnicity, race and age.

Recognising the role of pleasure also ties in with concerns about whether anthropologists, or researchers in general, inflate or deflate the seriousness of drug-related problems, as we explore later. A heavy focus on pleasure may ignore health and social risks – and vice versa. Finding balanced analyses is important.

Everyday Lows: Relieving Stress

Despite the global appetite for enhancing performance and increasing energy in industrial and post-industrial contexts, drug consumption for relaxation has not disappeared. Many drugs can serve as either stimulants or depressants, depending on the cultural context and individual's mindset (Zinberg's *set* and *setting*) when consuming. It is worth repeating what Hardon and Sanabria have emphasised that 'there is no pure (pharmaceutical) object that precedes its socialization and interpretation' (2017: 118). We take that to mean that just because we know what a particular substance does to people in one context does not allow for generalising about its social, cultural or even health effects in others. Users report that alcohol, for example, can both energise and relax, as can many other substances. Khat-chewing sessions notably contain moments of euphoria and deep contemplation, and the sequence of moods within sessions is culturally scripted in Yemen (Kennedy 1987): the first effect is a euphoric high, characterised by flowing conversation. The latter part of the session, once the high is considered to have worn off, is meant for quiet, internalised reflection.

This section will focus on alcohol, which is pharmacologically identified as a depressant. Other substances could fit into this category too, however, such as cannabis and kava (a drink made from the root of the *Piper methysticum* plant that is native to the western Pacific Islands [Perminow 1995]).

Cultural and Social Contexts of Drinking

Anthropologists studying alcohol consumption have taken different approaches in the vast literature on it, and we have mentioned key work already in Chapters 1 and 2. One focus of writing has been on cultural and social contexts of consumption. Early publications chronicled drinking patterns cross-culturally. MacAndrew and Edgerton's (1969) *Drunken Comportment* made the important point that the effects of alcohol are culturally constructed and not determined by their chemical properties. It was an argument rejecting popular beliefs that alcohol's effects are universally identical – what we have called *pharmacological determinism*. In his classic analysis of drinking patterns among the indigenous Camba of Bolivia that was originally published in 1958, Dwight Heath argued that not only are drinking patterns culturally and historically particular, but that the physiological effects can also vary. In the 1950s, he noticed that people drank distilled spirits heavily in a 'highly stylized manner' (2004: 121) on a weekly basis at fiestas, but that it did not lead to the stereotyped loss of inhibitions a Western observer might expect. He wrote that: 'drunken behavior ... did not evoke any special comment because it differed so little from sober behavior. It was extremely rare that any Camba, drunk or sober, should show any aggression' (ibid. 122) Furthermore, no one complained about hangovers.

Others have written about highly regulated and ritualised drinking patterns, both in contemporary and traditional contexts, emphasising their role in social integration. Donner (1994) wrote about consumption on the Solomon Island atoll of Sikaiana, where drinking what they call *toddys* (a fermented drink made from the sap of coconut shoots) in both informal contexts and on the occasion of religious holidays had traditionally been restricted to men only, but that had changed by the early 1980s. Po et al. (2020) wrote about the integral part alcohol played in hosting guests and in sharing among kin and social networks in northern Vietnam among Hmong and Yao ethnic minorities, with 'home-distilled alcohol preferred as an indicator of deep respect and connection given the cultural value it holds as well as the time and labour input its production requires' (402).

Drinking and Identity

At the same time as alcohol facilitates social interactions, it is, as we saw for tea, a marker of identity. Gurr (2019) wrote about the association of substance use with political affiliation in the context of Brazil. Members of Brazil's Landless Rural Workers' Movement (MST) associate MST membership with smoking and drinking alcohol distilled from sugarcane. Gurr (2019) wrote that 'Drinking [Chachaca] Socialista ... was a means to support their comrades' venture in sustainable agriculture' (696) and that it defied traditional sanctions against women drinking in public. Drinking is also often associated with gender identities. Sugg (1996) documented changing gendered dynamics of ritualistic and social beer drinking in Botswana. Brewing beer in southern Africa dates at least back to the days of Great Zimbabwe. In the pre-capitalist period, people largely considered alcohol consumption to be a masculine behaviour in which elderly women took part (it was considered an age-appropriate masculine thing for them to do). Suggs (1996) traced how drinking patterns have changed in the transition from an agricultural to a capitalistic, commodity-based society. Local people in the town studied identified bars as men's spaces and the home as women's space. Women were more likely to drink in public if they had an independent source of income. For men, drinking was an expression of an adult masculine identity. Elite men tended to drink in bars, while lower status men drank at less expensive outdoor stands or in more relaxed informal spaces, where men tended to consume higher quantities of alcohol. Suggs explained that as alcohol became commoditised – a product to be paid for with cash as opposed to brewed within the home – patterns of consumption changed. Whereas older women tended to drink in pre-capitalist times (when they did not have to pay for alcohol with cash), younger women who had access to cash began drinking more with the commoditisation of alcohol. While older men used to drink more publicly in pre-capitalist times, younger men dominated the bars.

In the UK, pubs and taverns have long been places where people, especially men, come together to socialise and share information. As in Botswana, the pub, as a drinking establishment, serves as a 'third place' (Oldenburg 1999) – an informal gathering place that is between work and home, where people share ideas, nurture social connections, and where social hierarchies may become somewhat levelled. In studying drinking patterns of Irish men in London, Tilki (2006) found the tavern to play an economic role in connecting people to contractors looking for labourers as well as a way to stay in touch with the cultural practices of the places they left back in Ireland. Tilki (2006) found drinking heavily to be associated with masculinity. She notes that it is common in Ireland that one's first alcoholic drink in a pub is celebrated as a rite of passage into acceptance into male companionship.

Alcohol use accompanies and symbolically demarcates non-binary gender expressions as well. Yuen (2020) describes the role of drinking parties for the female-to-male (FTM) transgender community in Japan. These events, called *ofukai*, are part of a cultural scene that is 'organized predominantly to provide a space for FTM trans people (and their partners) to socialize over drinks and food in a (semi-)private and relaxed setting'. Yuen argues that these events 'both build a sense of community and foster the formation of a (sub)public space for the expression of gender/sexual personhood by FTM people and their partners – or, in other words, to enact transgender cultural citizenship'. This is important for the rights of sexual citizenship through consumption in a country with conservative views of trans people.

Drinking and Conflict

In addition to focusing on social integration, many anthropologists have written about how drinking is often fraught with ambivalence and is a source of conflict within communities. This is particularly noticeable where drinking has been introduced into communities through colonisation, when drinking becomes disassociated with traditional contexts, or when people consume alcohol as an escape from oppression or meaninglessness. Robbins (1977) compared what he identified as a well-integrated form of alcohol consumption (a fermented banana beer) and a recently developed distilled version of it among the Baganda in Uganda. He tested the hypothesis that a more thoroughly socially integrated form of alcohol (banana beer) would have less problematic drinking associated with it. The beer is legal and produced at home, while the distilled version is illegal and produced by individuals working alone. He found the hypothesis to be mildly supported, in that people reported more social reasons for drinking the beer and more reasons associated with appeasing psychological problems for drinking the distilled spirit.

Spicer (1997) noted that anthropologists in the 1960s through the mid-1980s tended to write about the drinking in Native American communities from a functionalist perspective – to express values or assert identity or relieve stress, for example. Spicer responded to Room's (1984) call to acknowledge negative effects of alcohol consumption as well. He complexified his analysis of alcohol consumption, noting that

> drinking is at once recognized as a means of articulating core values *and* vilified as an alien and degrading influence; it is simultaneously something to which people are drawn *and* by which they are repelled; and it is associated with some of the best *and* some of the worst in contemporary American Indian life.
>
> (307, emphasis in original)

He investigated the paradox of people consuming alcohol despite having negative opinions of it, considering how drinking both strengthens relationships with others and at the same time has the potential to disrupt them. In so doing, he urges against a facile functionalist interpretation of the role of alcohol in any social setting.

Movements prohibiting or condemning alcohol reveal poignant examples of differences of opinion within cultural settings. Temperance movements, which were common in England, Australia, New Zealand and the US in the 1800s and early 1900s, brought differences of opinion into the legal sphere. They culminated in Prohibition banning production, sale and consumption of alcohol from 1920 to 1933 in the US, though that only made the production, trade and consumption of alcohol go underground. Marshall and Marshall (1990) document the women's temperance movement (a temperance movement advocates for moderate alcohol consumption or total abstinence) in the island of Truk in Micronesia, when women publicly condemned the negative effects of drinking in between 1976 and 1985. In so doing, they joined temperance coalitions throughout the Pacific Islands. The women of Truk petitioned local officials, resulting in a prohibition of alcohol in one municipality. In another case, Christine Eber's (1995) book about women and alcohol in a highland Mayan town in Chiapas, Mexico, discusses the numerous ways that women have struggled to contain the negative effects of alcohol in their communities. While drinking has a place in religious ritual, many people drink in ways that are physically, emotionally and economically destructive to family and community life. One of women's strategies is to join Protestant churches that discourage drinking. In a later work, Eber (2001) notes that both men and women who join the Zapatista democracy movement 'reject alcohol as a symbol of political and economic domination' (abstract).

Anthropology and Drug Harms

Many anthropologists studying substance use have sought to contribute to public health responses to them, recognising the harms that can revolve around these substances (Marshall et al. 2001). Merrill Singer (1986) has been a pioneer in locating the anthropology of drugs within a political economic approach that questions the structural factors that contribute to problematic outcomes. As we have discussed, this critical medical anthropology approach examines social and structural determinants of health – the role of dominant cultural actors (e.g. laws and policies, as well as colonial remnants and multinational corporations) in shaping access to psychoactive substances, and thereby creating conditions for problematic and disruptive consumption. This provides a logical transition to Chapter 6, which focuses on drug dependence – what people often refer to as 'addiction' or 'abuse'. While we deconstruct these charged concepts, we also recognise the power of culturally situated chemical substances to change, and even shatter, lives. As in this chapter and its focus on how stimulants and alcohol can not only bind us together but also break us apart, we seek, along with Room et al. (1984), to find a balance between problem deflation and problem inflation. The line is often blurry between culturally acceptable consumption and consumption deemed to be problematic, and there will always be different perspectives, even within a group sharing many cultural practices.

Notes

1 See this WHO fact sheet on tobacco: www.who.int/news-room/fact-sheets/detail/ tobacco (accessed November 2022).
2 Report available online: www.amnesty.org/en/latest/news/2020/07/iran-man-executed-for-drinking-alcohol/?__cf_chl_jschl_tk__=pmd_IppWn0iuAW0xiNCD OWdI7DTmJbJhxdoj80iYuFthxGQ-1630414002-0-gqNtZGzNAiWjcnBszQiR (accessed November 2022).

Works Cited

Alderete, Ethel, Pamela I. Erickson, Celia P. Kaplan, and Eliseo J. Pérez-Stable. 2010. "Ceremonial Tobacco Use in the Andes: Implications for Smoking Prevention Among Indigenous Youth." *Anthropology & Medicine* 17 (1): 27–39.
Allen, Catherine J. 1988. *The Hold Life Has: Coca and Cultural Identity in an Andean Community*. Washington, DC: Smithsonian Institution Press.
Amnesty International. 2020. *Iran: Man Executed for Drinking Alcohol*. Amnesty International. www.amnesty.org/en/latest/news/2020/07/iran-man-executed-for-drinking-alcohol/?__cf_chl_jschl_tk__=pmd_IppWn0iuAW0xiNCDOWdI7DTm JbJhxdoj80iYuFthxGQ-1630414002-0-gqNtZGzNAiWjcnBszQiR

Bell, Kirsten, and Simone Dennis. 2013. "Towards a Critical Anthropology of Smoking: Exploring the Consequences of Tobacco Control." *Contemporary Drug Problems* 40 (1): 3–19.

Bevan, Imogen. 2016. "E-cigarettes:Smoking Pleasure Reinvented? The Many Faces of Harm Reduction in France." *Contemporary Drug Problems* 43 (3): 228–241.

Bourdieu, Pierre. 1979. *Distinction*. London: Routledge.

Bourgois, Philippe I. 1995. *In Search of Respect: Selling Crack in El Barrio*. Cambridge: Cambridge University Press.

Carrier, Neil. 2007. *Kenyan Khat: The Social Life of a Stimulant*. Leiden: Brill.

Chapman, Christopher R. 2020. "Searching for a Feeling Once Felt: Narratives of Alcohol and Health among Japanese Immigrants in Hawai'i." *Anthropology & Medicine* 27 (3): 300–314.

Cobo, B., and R. Hamilton. 2010. *Inca Religion and Customs*. Austin, TX: University of Texas Press.

Cohen, Anjalee. 2014. "Crazy for Ya Ba: Methamphetamine Use Among Northern Thai Youth." *The International journal of drug policy* 25 (4): 776–782. https://doi.org/10.1016/j.drugpo.2014.06.005

Cusack, Tricia. 2014. *Regulation and Excess: Women and Tea-Drinking in Nineteenth-Century Britain*. Dublin: Dublin Institute of Technology, School of Culinary Arts & Food Technology.

Cusicanqui, Silvia Rivera. 2005. *Invisible Realities: Internal Markets and Subaltern Identities in Contemporary Bolivia*. Amsterdam/Quezon City: South-South Exchange Programme for Research on the History of Development.

d'Abbs, Peter. 2019. "Tea Art as Everyday Practice: Gongfu Tea in Chaoshan, Guangdong, Today." *Asia Pacific Journal of Anthropology* 20 (3): 213–231.

Donner, William W. 1994. "Alcohol, Community, and Modernity: The Social Organization of Toddy Drinking in a Polynesian Society." *Ethnology: An International Journal of Cultural and Social Anthropology* 33 (3): 245–260.

Douglas, Mary. 1987. *Constructive Drinking Perspectives on Drink from Anthropology*. London: Routledge.

Douglas, Mary, and Baron C. Isherwood. 1996. *The World of Goods: Towards an Anthropology of Consumption*. New York: Routledge.

Drucker-Brown, Susan. 1995. "The Court and the Kola Nut: Wooing and Witnessing in Northern Ghana." *The Journal of the Royal Anthropological Institute* 1 (1): 129–143.

Eber, Christine. 1995. *Women and Alcohol in a Highland Maya Town: Water of Hope, Water of Sorrow*. Austin, TX: University of Texas Press.

———. 2001. "Take My Water': Liberation Through Prohibition in San Pedro Chenalhó, Chiapas, Mexico." *Social Science & Medicine* 53 (2): 251–262.

Eriksen, Thomas Hylland. 2016. *Overheating: An Anthropology of Accelerated Change*. London: Pluto Press.

Garriott, William. 2013. "Methamphetamine in Rural America: Notes on Its Emergence." *Anthropology now* 5 (1): 27–35.

Gebissa, Ezekiel. 2010. *Khat in Ethiopia: Taking the Place of Food*. Trenton, NJ: Red Sea Press.

———. 2012. "Khat: Is It More Like Coffee or Cocaine? Criminalizing a Commodity, Targeting a Community." *Sociology Mind* 02: 204–212.

Geertz, C. 1973. *Thick Description: Toward and Interpretive Theory of Culture*. New York, NY: Basic Books.

Gezon, Lisa L. 2012. *Drug Effects: Khat in Biocultural and Socioeconomic Perspective.* Walnut Creek, CA: Left Coast Press.

Gudata, Zerihun Girma, Logan Cochrane, and Gutema Imana. 2019. "An Assessment of Khat Consumption Habit and its Linkage to Household Economies and Work Culture: The Case of Harar City." *PLOS ONE* 14 (11): 1–17.

Gurr, Mel. 2019. "Celebratory Socialism: Subcultural Politics of Dancing, Drinking, and Hooking Up Among Youth of Brazil's MST." *Journal of Latin American & Caribbean Anthropology* 24 (3): 690–708.

Hardon, Anita, and Emilia Sanabria. 2017. "Fluid Drugs: Revisiting the Anthropology of Pharmaceuticals." *Annual Review of Anthropology* 46 (1): 117–132.

Heath, Dwight B. 2004. "Camba (Bolivia) Drinking Patterns: Changes in Alcohol Use, Anthropology and Research Perspectives." In *Drug Use and Cultural Contexts "Beyond the West": Tradition, Change and Post-Colonialism*, edited by Ross Coomber and Nigel South, 119–136. London: Free Association Books.

Helme, Donald W., Edward Morris, Ana de la Serna, Carina Zelaya, Carrie Oser, and Hannah K. Knudsen. 2021. "Country Boys Spit and Dip': Masculinity and Rural Adolescent Smokeless Tobacco Use." *Journal of Men's Studies* 29 (2): 213–234.

Hirsch, Eric. 2007. "Betelnut 'Bisnis' and Cosmology: A View from Papua New Guinea." In *Consuming Habits: Global and Historical Perspectives on How Cultures Define Drugs*, edited by Jordan Goodman, Andrew Sherratt and Paul E. Lovejoy, 86–97. New York: Routledge.

Kan, Paul Rexton. 2009. *Drugs and Contemporary Warfare.* Sterling, VA: Potomac Books.

Kennedy, John G. 1987. *The Flower of Paradise: The Institutionalized Use of the Drug Qat in North Yemen.* Dordrecht: D. Reidel Publishing Company.

Kohrman, Matthew. 2004. "Should I Quit? Tobacco, Fraught Identity, and The Risks of Governmentality in Urban China." *Urban Anthropology and Studies of Cultural Systems and World Economic Development* 33 (2/4): 211–245.

Lovejoy, Paul E. 2007. "Kola nuts: the coffee of the central Sudan." In *Consuming Habits: Drugs in History and Anthropology*, edited by Jordan Goodman, Paul E. Lovejoy and Andrew Sherratt, 98–120. New York: Routledge.

Lowry, David Shane. 2017. "Redpilling: A Professional Reflects on White Racial Privilege and Drug Policy in American Health Care." *Journal of Ethnicity in Substance Abuse* 17 (1): 50–63.

Lukasz, Kamienski. 2016. *Shooting Up: A Short History of Drugs and War.* New York, NY: Oxford University Press.

MacAndrew, Craig, and Robert B. Edgerton. 1969. *Drunken Comportment.* Chicago: Aldine.

Mak, Veronica Sau-Wa. 2021. "The Heritagization of Milk Tea: Cultural Governance and Placemaking in Hong Kong." *Asian Anthropology* 20 (1): 30–46.

Marshall, Mac. 1979. *Beliefs, Behaviors, and Alcoholic Beverages: A Cross-Cultural Survey.* Ann Arbor, MI: University of Michigan Press.

———. 2013. *Drinking Smoke: The Tobacco Syndemic in Oceania.* O'ahu: University of Hawai'i Press.

Marshall, Mac, Genevieve M. Ames, and Linda A. Bennett. 2001. "Anthropological Perspectives on Alcohol and Drugs at the Turn of the New Millennium." *Social Science & Medicine* 53 (2): 153–164.

Marshall, Mac, and Leslie B. Marshall. 1990. *Silent Voices Speak: Women and Prohibition in Truk.* Belmont, CA: Wadsworth Publishing Company.

Masquelier, Adeline. 2013. "Teatime: Boredom and the Temporalities of Young Men in Niger." *Africa: Journal of the International African Institute* 83 (3): 470–491.

Mauss, Marcel. 1925. *The Gift*. London: Routledge.

Moe, Thida, Boonmongkon Pimpawun, Wang Xiaochuan, Phukao Darunee, Timo T. Ojanen, and Thomas E. Guadamuz. 2017. "A Critical Ethnographic Study on Betel Quid Dependence Among Young Men in Mandalay, Myanmar." *Asia-Pacific Social Science Review* 17 (2): 239–248.

Nichter, Mimi. 2015. *Lighting Up: The Rise of Social Smoking on College Campuses*. New York: New York University Press.

Nutt, David J., Leslie A. King, and Lawrence D. Phillips. 2010. "Drug Harms in the UK: A Multicriteria Decision Analysis." *The Lancet* 376 (9752): 1558–1565.

Ohler, Norman, and Shaun Whiteside. 2017. *Blitzed: Drugs in the Third Reich*. Boston, MA: Houghton Mifflin Harcourt.

Oldenburg, R. 1999. *The Great Good Place: Cafe's, Coffee Shops, Community Centers, Beauty Parlors, General Stores, Bars, Hangouts, and How They Get You Through the Day*. New York, NY: Marlowe & Company.

Perminow, Arne Aleksej. 1995. "'Recreational' Drinking In Tonga." *Canberra Anthropology* 18 (1–2): 119–135.

Po, June Y. T., Jennifer C. Langill, Sarah Turner, and Jean Michaud. 2020. "Distilling Culture into Commodity? The Emergent Homemade Alcohol Trade and Gendered Livelihoods in Upland Northern Vietnam." *The Asia Pacific Journal of Anthropology* 21 (5): 397–415.

Race, K. 2009. *Pleasure Consuming Medicine: The Queer Politics of Drugs*. Durham, NC: Duke University Press.

Robbins, Michael C. 1977. "Part One: Problem-Drinking and the Integration of Alcohol in Rural Buganda." *Medical Anthropology* 1 (3): 1–24.

Room, Robin. 1984. "Alcohol and Ethnography: A Case of Problem Deflation?" *Current Anthropology* 25 (2): 169–191.

Sachedina, Amal. 2019. "The Politics of the Coffee Pot: Its Changing Role in History-Making and the Place of Religion in the Sultanate of Oman." *History & Anthropology* 30 (3): 233–255.

Schaeffer, Joseph. 1975. "The Significance of Marihuana in a Small Agricultural Community in Jamaica." In *Cannabis and Culture*, edited by Vera Rubin, 355–388. The Hague: Mouton Publishers.

Shyrock, Andrew. 2004. "The New Jordanian Hospitality: House, Host, and Guest in the Culture of Public Display." *Comparative Studies in Society and History* 46 (1): 35–62.

Singer, Merrill. 1986. "Toward a Political-Economy of Alcoholism: The Missing Link in the Anthropology of Drinking." *Social Science and Medicine* 23 (2): 113–130.

———. 2008. *Drugs and Development: The Global Impact on Sustainable Growth and Human Rights*. Long Grove, IL: Waveland Press.

Spicer, Paul. 1997. "Toward a (Dys)functional Anthropology of Drinking: Ambivalence and the American Indian Experience with Alcohol." *Medical Anthropology Quarterly* 11 (3): 306–323.

Suggs, D, and Mosadi Tshwene. 1996. "The Construction of Gender and the Consumption of Alcohol in Botswana." *American Ethnologist* 23 (3): 597–610.

Tilki, Mary. 2006. "The Social Contexts of Drinking Among Irish Men in London." *Drugs: Education, Prevention & Policy* 13 (3): 247–261.

Ting, Liu. 2017. "Tobacco Growing and Cultural Impacts on Smoking Among Ethnic Minority Women in Yunnan, China." *International Journal of Business Anthropology* 7 (1): 99–112.

Towler, Solala. 2010. *Cha Dao: The Way of Tea, Tea As a Way of Life*. Philadelphia, PA: Jessica Kingsley Publishers.

Vagins, Deborah J., and Jesselyn McCurdy. 2006. *Cracks in the System: 20 Years of the Unjust Federal Crack Cocaine Law*. New York: American Civil Liberties Union.

Volkow, Nora D., Gene-Jack Wang, Frank Teland, Joanna S. Fowler, Jean Logan, Millard Jayne, Yeming Ma, Kith Pradhan, and Christopher Wong. 2007. "Profound Decreases in Dopamine Release in Striatum in Detoxified Alcoholics: Possible Orbitofrontal Involvement." *Journal of Neuroscience* 27 (46): 12700–12706.

Wang, Chuanfei. 2021. "Creating a Wine Heritage in Japan." *Asian Anthropology* 20(1): 1–16.

World Health Organization. 2022. *Tobacco*. World Health Organization. www.who. int/news-room/fact-sheets/detail/tobacco

Yuen, Shu Min. 2020. "Unqueer Queers – Drinking Parties and Negotiations of Cultural Citizenship by Female-to-Male Trans People in Japan." *Asian Anthropology* 19(2): 86–101.

Zinberg, Norman. 1984. *Drug, Set, and Setting: The Basis for Controlled Intoxicant Use*. New Haven, CT: Yale University Press.

6 Perspectives on Addiction in Anthropology

Drugs can help us in our lives (stimulating us, soothing us, enhancing social relationships), but there appear to be thresholds after which these same substances harm us. Instead of us consuming them, in some ways they seem to consume us: the power in the relationship appears to shift from the consumer to the drug. In this chapter, we look at power and agency in relation to drugs, focusing on discourses of addiction. The concept of addiction raises key ideas about the power of the drug over the consumer, as well as linking to ideas of free will, responsibility and control and choice and morality. As we will see, anthropologists have contributed much to the study of addiction and, in particular, to the study of the lives led by addicts. Anthropologists' work has played an important role in both thinking through theoretical questions about such issues as the power of material items generally to shape our lives (new materialism), the role of political and economic dynamics to shape individuals' experiences (critical medical anthropology) and the discursive construction of a phenomenon that has significant cultural, social and experiential ramifications. This chapter focuses on drugs from the perspective of politico-cultural constructions and individual experiences of 'harm' or 'problem' use – a focus that is dominant in academic studies of drugs, as is evident in a search for textbooks on drugs.

Anthropologists deconstruct a pathologizing view of drugs, emphasizing instead that drugs also bring pleasure and positive social conviviality. They are also sceptical of labels of 'addiction' or 'addictive' substances as they emerged as constructs in particular historical and cultural contexts and come with much ideological baggage. On the other hand, anthropologists recognise the very real potential of drugs to ruin lives, albeit a potential that emerges within particular socio-cultural and political contexts or assemblages. As Bourgois (2018: 387) noted,

> anyone who has experienced on an embodied level the mystery of 'addiction', whether personally through uncontrollable emotional cravings or manic ecstatic/soothing epiphanies followed by torturous withdrawals,

DOI: 10.4324/9781003109549-6

or through the loss of a family member or loved one, knows how seriously one has to take the pharmacological power of drug effects.

Yet, he notes, we cannot ignore 'the socio-cultural and political-economic "determinants" of drug effects' (2018: 387). To this effect, anthropologists, including Bourgois, have also meaningfully contributed to public health initiatives to conceptualise, implement and assess programs to mitigate suffering around addictive states. This chapter explores the meaning of 'addiction' and 'dependence' in historical and cultural contexts, considering both cultural constructions and biophysical aspects of the drug chemicals. It presents anthropological approaches to the study of addiction and examines case studies of specific substances.

Agency and Power: The Notion of Addiction

People tend to see substances labelled as 'drugs' as especially potent things, as things that have agency, or the ability to act independently, outside of the way they are culturally constructed. This phenomenon may be most obvious in concepts of addiction or dependence, where the substances are seen to take agency from the consumer. One way this happens is when users explicitly give substance agency, as in the case of Carrier's friend Nico when talking about khat and *handas* – a Kenyan term for the 'high' of khat. Nico would often personify *handas* through giving it agency rather than him in explaining, for example, why he does not like chewing khat in a cold climate: *handas does not like the cold*. For Nico, *handas* came to life as a trickster-like character that can bring pleasure, but that can also deceive. If Nico did something foolish or forgetful while under the influence, he would blame *handas*.

While there was some comic intent in this playful personification of *handas*, this tendency to give agency to drugs is common and significant. In the UK and US, alcohol has been personified as John Barleycorn as early as the 1600s. This fictional character has continued to appear in folklore, poetry, fiction and song since then. The ability of opium-based drugs to seize power and agency was also well known in the nineteenth century, and its agency was especially noted in Thomas De Quincey's famous *The Confessions of an English Opium Eater* (1822) who presented opium as the true hero in the story (1985 [1822]). Historian Timothy Hickman explains that through this

> the book's narrator, the English Opium Eater of the title, lost possession of his own story as the opium itself seized narrative agency. The Opium Eater had come under the power of an outside force – an irresistible urgency that was somehow located in the opium.
>
> (Hickman 2022: 217)

This idea of drugs as possessing agency invites us to think about the role of 'free will' in drug consumption, and even 'responsibility': how responsible are we for things we do *under the influence*? This chapter examines various factors that can hamper the ability of individuals to make whatever decisions they want, including chemical composition, social relationships, cultural norms and political-economic structural factors. Recognizing these factors is essential to creating and implementing effective addiction treatment initiatives.

History of 'Addiction'

Addiction is now a globalised term and concept, being used in popular and medical discourse throughout the world, but its origins are historically and culturally bound to the industrialising societies of the Americas and Europe and have a focus on individualism that has been exported elsewhere. Addiction comes from the Latin word *addictio*, 'the technical Latin term for the judicial act by which a debtor was made the slave of his creditor' (Rosenthal and Faris 2019), and the *addictus* was the person bound over in this way, sometimes as result of gambling debt. Similarly, addict as a verb became an English legal term in the sixteenth century that 'described the legal action of a court when it decreed a duty or a practice for a person to carry out, usually against their will' (Hickman 2022: 226). The final clause of that last sentence is important, given how addiction as related to drugs is often seen as a *disease of the will* (Valverde 1998). Addiction also had another meaning in early modern England, however, of devoting oneself to something or someone, as Rebecca Lemon has written about (Lemon 2018). As Hickman describes (2022), these different resonances of the term are still important today given their ambiguities in the attribution of responsibility. While many think addiction should be seen as a disease and hence moral judgement suspended as people are addicted against their will, the notion that some addicts hold responsibility for devoting themselves to the substance in question shows how moral judgement is still a factor in the use of the term.

The idea of addiction in relation to drugs is relatively recent and grew out of concern for habitual drunkenness beginning in the seventeenth century, demonstrated in the pamphlets and sermons of moralists such as Increase Mather. Mather and other Puritans used the term 'addiction' as was common at that time, to refer to an attachment with neither positive nor negative connotations. Mather decried 'drunkenness as a sin, an evil propagated by the Devil, most certainly a bad choice, but not a disease' (Rosenthal and Faris 2019: 445).

In earlier centuries in Europe (and perhaps elsewhere), drinking alcohol was common, even among Puritans. Drunkenness was an expected aspect of society, sometimes unfortunate, other times comic, but always seen as something the drinker desired and chose. People who drank habitually were called drunkards and were not socially stigmatised as a group until the 1700s, when alcohol came into focus as a socially destructive substance. It is important to note that concern about drunkenness correlates with globalization and mass production and dissemination of cheap distilled alcohol. The prevailing ideology in the 1700s was that rational people would give up drinking when they realised its harm. That some people refused to give it up suggested that drinking to the point of drunkenness was something irrational and beyond their control. This ushered in a new meaning for the term 'addiction' by the late 1700s. In the nineteenth century, temperance movements arose first in the US and then spread to the UK, other European countries, India and parts of Africa. The goal of these movements was at first to eliminate liquor consumption and to promote abstinence from all alcohol. Tracing the history of the concept of addiction, Levine (1978) found that people in the American nineteenth century temperance movement found alcohol itself to cause the addiction, while after alcohol Prohibition (Prohibition lasted from 1920 to 1933 in the US), the cause was thought to lie within individual bodies rather than in the alcohol itself: they posited that some bodies react differently to alcohol. Both schools of thought were different from previous ones in positing that quitting alcohol is not a choice – at least not for some people.

The first systematic conceptions of alcohol addiction as a disease – as a condition that was beyond individual choice – were laid out by reformers and physicians in the mid-to-late 1770s in the US and dominated temperance thought in the 1800s. Dr. Benjamin Rush – considered the founder of the temperance movement – described addiction as a 'disease of the will' that one is unable to refrain from due to a loss of control (Levine 1978: 152). Furthermore, it is a condition that threatens society in the form of crime, poverty and insanity. This was seen as especially troubling in an era of industrial capitalism and growing pressure for workers to be increasingly productive (see Chapter 5): loss of control in relation to alcohol was seen by some as incompatible with the need for a work ethic. In keeping with changing concepts of addiction, increasing numbers of drinkers began claiming that they had no control over their drinking behaviour. In response, Rush and other temperance organizations supported efforts to develop asylums for reforming drunkards. Toward the end of the 1800s, this idea of loss of control co-existed with a loss of sympathy for the habitual drunkard. According to Levine, 'The drunkard came to be viewed less and less as a victim, and more and more as simply a pest and menace' (162).

As well as alcohol, opium came under scrutiny as a substance capable of leading people astray through habitual use. Opium was readily available as a medicine in the eighteenth and nineteenth centuries in England, the US and elsewhere, and doctors regarded it as one of the most useful treatments for a range of ills, including for pain relief, insomnia and stomach problems (Hickman 2022). Indeed, much habitual use of opium emerged through *iatrogenic* means, that is to say, as a result of an initial prescription for medical purposes (and this remains the case today with much opiate usage, especially in North America). Opium usage in the early nineteenth century is associated strongly with the likes of Samuel Taylor Coleridge and Thomas De Quincey, famous literary figures whose experiences with opium shaped their writing, explicitly in the case of De Quincey in his *Confessions of an Opium Eater*. Yet opium was used much more widely, and for some consumers, dosing with this unrestricted medicine became a chronic practice, so much so that the medical profession in Europe and North America became concerned that, like alcohol, opium use had the potential to become habitual beyond any medical benefit. Opium consumption began to seem something sinister, being often associated too with people on the margins of society, including Chinese migrants in the US and UK (Berridge 1999), while the legacy of the Opium Wars (see Chapter 3) also consolidated opium's image as a pernicious, habit-forming drug. In this way, opium became one of the first substances associated with the emerging concept of drug addiction.

International measures to suppress opium grew strong in the twentieth century, and aside from medical use as an anodyne, its use – and use of related opiates – became seen as beyond the pale in much of the world. Given that alcohol was consumed so widely throughout much of global society, the drinking practices of the mainstream had to be separated from those whose drinking was problematic for them and wider society. With the organization of Alcoholics Anonymous in the 1930s, the concept of alcoholism as an addiction that affects only some drinkers of alcohol became the norm. This served the purpose of accepting some social drinking while condemning forms considered to be excessive. In this view, people labelled 'addicts' have a disease that prevents them from making good choices, a view promoted by Jellinek (1960), a physiologist and alcohol researcher, who was an intellectual leader in shaping public responses to alcohol consumption. From its beginning, this idea has been central to Alcoholics Anonymous' 12 Steps Program for recovery. In this model, abstinence is the only solution to treat alcoholism, since alcoholics are seen as incapable of moderate consumption. This disease concept was soon applied to other drugs too. By invoking idea of a 'disease', advocates argue that addicts are not chronic consumers because they are immoral or inherently criminals, but rather through something out of their control.

This distinction between heavy drug users as medically diagnosable 'addicts' as opposed to criminals has shaped drug policy (which we explore in detail in Chapter 8): criminals are incarcerated, while addicts undergo treatment. In the criminal model, government resources are used to fund enforcement of illegal drug use; in the addiction model, resources are directed toward 'harm reduction' techniques, including needle exchanges (Klein et al. 2004). Critics of the criminal model argue that incarceration will only exacerbate drug use problems and perpetuate racialised criminal profiling. Critics of the harm reduction model come from two fronts. Some fear that harm reduction condones illegal behaviour. Others note that, while it purports to champion humane practices, it is not value-neutral and results in enhanced social control (Campbell and Shaw 2008).

In the late twentieth century, the term 'addiction' came under scrutiny. Because of the negative connotations associated with the word, the World

Health Organization (WHO) switched from talking of 'addiction' to 'dependence syndrome' in 1964. Psychologists also found the meaning of the word 'addiction' to be too ambiguous to be included in the American Psychiatric Association (APA)'s Diagnostic and Statistical Manual of Mental Disorders (DSM) between 1980 and 2000. It was added to the DSM-5 in 2013 in the category of 'Substance-Related and Addictive Disorders', yet it was not used to refer to substance use, again because of the ambiguity and negative connotations. Rosenthal and Faris (2019: 447) point out this 'strange ambivalence' regarding substance use and claim that 'without a clear way to "pin down" its clinical usage and define it properly, it will continue to hinder our understanding'. In the psychological literature today, it is common to see problems related to substance use as 'substance use disorders', or SUDs. This term is meant to capture biosocial factors: both *social problems* associated with use and dependence (legal, interpersonal, economic) and *physiological reliance* on substances.

All the above ways of conceptualising relationships with drugs link consumption with the individual, either through personal choice or loss of control of self. Another way of looking at it considers structural factors that shape individual decisions – what Levine (1978) calls a 'postaddiction model' of substance problems. In this case, social and structural dynamics frame and create a context for problematic substance use. He gives the case of drunk driving, suggesting that it is as much a problem of available transportation as it is a function of substance consumption. The practical significance is in finding solutions: does one increase rehabilitation efforts or seek innovative ways of implementing new forms of transportation to accommodate drinkers? We will be exploring the structural factors in problematic substance use later in this chapter, as this perspective has been a major contribution by anthropologists.

This short introduction to the history of the concepts of addiction and related ones such as alcoholism are very potent in themselves. Like the word 'drug', they are highly loaded with meanings, usually ones quite negative. The label of 'addict' is one that can itself have implications for people's relationships with drugs. For example, notions that substances like alcohol or opiates are addictive seem to have the power to generate more alcoholism and addiction as people's beliefs in this regard can act as self-fulfilling prophecies, while 'cultures in which people do not believe drugs can cause the "loss of control" exhibit far less uncontrolled drinking' (Reinarman and Granfield 2015: 14–15). Indeed, 'addiction' and 'alcoholism' are *cultural constructs* formed at a particular time in particular types of industrialising countries. The concepts interact in complex ways with actual patterns of drug use and drug harms. This is not to deny the reality of addiction or alcoholism for many people who feel their drug use is out of control: 'just because "loss of control" is a cultural construct does not imply that users' feelings of "loss of control" are any less acute or troubling or worthy of assistance' (ibid.). Addiction as a concept has also been globalised through popular culture and the internationalisation of drug law and forms of treatment. The lives of people throughout the world are being shaped through ideas of addiction and ideas of how addicts should be treated (for example through medicalisation or through criminalisation), as Raikhel and Garriott show in their volume *Addiction Trajectories* (2013).

Complicating Addiction

In this section, we examine three different theories of addiction: a neuroscience medical disease model, a cultural meaning and social interaction model that includes mental health considerations (or socio-cultural model for short) and a structural/political-economic model.

Neurobiological/Disease Models

The medical model of addiction holds that it is a disease that can be understood through biophysical evidence and over which individuals have little control, but where medical interventions can provide effective treatment. One of the key features of this model is the idea of withdrawal, or, the notion that unpleasant and even dangerous symptoms await those who try to quit. This is especially associated with 'cold turkey' opiate withdrawal, which the American writer of the Beat generation, William S. Burroughs (2012 [1959]) associated with goose pimples and a sensation of a 'cold burn'. Some drugs are described pharmacologically as producing physical addiction, where the body becomes dependent on it for baseline functioning, producing withdrawal when it is no longer in the system. Substances producing physical withdrawal symptoms of this sort include opiates and opioids (drugs made from poppies or their chemical compounds – including morphine, heroin, fentanyl, OxyContin and Percocet), barbiturates ('downers'), and benzodiazepines (Valium and Xanax). Others like cocaine are considered to be psychologically but not physically addictive, but nevertheless also hard to quit because of the pleasurable feelings they produce.

Disease models of addiction have recently focused strongly on the brain, with addiction described as a CRDB: a 'chronic relapsing disease of the brain'. The idea is that habitual consumption of drug compounds causes changes in brain structures and functioning that lead the addict to become susceptible to craving and relapse when they encounter cues. The power of this idea partly lies in its visual representation through neuroimaging technology which has been used to produce colourful images of brain scans that suggest stark contrasts between the addicted brain and control images. Such imagery can be convincing, allowing us to *see* addiction. Yet it is important to remember that such images are highly processed and mediated by technology and by the choices made by research scientists developing the imaging techniques and policy advocates who use them: anthropologist Joseph Dumit has written a critical work on such technology and its social uses (Dumit

2004). Historian Timothy Hickman has also written critically about the use of such imagery in supporting ideas of addiction as a brain disease (Hickman 2014) and highlights how the notion of the *hijacked brain* has also supported these ideas. This metaphorical usage of 'hijacking' to describe potential effects of drugs on the brain came into vogue in the late 1990s, gaining increasing potency as verbal imagery following the 9/11 attacks and efforts by the US Drug Enforcement Administration to link drugs and terrorism (ibid. 222).

Advocates again argue that such a model should increase sympathy for consumers as addiction and difficulties of escaping it are framed as beyond conscious choice and so beyond the moral sphere. However, as Nancy Campbell shows (2010), even this model of addiction can struggle to rid addiction discourse of moral judgements. Also, while addiction treatment is based now mainly on a disease model, which moves away from drug-taking as conscious choice, criminal justice measures are still based on the notion that consumers of illegal drugs are making unlawful choices. One study found that criminal defence attorneys were more likely to embrace the disease model (and accept that their clients have little willpower in their drug use) than physicians, who overall still embraced the medical model but were more likely to ascribe control to the users. The study authors' objective was less about whether the CRBD is scientifically correct than to study the CRBD model's ability to increase referrals to and engagement in treatment programs (Avery et al. 2020).

Regarding neuroscience, there exists potential for anthropologists and neuroscientists to work together, considering the plasticity of the brain: that is to say, how malleable it is and susceptible to wider influence. Daniel Lende is a pioneer of *neuroanthropology*, a field that aims to bridge neuroscience and anthropology. He has pointed out the complexity of addiction at the neurological level, writing: 'The parts of the brain where addiction happens are not single, isolated circuits – rather, these areas handle emotion, memory, and choice, and are complexly interwoven to manage the inherent difficulty of being a social self in a dynamic world' (Lende 2012: 342). He looks at repetition of behaviour (of drug use in this case) and how it affects neural pathways in the brain, considering how incentive salience (that is to say, *craving*) becomes habitual within cultural, social and institutional environments. In this way, he and other neuroscience researchers have moved away from a reductive model of addiction that places it all within the brain, highlighting the importance of socio-cultural processes and contexts for understanding neural functioning.

Reinarman and Granfield (2015: 7) convey well the need to place addiction within much wider assemblages than the brain alone in the following quotation:

> Biology cannot eclipse culture because it always operates within and in interaction with culture. The brain is an infinitely complex set of systems that serve as a reflexive repository of lived experiences. Brains

are embedded in bodies, and bodies in turn in families, and families are nested in communities and in particular niches in the wider social structure. These things shape the conditions under which drug users live, and thus impinge upon their psyches, their situations, and their practices. If we reduce the aperture of attribution through which we view addiction so that only individual brain activity comes into view, we sever the brain from the webs of meaning in which it is enmeshed and through which its inputs flow.

Cultural Meaning and Social Interaction Model of Addiction

The model of addiction as brain disease is appealingly simple, but flaws can easily be spotted since broad cultural factors play a role in addictive drug consumption behaviour. For example, people in the UK switched more rapidly from cigarette smoking to vaping than to nicotine patches as an alternative and potentially safer route of administration of nicotine. A nicotine patch can give the body the apparently addictive compound – nicotine – but cannot replicate the other 'hits' that cigarettes offer consumers. These include the materiality or feel of the cigarette (smokers often talk of the act of holding the cigarette as important in giving them something to do with their hands), the element of conspicuous consumption (as some smoke to convey certain meanings or a particular image of themselves) and how smoking can bind people together (through sharing cigarettes or sharing the activity of smoking, or through sharing a culture of smoking). Vapes can fulfil in similar ways these aspects of smoking in a way that patches cannot, partly explaining their efficacy in smoking cessation (although worries remain about the dangers of vaping itself [see, for example, Hamberger and Halpern-Felsher 2020]) Furthermore, evidence suggests that certain drugs, even when consumed in the same way (route of administration), are more addictive in some social and historical circumstances than in others. The lack of direct correlation between incidence of addiction and drug taken further reinforces the argument that other factors come into play (Heyman 2009), just as with the example of smoking.

We introduced the terms *drug, set, and setting* (Zinberg 1984) in Chapter 1. Recall that '*drug*' refers to the chemical, pharmacological and biological aspects of a substance. While the theory of new materialism would rightly ask us to take chemical potency seriously (in the case of smoking, nicotine does have some agency), we also need to consider the effects of the particular individual consumer and the social environment – or *set* (individual mindset) and *setting* (the socio-cultural context). Taking those three factors together means rejecting what we have called *pharmacological determinism*, or the idea that pharmacological properties alone explain drug-related experiences and behaviour. We could add that they also mean rejecting genetic and neurobiological determinism for the same reasons. In other words, seeing a brain scan does not tell us everything about how that person feels or acts under the influence of a particular chemical, or even if they exhibit factors described as addictive, or associated with an SUD. The socio-cultural model seeks to understand addiction and SUDs by examining how cultural meanings and social interactions shape the chemical experiences in question. As we will see below, anthropologists contribute to this through in-depth ethnographies of substance use.

Structural/Political-Economic Model of Addiction

In this model, we consider the ways that power, politics and economics shape patterns of substance use problems through the way they structure our lives and life chances. The psychologist Bruce Alexander criticised animal studies of addiction. Classic studies, based on laboratory experiments, showed that, given access to opiates (heroin and morphine), animals (monkeys and rats in particular) would self-administer frequently, to the detriment of their own health (Alexander 2008: 194). Instead of seeing drug use as an addiction deriving from the substance itself, he studied the context in which the addictive substances were taken. He proposed that these highly social animals self-administered drugs as a response to the stress of their environment, being housed individually in metal cages with surgical implants enabling them to self-inject. He proposed that those experiments 'may show nothing more than that severely distressed animals, like severely distressed people, will seek pharmacological relief if they can find it' (ibid.). He tested that hypothesis through a set of experiments in what came to be called 'Rat Park'. Rat Park was not your typical cage: it was large, scenic and peaceful, with 16–20 rats housed together. Alexander and his collaborators found that the Rat Park rats consumed far less morphine (dissolved in water bottles) than those in small individual cages, even when the morphine water was sweetened and even when the rats had been given morphine before entering the experiment to give them a craving for it. Alexander concluded that opioid drugs do not have 'an irresistibly addictive quality, even for rats' (ibid. 195). Stressful environments (resulting from structural factors, such as poverty) are a greater cause of addiction than the drug itself.

Alexander identified the cause of addiction in what he calls a 'dislocation theory of addiction'. In this model, he cites the human need for identity and a meaningful, interdependent set of social relationships. He argues that addiction is a response to modernity and globalisation, the coming of industrial capitalism and its rupturing of social ties. We live in a form of society where many people feel marginalised and dispossessed, either financially or spiritually, and where they seek respite or even escape in drugs. It is this lack or loss of connection that he calls 'dislocation', which can result in self-destructive behaviours and even suicide. While dislocation can happen in any society, he proposes, based on his research in Vancouver, that it is particularly likely in a 'globalising free-market society', where laws encourage competition, grow global economic markets (as opposed to building local communities) and protect private property. While dislocation is particularly prevalent among the poor, it occurs in all segments of society, and addiction of all sorts (gambling, gaming, shopping etc.) is a way of adapting to it.

Alexander's analysis is somewhat extreme in moving causality so far from the chemistry of drugs themselves. He might be said too to romanticise the past, suggesting drugs were unproblematic in other societies and at different times in history. But his research presents strong evidence that drug chemistry does not in itself determine the nature of addiction – in other words, it cautions against pharmacological (or chemical) determinism. And indeed, in certain cultural and historical contexts, people have given up even strong opiates without much difficulty (the heroin-using US soldiers in the Vietnam War being the classic example that we discussed in Chapter 1), and many people discontinue problematic drug use despite satisfying alternatives. Heyman, also a psychologist, argues (2009) that there is no simple dichotomy between drug addiction being a disease and being choice-based criminal activity. He challenges a simple medical model that does not acknowledge the ways that psychological states affect neurological biological processes. In his view, the best way to tackle problematic drug use is to recognise the agency of users by identifying consumption as a choice, but not a criminal one. He argues that providing healthy and meaningful social, economic and cultural alternatives – as is the case with Alcoholics Anonymous which provides a meaningful community (despite the disease discourse it embraces) – is more effective than treating it in a medical context as a disease.

Studies of alcohol use in indigenous communities provide other cautions against pharmacological determinism. While it has been common to identify genetic predisposition for chemical abuse as the cause of high levels of alcohol use in indigenous communities, other research has revealed the social conditions that have shaped and exacerbated its use. Beauvais (1998) found that social and historical factors explained Native American drinking better than an argument about genetic disposition to chemical abuse. Before their encounter with Europeans, Native Americans lacked familiarity with alcohol stronger than fermented beverages. European traders pushed Native American alcohol consumption by using it as a medium of trade (instead of currency). The traders often encouraged drinking during trade negotiations to better take advantage of them. Furthermore, extreme intoxication was modelled by the traders and other colonists themselves, who often drank heavily. These factors contributed to an epidemic of socially and personally destructive alcohol consumption.

In response to arguments identifying genetic causes of Native American alcoholism, anthropologists have often defended Native American drinking as socially functional as a shaper of identity or as an escape from the ills of centuries of domination. Paul Spicer (1997) noted, however, that even if alcoholism is a social rather than a genetic phenomenon, it does not follow that alcohol use is culturally positive. Following Room (1984)'s criticism of problem deflation, Spicer argued that it is not only inaccurate but harmful to ignore the destructiveness of alcohol consumption in some contexts. Based on his research with Native Americans in an urban setting in Minnesota, US, Spicer pointed out an ambivalent, complex relationship with drinking, as testimonies from people who were currently drinking revealed that drinking facilitated community with some people while destroying relationships with others – in particular one's children and elders. Spicer wrote that 'it is testimony like this that should give us pause when we discuss the culturally integrated nature of Indian drinking' (312). It suggests what we know about any other cultural context, which is that culture is not homogeneous and that even single individuals have mixed and sometimes contradictory feelings. Culturally integrated or not, we see that social contexts profoundly shape patterns of drinking that cannot be explained simply by the fact of the substance itself. But it also does not mean that consumption is always socially or individually positive.

The structural model of addiction identifies causality of addiction in the broad socio-political contexts that shape access to drugs, the geographies of their use, policies that codify what kind of drug use is dangerous and should be treated or punished, as well as psychological factors that might make them attractive (such as mental health explanations and Alexander's dislocation theory). In all this, the structural model does not stop with individual choice but examines the conditions that shape this choice, thus aligning with Critical Medical Anthropology and its focus on the wider structures of medical and health inequalities that often constrain the choices people can make (Singer and Baer 2018).

The Anthropology of Addiction

Ethnographies of Addiction

Anthropology is well placed to help better understand addiction from emic and critical perspectives, showing the importance of culture and sociality to understanding its expression. Prior to the mid-twentieth century, few anthropologists wrote about drug addiction. This makes sense, as anthropology's focus was on understanding normative patterns of consumption, defending seemingly nonsensical or irrational practices as socially and culturally functional. One interesting early example of an anthropologist grappling with the theme of addiction was Gregory Bateson's work on alcoholism and Alcoholics Anonymous (1971). In essence, it looks at how drinkers get into impossible situations whereby they attempt to demonstrate their power over alcohol by consuming large amounts while drinking socially (often a competitive process) without succumbing to the effects, yet when they almost inevitably do get drunk those around them push them to show more 'self control'. Later on, however, pride pushes them back to drinking in something of a vicious cycle. Bateson argued that in some ways being drunk was a corrective to a Western epistemology whereby people were seen as separate from the world, as beings in charge of their own destiny, an epistemology in which a myth of willpower and control could take root. In Bateson's analysis, submitting to the power of alcohol corrects this, and Alcoholics Anonymous gains much of its efficacy through pushing the alcoholic to admit their powerlessness. This work is highly evocative, and it speaks to a wider anthropological interest in personhood, contrasting Western individualism and collectivistic and interconnected conceptions of what it is to be human in other cultural contexts. In this way, it is a good example of how alcoholism – and addiction more generally – can speak in interesting ways to wider sociocultural ideas about what it is to be human.

Beyond Bateson's paper, anthropologists began to produce ethnographies in the 1960s and 1970s that focused on street addicts especially in the US, foregrounding the lives and experiences of heroin users – especially the *business* of being an addict (Preble and Casey 1969). In his book, *Ripping and Running*, Michael Agar (1973), for example, argued that, contrary to popular stereotypes, heroin addicts were generally not 'escapists' (a common trope in discourse about drugs) living in an intoxicated bubble. They live incredibly busy lives as they endeavour to gain access to their drugs of choice. In a linguistic study of addicts, he noted that they had developed a rich vocabulary and alternated between *hustling* (getting money through casual labour or petty theft), *copping* (obtaining a supply of heroin) and *getting-off* (using the drug and feeling its effects). Such ethnographies joined literary portrayals of addiction at the time that depicted heroin use, for example, as a way of life (Burroughs 1959). These ethnographies not only helped in understanding the heroin economy on the street but also the values and meanings of life as an addict. It followed in the tradition of anthropological works that humanise the Other. More recent ethnographies also highlight just how busy heroin users must be as hustlers to obtain their heroin supplies. Mark Hunter's work on heroin users in South Africa takes up the theme of hustling, as users work hard in South Africa's informal economy – doing casual work like washing cars – or in the illicit economy to secure money for their supply (Hunter 2020).

While addiction happens in all segments of society, many studies have focused on marginalised populations whose drug habits have been considered socially problematic, including street addicts, the homeless and poor people in general. For example *Righteous Dopefiend* by Bourgois and Schonberg (2009) is a moving presentation of the lives of heroin and other drug addicts living on the streets of San Francisco. In this book, Bourgois and Schonberg show the complexity of social relationships, demonstrating how gifts of heroin and other forms of aid and protection bond homeless addicts into social networks. They show the importance of reciprocity, linking with Marcel Mauss' (1925) observations of the importance of gifts in social life (see also Chapter 5). These bonds of sociality create meaning among people cast out from the mainstream economy and society. A similar analysis is presented by Stephen Wakeman (2016), who argues that a 'moral economy' of heroin consumption among older users in the northwest of England helps explain its appeal in the England of the years following the financial collapse of 2008 where the UK government had responded with austerity measures that gutted public services through funding cuts. This moral economy of exchange and support created meaningful social bonds for the marginalised in this political-economic context. However, such social bonds can further reinforce their marginalization from wider society. Such ethnographies are highly nuanced, showing how rich with meaning and sociality are the lives of addicts, yet also how this meaning and sociality can lead to further harms.

Political Economies of Addiction

The focus on marginal populations led to Critical Medical Anthropology analyses of the relationships between political-economic structural disadvantages and addiction. On the one hand, the illegal status of drugs leads to a myriad of risks to the user, even once they have stopped using drugs. These include prison terms, criminal records that make it difficult to find housing or employment, lack of opportunity to build capital to support financial independence, health effects of either poor healthcare or co-morbidity (diseases stemming from drug use, as in lung cancer from tobacco use) and so on. On the other hand, some have argued that the derision with which people look down on drug users actually serves the function of bolstering mainstream cultural values, making drug addicts easy targets for blame for social problems. Singer and Page (2014) extend this line of thought in *The Social Value of Drug Addicts*, showing how productive this stigmatised group is in terms of generating cheap, docile labour (as many incarcerated drug users work for low wages within prisons), sensationalised figures for the media and arts, and useful examples of bad behaviour as societal scapegoats. In this way, addicts are highly productive members of society, albeit in a dark, sinister way, as they become exploited.

Embedded within political-economic critiques are anthropologists' and others' efforts at developing practical public health solutions. Anthropologists have been involved in doing drug ethnography with funding from the National Institute of Health with the explicit goal of identifying effective solutions to debilitating drug use. Many anthropologists, including Michael Agar, who wrote one of the first street ethnographies on heroin users (cited above), did government-funded drug ethnographies at the National Institutes of Mental Health (US) Clinical Research Center, National Institutes of Health and NIDA (Page and Singer 2010). During the AIDS epidemic, anthropologists helped understand how intravenous drug use contributes to the spread of HIV/AIDS. In these capacities, anthropologists advocate for qualitative research, because good drug research requires nuanced and sensitive knowledge not accessible through questionnaires (ibid. 67). To this day, many anthropologists around the world work in and for addiction programs in different parts of the world. For example the late Susan Beckerleg researched heroin addiction in Kenya as an anthropologist, and she also worked for a pioneering harm reduction organization called The Omari Project in Malindi (Beckerleg 2001). This organization sought to provide clean needles in an area with high rates of blood-borne diseases, such as HIV/AIDS, and was named after the first person in Malindi to die from using a contaminated needle.

Addiction and Treatment as Cultural Constructions

Because of the potential of harm in labelling, anthropologists have joined psychologists and others in critiquing the very concept of addiction. In this regard, they resist a facile labelling of drug use as pathological. This links to the work of American psychologist Carl Hart, who wrote a recent book entitled *Drug Use for Grown-Ups* (2021) that speaks candidly of his own use of heroin and other drugs. He makes a case that even drugs like heroin – so-called *hard drugs* associated with addiction – can be used in controlled ways, especially when used by people like himself with relatively stable lives. This is not to deny the problems associated with drugs but to push back at public health and popular culture framings that suggest all or most drug use is pathological. While certain assemblages of drugs, ideas about drugs, social networks and political-economic conditions can lead to harm, others can be relatively innocuous or even beneficial.

In addition to needlessly vilifying many instances of drug use, social scientists have shown that addiction science is not neutral but links to the political economy of drugs and drug treatment. Raikhel and Garriott (2013) demonstrate the many 'trajectories' of addiction and addicts as people interact both with drugs and with the forms of treatment and punishment that ideas of addiction have generated. They present addicts as both *agents* navigating assemblages of drugs, social networks, forms of treatment and punishment and as *objects of knowledge* for law enforcement and for the science of addiction. Addicts have choices, but those choices are framed within particular legal and scientific structures. In another critical analysis of addiction, Carr (2010) traced the politics of talk therapy addiction treatment, which focuses on 'healthy' language more than it encourages actual reconfigured relationships with drugs. In sum, these studies reveal that addicts live highly complex lives amidst constantly evolving notions of what addiction is and what social purposes it serves.

Perhaps the most moving recent ethnography of addiction is that by Angela Garcia (2008), called *The Elegiac Addict*. In this essay, Garcia focuses on Hispanic addicts in New Mexico. In a chilling narrative, she told the story of Alma Gallegos, who died from a heroin overdose during a 'relapse' from drug rehab in northern New Mexico, a state in the US southwest. Garcia wrote about the confluence of histories of land loss and domination with experiences of generational suffering and mourning, often manifest in harmful drug use. Garcia links the lives of addicts to the themes of escapism and dispossession, describing the centuries of loss felt by the people of the region, loss that provides a context for high rates of addiction in this area. In addition to chronicling generational desperation, she identifies how contemporary ideas about and practices of addiction treatment actually reinforce addiction. She writes how the notions of time – of the 'vicious cycle' that predicts relapse – in some ways reinforce the hopelessness they feel and perpetuates this cycle. Medical ideas about addiction as a chronic, relapsing disease powerfully shape outcomes. The full complement of contradictory ideas about addiction confront and further marginalise them, as their encounters with law enforcement follow the logic that they are immoral law-breakers, with all the consequences therein. In such tragic circumstances, Garcia argues that the discourse of addiction can be a self-fulfilling prophecy.

Case Studies

Khat

Looking at case studies of particular drugs in context allows us to deconstruct how the concept of addiction is used in regard to particular substances. Both authors of this text have studied khat – Carrier in Kenya and Gezon in Madagascar. Carrier's work has looked at how British attempts to ban khat in colonial Kenya were counterintuitively undone by their promotion of the idea of it being addictive and withdrawal from it being dangerous (Anderson and Carrier 2009). By the time the British became interested in khat in Kenya in the 1930s, the concept of addiction was thoroughly globalised, and khat became conflated in the minds of some of the British administrators with drugs such as opium. While wanting to ban what they saw as a corrupting influence on the population, the British were also concerned that as an 'addictive' drug, there was a possibility that consumers would experience dangerous withdrawal symptoms if they simply stopped chewing. For this reason, they introduced a scheme whereby self-declared 'addicts' could obtain supplies of khat through the British administration to prevent withdrawal. Unsurprisingly, many khat consumers declared themselves addicted to get their khat courtesy of the colonial state.

Although legal and often socially validated in key countries of consumption such as Kenya and Ethiopia, perceptions of khat globally are still often coloured by its reputation as an addictive drug. Indeed, it is often described as addictive in media coverage and by those campaigning against it. Countries where much khat is consumed, such as Yemen or Djibouti, are sometimes viewed as addict nations (for example, see Weir 1985: chapter 4) based on the logic that nothing other than addiction would lead so many people to spend so much time chewing the leaves and stems of khat. Yet most research on khat suggests evidence for it being addictive is ambiguous at best (Odenwald et al. 2020). There are withdrawal effects, including lethargy and vivid dreams, but overall, these appear relatively minor compared with those of opiates. In the 1980s, researchers suggested that long-term Yemeni chewers who move abroad to countries where they have no access to khat have little trouble adjusting to a khat-free environment (Weir 1985: 49). This is reminiscent of the research into US soldiers who used heroin in Vietnam and how few of them maintained a heroin habit once back in the US, such was the change in context (Robins et al. 1974).

This is not to say that there are no risks of dependency upon khat. Indeed, there are those who feel themselves drawn to khat-chewing sessions, often despite pressure to quit by family and friends. However, rather than being pushed by some 'addictive qualities' of the substance itself, it appears in contexts such as Yemen and Djibouti that it is the social institution of the khat-chewing session that people become dependent upon, rather than the plant itself, as Weir emphasised in her ethnography of Yemen (1985). So much of life is centred around the substance in those countries, that even those not keen on the effects get drawn to such sessions. In contexts such as the Somali diaspora in the UK – members of which often experience marginalisation and suffer from trauma – khat-chewing places (known as a *mafrish*) became places where chewers could feel comfortable not just through experiencing the familiar effects of khat, but also in the company of fellow Somalis insulated from the often difficult and unfamiliar environment of British cities. Of course, spending much time chewing khat in such places could lead to further marginalisation. Understanding 'addiction' in the case of khat requires understanding a much wider assemblage beyond the substance – drug, set and setting – and exploring how consumption can become institutionalised within a society. Ethnographies such as Weir's (1985) can play important roles in elucidating the social underpinnings of drug usage that might be classed as exhibiting dependency.

Tobacco

Tobacco provides a contrast with khat because although its negative health consequences are well documented, it is relatively socially acceptable in most contexts where it is smoked. Tobacco also raises questions about the chemical power of a substance, reminding us that while pharmacological determinism is misleading and even harmful to users, we must also take seriously the power of the chemical to affect one's agency, or ability to choose – we need to see the substance in *biocultural* or *biosocial* perspective. Despite the severe negative health impact of tobacco, it is a drug that is hard to quit once one is addicted to it. Most people who smoke wish to quit, and 80% of people who try to quit on their own start smoking again within a month. Only 3% remain tobacco-free six months later (Benowitz 2009). Much of the toxicity of tobacco is related to smoking it (such as lung cancer), although there are health risks associated with heated tobacco products, including vaping (which are not yet well-understood), and smokeless tobacco products (cancer, heart disease, dental disease).

It is nicotine that causes dependence and addiction. Studies of brain images show that the introduction of nicotine dramatically increases brain activity in several areas, including the prefrontal cortex – the part of the brain associated with processing information and the ability to plan, organise and control our behaviour (Volkow et al. 2004). Like many other psycho-active substances, nicotine also releases dopamine, a neurotransmitter in the brain that allows us to feel pleasure and motivation. People who take nicotine repeatedly develop tolerance for it, meaning that the brain adapts to it and begins to need it to feel 'normal'. What that means is that the dopamine-related feeling of pleasure and motivation becomes lost when someone stops using nicotine. In essence, nicotine tolerance makes our brain lose the ability to regulate pleasure and motivation on its own. When attempting to quit, the nicotine-tolerant person experiences withdrawal symptoms, such as anxiety and stress – leading most to resume consumption of nicotine.

However, in addition to the pharmacological activity, habitual social behaviours and cultural meanings underpin why people have a hard time quitting: people associate tobacco use with specific times, places and moods for example. People also develop meaningful connections with the sensory aspects of smoking that make it hard to quit: the feel of the cigarette in one's hands and mouth, the smell, the taste and so forth. Programs aimed at helping people quit (tobacco cessation programs) need to take these factors into consideration, too. As mentioned earlier in this chapter, these factors become evident where the efficacies of vaping and nicotine patches are compared. Again, anthropological studies of drug use are imperative (Benowitz 2009), and work such as Andrew Russell's on tobacco that puts the agency of tobacco into the wider assemblage of socio-cultural factors is important (Russell 2019). Mark Nichter and his associates have studied cultural contexts of implementing cessation programs in many countries, including India, Indonesia and Turkey (Nichter et al. 2010, Nichter et al. 2017). Tobacco addiction can also be seen through a Critical Medical Anthropology lens, one that shows how tobacco dependency often accompanies poverty, and indeed tobacco firms are known to promote their products aggressively in poorer countries as the market for cigarettes declines in wealthier ones, what Singer refers to as 'drugging the poor' (Singer 2008)

Opioids

In a final case study, we look to opioids to examine not only the power of the chemical (most poignantly in causing death), but also to trace this epidemic to structural violence, considering social determinants of health. We could take any number of drugs as case studies here, including methamphetamines and crack cocaine, and maybe you will follow up on these in your own research. First, we review definitions: an opiate is a term for chemical compounds found naturally in the poppy plant and that are refined into heroin, morphine and codeine. The term 'opioid' refers to both natural opiates and ones that are made in a laboratory with the same chemical structure – called synthetic compounds. Semi-synthetic opioids include oxycodone and hydrocodone. Fully synthetic opioids include tramadol and fentanyl. Used medically, they are prescribed for reducing pain. They also cause feelings of euphoria, which partly explains why so many people, especially poor and marginalised (Bourgois' [2018] *lumpen*) ones, become addicted.

Unfortunately, taking too much can lead to lethal overdose. The WHO reports that 70% of drug use deaths are due to opioid use. Fentanyl is a particularly potent synthetic opioid, about 50–100 times more potent than morphine.[1] Fentanyl, in addition to being used legally in anaesthesia, is also added to other drugs, such as heroin, to increase its potency. It is also used in counterfeit prescription pills sold as drugs like oxycodone and Adderall. In concert with the high demand for illegally obtained but legally produced opioids (especially OxyContin) in the US, Mexican and Chinese cartels began making counterfeit pills with fentanyl, leading to a spike of overdose deaths starting in the late 2010s (Bourgois 2018).

The trajectory of the current opioid epidemic is somewhat unique, partly because pharmaceutical companies and not illegal drug cartels are at its origin. What started as a wonder drug for pain ended up being vastly over-prescribed, and pharmaceutical companies as well as pharmacies are being held responsible for their role in its distribution. Another reason is because of the communities it has hit, which include both poor and middle-class ones. It has been particularly associated with white communities, and some have argued that that has shaped public perception and medico-legal responses to it. As Mendoza et al. (2018: 242) argue:

> The rise of opioid abuse among Whites has resulted in popular narratives of victimization by prescribers, framing of addiction as a biological disease, and the promise of pharmaceutical treatments that differ from the criminalizing narratives that have historically described urban Latino and black narcotic use.

According to this argument, the more favourable perception of prescription opioid drug addicts than, say, heroin addicts is linked to race and class. The relatively compassionate treatment of opioid addicts highlights the structural violence and even racism in the systematic, systemic marginalization of those addicted to other substances – the violence that sends them to prison, an act that has ripple effects into every other area of their lives and reinforces structural inequalities.

Anthropology and Drug Potency

Anthropologists studying problematic drug use have been more comfortable with approaches that link addiction to cultural meanings as well as to marginality and structural violence than with approaches more focused on the power of the substance and the brain. But anthropologists now are interested in integrating cultural and biological perspectives, combining the materiality of the drugs with cultures and social lives of consumption. For example, it is important to recognise that opiates have the capacity for the relief of physical and mental pain, as well as the capacity to bring social as well as individual pleasure. These are key factors motivating dangerous and illegal use, which in turn reinforces structural inequalities and dislocation. Regarding neuroscience, anthropologists and neuroscientists have begun to work more closely in understanding drug effects, highlighting the plasticity and malleability of the brain. The brain and its neurochemistry are not deterministic but, like drugs themselves, are bound up in society and culture.

Returning to the theme of power by way of a conclusion, we see how anthropology is never content with simplistic notions of drugs as chemical enslavers that hold us in thrall even at the expense of our lives. Anthropologists show how drugs and our addictions to them are enmeshed in powerful webs of sociality and meaning, as well as in powerful political and economic structures. In recognizing this, potency is taken from the drugs themselves and shown to spread through much broader and more complex circuits. Perhaps anthropology in this way does not *problem deflate* in relation to drugs and addiction, but *problem inflates*? If only an addict's problems were simply related to a troubled relationship with a chemical substance, then that would be relatively straightforward to treat. Instead, addiction relates to much wider and much more intractable problems and challenges, including poverty and inequality.

Note

1 See WHO factsheet on opioids available online: www.who.int/news-room/fact-she ets/detail/opioid-overdose (accessed November 2022).

Works Cited

Agar, Michael. 1973. *Ripping and Running: A Formal Ethnography of Urban Heroin Addicts*. Princeton, NJ: Seminar Press.

Alexander, Bruce K. 2008. *The Globalization of Addiction: A Study in Poverty of the Spirit*. Oxford: OUP Oxford.

Anderson, David, and Neil Carrier. 2009. "Khat in Colonial Kenya: A History of Prohibition and Control." *Journal of African History* 50 (3): 377–97.

Avery, Joseph J., Jonathan D. Avery, Joseph Mouallem, Adam R. Demner, and Joel Cooper. 2020. "Physicians' and Attorneys' Beliefs and Attitudes Related to the Brain Disease Model of Addiction." *The American Journal on Addictions* 29 (4): 305–312.

Bateson, Gregory. 1971. "The Cybernetics of "Self": A Theory of Alcoholism." *Psychiatry* 34 (1): 1–18.

Beauvais, Fred. 1998. "American Indians and Alcohol." *Alcohol Health & Research World* 22 (4): 253.

Beckerleg, Susan. (2001). "Counselling Kenyan heroin users: Cross-cultural motivation?" *Health Education* 101 (2): 69–73.

Benowitz, Neal L. 2009. "Pharmacology of Nicotine: Addiction, Smoking-Induced Disease, and Therapeutics." *Annual Review of Pharmacology & Toxicology* 49 (1): 57–71.

Berridge, Virginia. 1999. *Opium and the People: Opiate Use and Drug Control Policy in Nineteenth and Early Twentieth Century England.* New York, NY: Free Association Books Limited.

Bourgois, Philippe. 2018. "Decolonising Drug Studies in an Era of Predatory Accumulation." *Third World Quarterly* 39 (2): 385–398.

Bourgois, Philippe, and Jeffrey Schonberg. 2009. *Righteous Dopefiend.* Oakland, CA: University of California Press.

Burroughs, William S. 1959. *Naked Lunch.* New York, NY: Grove Press.

———. 2012. *Junky.* New York: Penguin Books Limited.

Campbell, Nancy. 2010. "Towards a Critical Neuroscience of 'Addiction'." *Biosocieties* 9 (1): 89–104.

Campbell, Nancy D., and Susan J. Shaw. 2008. "Incitements to Discourse: Illicit Drugs, Harm Reduction, and the Production of Ethnographic Subjects." *Cultural Anthropology* 23 (4): 688–717.

Carr, E. Summerson. 2010. *Scripting Addiction: The Politics of Therapeutic Talk and American Sobriety.* Princeton, NJ: Princeton University Press.

De Quincey, Thomas. 1985 [1822]. *The Confessions of an English Opium Eater.* Oxford; New York, NY: Oxford University Press.

Dumit, J. 2004. *Picturing Personhood: Brain Scans and Biomedical Identity.* Princeton, NJ: Princeton University Press.

Garcia, Angela. 2008. "The Elegiac Addict: History, Chronicity, and the Melancholic Subject." *Cultural Anthropology* 23: 718–746.

Hamberger, Eric Stephen, and Bonnie Halpern-Felsher. "Vaping in adolescents: epidemiology and respiratory harm." Current opinion in pediatrics 32, no. 3 (2020): 378.

Hart, Carl. 2021. *Drug Use for Grown Ups.* New York: Penguin.

Heyman, Gene M. 2009. *Addiction: A Disorder of Choice.* Cambridge, MA: Harvard University Press.

Hickman, Timothy A. 2014. "Target America: Visual Culture, Neuroimaging, and the 'Hijacked Brain' Theory of Addiction." *Past & Present* 222 (suppl_9): 207–226. https://doi.org/10.1093/pastj/gtt021

———. 2022. "Dangerous Drugs: From Habit to Addiction." In *The Oxford Handbook of Global Drug History,* edited by Paul Gootenberg, 213–229. Oxford: Oxford University Press.

Hunter, Mark. 2020. "Heroin hustles: Drugs and the laboring poor in South Africa." *Social Science & Medicine* 265: 113329.

Jellinek, Elvin Morton. 1960. *The Disease Concept of Alcoholism.* New Haven, CT: Hillhouse Press.

Klein, Axel, Marcus Day and Anthony Harriott. 2004. *Caribbean Drugs: From Criminalization to Harm Reduction.* London: Zed Books.

Lemon, Rebecca. 2018. *Addiction and Devotion in Early Modern England.* Philadelphia: University of Pennsylvania Press.

Lende, Daniel H. 2012. "Addiction and neuroanthropology." In *The Encultured Brain: An Introduction to Neuroanthropology*, edited by Daniel H. Lende and Greg Downey, 339–362. Cambridge, MA: MIT Press.

Levine, Harry G. 1978. "The Discovery of Addiction. Changing Conceptions of Habitual Drunkenness in America." *Journal of Studies on Alcohol* 39 (1): 143–174.

Mauss, Marcel. 1925. *The Gift*. London: Routledge.

Mendoza, Sonia, Allyssa S. Rivera, and Helena B. Hansen. 2018. "Re-Racialization of Addiction and the Redistribution of Blame in the White Opioid Epidemic." *Medical Anthropology Quarterly* 33 (2): 242–262.

Nichter, Mark, Mimi Nichter and Myra Muramoto. 2010. "Project Quit Tobacco International: Laying the Groundwork for Tobacco Cessation in Low–and Middle-Income Countries." *Asia Pacific Journal of Public Health* 22 (3): 181–188.

Nichter, Mimi, Asli Carkoglu, Mark Nichter, Seyda Ozcan, and M. Atilla Uysal. 2017. "Engaging Nurses in Smoking Cessation: Challenges and Opportunities in Turkey." *Health Policy* 122: 192–197.

Odenwald, Michael, Axel Klein, and Nasir Warfa. 2020. "Khat Addiction." In *Textbook of Addiction Treatment 2nd ed.*, edited by Giuseppe Carra, Nady el-Guebaly, Marc Galanter and Alexander M Baldacchino, 455–466. Milan: Springer.

Page, J. Bryan, and Merrill Singer. 2010. *Comprehending Drug Use: Ethnographic Research at the Social Margins*. New Brunswick, NJ: Rutgers University Press.

Preble, Edward, and John J. Casey. 1969. "Taking Care of Business – The Heroin User's Life on the Street." *International Journal of the Addictions* 4: 1–24.

Raikhel, Eugene, and William Garriott. 2013. *Addiction Trajectories*. Durham, NC: Duke University Press.

Reinarman, Craig and Robert Granfield. 2015. "Addiction Is Not Just a Brain Disease: Critical Studies of Addiction." In *Expanding Addiction: Critical Essays*, edited by Robert Granfield and Craig Reinarman, 1–21. London: Routledge.

Robins, Lee N., Darlene H. Davis, and David N. Nurco. 1974. "How Permanent Was Vietnam Drug Addiction?" *American Journal of Public Health* 64 (12): 38–43.

Room, Robin. 1984. "Alcohol and Ethnography: A Case of Problem Deflation?" *Current Anthropology* 25 (2): 169–191.

Rosenthal, Richard J., and Suzanne B. Faris. 2019. "The Etymology and Early History of 'Addiction'." *Addiction Research & Theory* 27 (5): 437–449.

Russell, Andrew. 2019. *Anthropology of Tobacco: Ethnographic Adventures in Non-Human Worlds*. London: Routledge.

Singer, Merrill. 2008. *Drugging the Poor: Legal and Illegal Drugs and Social Inequality*. Long Grove, IL: Waveland Press, Inc.

Singer, Merrill, and Hans Baer. 2018. *Critical Medical Anthropology, 2nd edition*. New York: Routledge.

Singer, Merrill, and J. Bryan Page. 2014. *The Social Value of Drug Addicts: Uses of the Useless*. New York: Routledge.

Spicer, Paul. 1997. "Toward a (Dys)functional Anthropology of Drinking: Ambivalence and the American Indian Experience with Alcohol." *Medical Anthropology Quarterly* 11 (3): 306–323.

Valverde, Mariana. 1998. *Diseases of the Will: Alcohol and Dilemmas of Freedom*. Cambridge: Cambridge University Press.

Volkow, N.D., Fowler, J.S., Wang, G.J. and Swanson, J.M., 2004. "Dopamine in Drug Abuse and Addiction: Results from Imaging Studies and Treatment Implications." *Molecular Psychiatry* 9 (6): 557.

Wakeman, S. 2016. "The Moral Economy of Heroin in 'Austerity Britain'." *Critical Criminology* 24: 363–377.

Weir, Shelagh. 1985. *Qat in Yemen: Consumption and Social Change*. London: British Museum Publications Limited.

World Health Organization. 2021. *Opioid Overdose*. World Health Organization. www.who.int/news-room/fact-sheets/detail/opioid-overdose

Zinberg, Norman. 1984. *Drug, Set, and Setting: The Basis for Controlled Intoxicant Use*. New Haven, CT: Yale University Press.

7 Drug Economies, Livelihoods and Development

While the earlier chapters of this book have mostly focused on drug consumption – whether everyday, ritualistic, or linked to addiction – this chapter turns to the role of drugs as crops and commodities. In short, it turns to the industry around drugs, an industry worth billions of dollars. Just like drug consumption, this industry has also been much sensationalised in popular culture, with tropes of cartels and violence dominating depictions of the drug trade. Drugs are indeed valuable commodities, but standard notions of the drugs industry need nuancing to give a more balanced perspective of the trade in psychoactive goods, especially as some of the most valuable are legal drugs rather than the prohibited substances that often feature in films and television programmes. Such nonpharmaceutical legal drugs (alcohol and tobacco, primarily) provide significant income to many, and then there is the multibillion dollar psychotropic pharmaceutical industry, which includes Valium, Adderall and OxyContin. Illegal drugs also often sources of income for many people, often those marginalised from 'legitimate' livelihoods.

In this chapter, we look at the production and trade of drugs (growing and selling them), considering the often-global impact of the drug industry for providing livelihoods to people who produce and trade drug substances. In doing so, we take on common assumptions that drugs are necessarily negative for development and propose that drug crops can provide an important source of livelihood under some circumstances, especially when it does not impede access to food and security. In all this, we show how anthropology and ethnographic research can help bring nuance to understandings of the role of drugs as crops and commodities, and how drug crops help reveal ambiguities in the very concept of economic *development*.

Drugs as Crops and Commodities

To get to their consumers, drugs travel through trajectories of production and trade, usually as commodities produced to be sold for livelihoods and profit. These trajectories are the commodity chains that drugs follow, chains

DOI: 10.4324/9781003109549-7

studied by anthropologists, especially in the last few decades and inspired by work such as Appadurai's *The social life of things* (1986) that we discussed in Chapter 2. Anthropologists and other researchers have studied the commodity chain of drugs of all types, including pharmaceutical medicines. Kristin Peterson's work is highly instructive here, looking at how pharmaceutical markets in Nigeria are shaped by many local, national and global dynamics, especially those linked to neoliberal economic reforms that hollowed out Nigeria's own pharmaceutical industry and set the context for a rise in fake medicines (Peterson 2014). Fake medicines have become a key concern in countries like Nigeria, as they are a grave risk to consumers given their limited efficacy. The profitability of legally prescribed pharmaceuticals in markets such as the US is a key factor in rates of addiction, especially in relation to opiate medicines, which is the focus of so much concern in North America. Synthetic opiates such as OxyContin and buprenorphine (used for treating opiate addiction) have proved some of the most profitable by creating dependencies that require long-term consumption (for an anthropological analysis, see Hansen and Skinner 2012). However, in this chapter, we will focus mainly on farmed drugs rather than synthetic or pharmaceutical ones.

In many ways, drugs are commodities just like any others. But they have some differences from other commodities that are worth noting. One aspect that makes drug commodities unique goes back to their pharmacologically documented and experienced chemical potency (see Chapters 1 and 2). But even more importantly, we argue, what makes some drugs distinctive as commodities is a poignant combination of their capacity to generate dependency and thus lock consumers into their purchase, and the consequences of their legal status: such drugs are lucrative and in constant demand. Philippe Bourgois (2018) proposes a pattern of what he calls 'predatory accumulation' to explain the money-making potential of drugs. Throughout history, drugs have enabled wealthy entrepreneurs and their governments to accumulate capital by facilitating and even creating drug markets that encourage addiction (drug production and sale) and preying on addicts through criminal justice and public health systems. A related feature that makes drug commodity chains stand out is their role in fuelling global integration historically. Psychoactive substances, such as tobacco, coffee, tea and sugar, were among the first globalised commodities (see Chapter 3).

Finally, the high value to weight ratio of drugs gives illegal drugs distinctive properties. That they are both small, relatively light-weight and highly profitable has made it easy and attractive to smuggle them, despite the high risks of personal harm and loss of revenue in the smuggling business (Van Schendel and Abraham 2005). In sum, the addictive potential of some drugs, their centrality to global economic and political integration, their sometimes illegal status, and their high value to weight ratio make them stand out from other commodities.

Dangerous Commodities?

Today, drug production and trade are usually associated with illicit commodities in the shadows of other global flows of goods, with 'kingpins' and desperate or foolish smugglers. Drugs are seen as a way to make money and make it quick. This is glorified through films like Scarface and Midnight Express, and more recently through the streaming shows *El Chapo* and *Orange is the New Black*. The financial opportunities that illicit drugs provide cannot be underestimated as a motivation for political manoeuvres and policy decisions around the world. Danger exists not only where people grow and take drugs, but also in the places the drugs flow through on the way, called transit hubs. Many countries in Africa, particularly West Africa, have been transit hubs for drugs destined for Europe. This threatens political and economic stability by diverting producers away from food crops and fishing, encouraging violent crime networks and governmental corruption (sometimes called narco-states), and introducing drug use, particularly among youth (Adeyanju 2020, Klantschnig 2016, Carrier and Klantschnig 2012).

Because the trade occurs in the shadows of the global economy, without government regulation, and because of the tremendous stakes, the illegal drug trade can be dangerous. It leads to repressive drug policies that criminalise people who risk life and limb to participate in the lucrative trade. However, it is important to remember that it is the illegal status of the substances being traded that is the most important factor in making them dangerous as trade commodities, not the substances themselves (although the substances aren't necessarily without harm).

However, not all drug trade is cartels and crime. Van Schendel and Abraham (2005) encourage us to think about not only legal status but also social acceptability. The lines between licit and illicit/legal and illegal are blurry, with unclear or unevenly enforced laws and with varying amounts of social acceptability. In other words, some drugs may be illegal but socially acceptable in some places and contexts. There are many places in the world where small-scale farmers grow and trade illegal or quasi-legal drugs (the latter are drugs whose legal status is ambiguous or fluctuates depending on context, see Carrier and Klantschnig 2018). These include substances such as khat, cannabis, opium poppies and coca in lower-risk scenarios, where making a living through local trade or for household consumption is locally accepted socially, as you will read about in the case studies later.

Furthermore, not all cartels and crime involve drugs. While drugs take on moralistic disapproval, and while they provide a poignant example of illegality, they are not the only illicit commodity, and so they are not the only commodity whose very trade presents danger: when traded illegally, wildlife, cattle, arms, diamonds and even people (through human trafficking) can generate similar dangers as drugs (van Schendel and Abraham 2005). Any commodity that is deemed to be illegal may take on the dangerous characteristics of illicit drugs, even something as seemingly innocuous as sugar in Somalia (Rasmussen 2017).

While illicit commodities have a lot in common in their tendency toward crime and violence, we must not forget that one of the dangers that unites licit and illicit drugs is the public health risk associated with many drug substances. The most lethal drug globally, in fact, is legal: tobacco takes about 8 million lives each year and is one of the leading causes of death globally. As we have seen in Chapter 6, the risk of chemical dependency – *addiction* – all along the commodity chain leads to a unique kind of devastation not only for the individuals who are addicted but also for the security and sustainability of the whole community. The public health risks increase in places where there is not a history of the use of the substance in question and therefore a lack of culturally prescribed ways of taking it to mitigate social and economic dysfunction associated with its use. The global commodification of drug substances has dramatically increased the health and social dangers associated with dependence.

Drugs and Livelihoods: Economic Development and Its Alternatives

The connections between drugs and making a living speak to issues of economic *development* and larger questions of the role or the potential role of drug production and trade in livelihoods and quality of life. The link of drugs with development – usually framed as a negative link – has grown strong in recent years, and work by anthropologist Merrill Singer (2008) summarises well many of the key developmental issues connected with drugs both licit and illicit, including violence and impacts on youth. Here we take a closer look at what economic development is, how anthropologists have studied it, and where drugs fit into it. The story of 'economic development' begins in the twentieth century, in particular, after WWII and a new global monetary system established in the Bretton Woods agreement in 1944. In this, the US, Canada, Australia, western European countries, and Japan came together to create the World Bank, which began by lending money to European countries. Soon after, it turned its sights to lending money to 'developing' or 'emerging market' economies in Asia, Africa and Latin America (most being former colonies) with the intention of bringing them up to the wealth and standard of living of Europe and the US. The Bretton Woods agreement also created the International Monetary Fund (IMF), designed to stabilise currencies and provide temporary assistance to countries with struggling economies. While global economies had been connected for centuries, and even millennia, the Bretton Woods agreement ushered in a new phase of global integration, underscoring the importance of profit-driven capitalistic economic development as a path to accumulation. It also accelerated globalisation and the heightened connections between economies and people through more highly accessible trade, travel and communication. In all this, development became measured through GDP (Gross Domestic Product) and per capita income, very economistic and reductive ways of measuring what is valuable to humanity.

However, some scholars have argued that not only does economic development not alleviate poverty in former colonies, but also it makes poverty worse. Dependency theory was first developed in the middle of the twentieth century (Wallerstein 1974, Frank 1967). At its core, dependency theory states that the wealth of the developed nations depends upon the resources gained at low cost from 'underdeveloped' countries. It is an unbalanced relationship and cannot be corrected under the current terms of trade in the global economy. The former colonies are considered underdeveloped *because of* the development of wealthy countries: the wealth of the few depends on the impoverishment of the many. Drug crops are among those cheap commodities that wealthy operators benefit from, and here we see an interesting nexus between the dependency of 'addicts' on particular substances and the economic 'dependency' that can develop in regard to drugs as commodities. Today, we can see this model exemplified in the legal trade in psychotropic substances (tea, coffee, sugar). While 'fair trade' models for coffee trading exist (Tucker 2017), farmers still receive a small fraction of the profit that is earned by traders and retailers. Profit and relatively inexpensive goods depend on the raw materials being produced at very low prices. No loans from the World Bank or elsewhere can fix the poverty of growers without either decreasing profit for the wealthy or charging significantly more for coffee.

Anthropologists have often been critical of 'development', citing negative impacts on the lives of actual people (Bodley 2014). Two kinds of scholarship have been labelled 'development anthropology' and 'the anthropology of development'. While the former engages with economic development on its own terms, the latter critiques its foundational assumptions. Indeed, scholars engaging in the anthropology of development critique the grounds and goals of 'development'. They identify paradoxes within its very framework, noting that the paradigm carries the seeds of its own inability to succeed in its stated goals. James Ferguson's (1994) *Anti-Politics Machine* presents a scathing criticism of the economic development paradigm, pointing out that the continued failure of development initiatives to bring about economic stability and raise quality of life is a result of 'a development discourse fantasy' that refuses to acknowledge the connection between poverty and larger questions of global resource allocation and the history of colonial imperialism. Arturo Escobar's (1995) *Encountering Development* explores 'development' as an ideology that actually ensures the impoverishment and oppression of people. He shows that insisting that peasants grow cash crops results in food insecurity, for example.

In considering how all this relates to drugs as a source of livelihood (licit and illicit) for many people, we should think critically about what 'development' actually means, and about who wins and who loses in the production and sale of psychoactive substances. The case studies below consider these issues in the context of specific drugs. The conclusion we draw from these case studies is that we have seen instances where drugs can be a robust source of livelihoods in some communities, whereas in others, their illegality, associated with physical and social violence as well as public health risks, can wreak havoc on people and communities. In many cases, we will learn that there is not an easy answer due to the complexity of the dynamics: as in most situations in life, there are costs and benefits. For each one, we will identify how it is produced and traded, and then analyse it by considering its risks and opportunities. We begin with a substance that is legal but controlled in many national contexts: tobacco. We continue with a quasi-legal crop, khat, and conclude with opium, which is widely illegal and heavily controlled.

Case Studies

Tobacco

Legal Status and Public Health

Tobacco is a drug that helped shape the contours of the globalised world as we know it today (Chapter 3). It was important in fuelling the early capitalist engines of mass production and in creating a dedicated industrial working class. It is now a major global crop. Tobacco production is legal everywhere it is grown, although in nearly every country there are restrictions and laws governing its manufacture, labelling, advertising and marketing (particularly to youth), and legal age of use. There are also laws regulating where and if people can smoke in public places. The World Health Organization (WHO), with 181 signatory countries (covering more than 90% of the world's population), adopted the Framework Convention on Tobacco Control (WHO FCTC) in 2003. This legally binding treaty includes measures for reducing demand (fewer people smoking) and the supply of tobacco products. It encourages the implementation of tobacco cessation programmes (including nicotine replacement therapies) and by monitoring policies that regulate tobacco use and prevention policies, ban tobacco advertising and implement taxes on the sale of it.

The enforcement of these laws is often difficult, especially in countries where law enforcement does not receive adequate funding. Another challenge is that the tobacco industry 'has a long history of systematic, aggressive, sustained and well-resourced opposition to tobacco control measures' (WHO 2019 Report Global Tobacco Epidemic, p. 60). Some common tactics taken by the tobacco industry include using front groups to make it seem like pro-tobacco stances are more popular than they are, 'making unproven claims and discrediting proven science; exaggerating the economic importance of the industry, intimidating governments with litigation or the threat of litigation' (WHO, p. 61). Anthropologists Otañez and Glantz (2009) document how tobacco companies have used visual imagery to undermine health policy. Benson (2012) tells how tobacco companies pursue social responsibility causes, including education initiatives, to deflect criticism of their support for tobacco expansion. Stebbins (2001) has documented the aggressive techniques used by tobacco companies to gain access to South American markets, especially since the market for cigarettes was shrinking in wealthy countries. Anthropologists Russell et al. (2015) show how Philip Morris International (PMI) tried to keep the South American country of Uruguay from enacting legislation to curb the use of tobacco.

Korhman and Benson (2020), in their review of tobacco studies in anthropology, pointed out that there has been some resistance to seeing tobacco through the lens of Big Tobacco and negative public health outcomes. They identify authors who wish instead to examine it as a lived experience of pleasure in consumption, untarnished by the politics and moralism that have been prevalent in the literature on tobacco (Bell and Dennis 2013). While Kohrman and Benson agree that tobacco is a complex social phenomenon, they express concern that these scholars seem to mirror the rhetoric used by the big tobacco companies. There are indeed scholars who look both at people's lived experiences of pleasurable consumption and the politics of exploitation and the health concerns of tobacco. Mimi Nichter's book, *Lighting Up* (2015), does that, using insights into why and how people consume to effect better public policy and intervention programmes aimed at smoking cessation.

Tobacco Farming

There are multiple steps to producing tobacco products for consumption, including planting, harvesting, curing, sorting, packaging and shipping it to manufacturers, who turn it into products people consume, including cigarettes, pipe tobacco and chewed tobacco products. This section will focus on the processes before it gets sent to factories for processing. Tobacco is grown in over 120 countries. China, Brazil, India, Zimbabwe and the US are the largest producers (in that order), producing about two-thirds of the world's tobacco crop (De Lorenzo 2021). The global tobacco crop is worth about US $20 billion. That amount, however, is just a small fraction of what is generated from the manufacture and sale of tobacco products. In that sense, tobacco is like other commodities, where the primary producers earn fractions of what is made after value is added through processing, turning it into a consumable product. The global market is dominated by a small number of corporations, sometimes referred to as Big Tobacco, that earn the largest share of the overall tobacco profits.

While numbers and statistics paint a broad picture of tobacco production, ethnographic research into the lives of farmers reveals the processes of tobacco growing as well as the meanings surrounding tobacco farming and the social norms (including gender, ethnicity and social class) that shape decisions and lived experiences. Wherever it is grown, it is a labour-intensive crop that includes planting, cutting, drying and packing. Temporary migrant

labour on tobacco farms is common around the globe, particularly at specific times of the growing season. In the US, Singer (2008: 45) recalls that
the labour-intensiveness of tobacco growing fuelled the slave trade. Today,
that role has been increasingly filled since the 1970s by temporary migrant
labourers from the Caribbean and Latin America. Labour conditions for
migrant and seasonal workers tend to be difficult wherever they are found.
In Brazil, where China's market share of tobacco went from 1% of Brazil's
exports in 1997 to more than 19% in 2019, investigative reports suggest that
labour conditions are deplorable on contract farms that hire labourers, with
one outlet calling out instances of 'modern day slavery', since some farm
owners reportedly do not pay their labourers.[1]

Some studies found there to be ethnic tensions on tobacco farms. Michael
Duke (2011) documented labour conditions in the Connecticut River
Valley of the US, where shade tobacco is grown for making cigar wrappers.
After WWII, there was a labour shortage, and temporary labourers started
coming from Jamaica, Puerto Rico and later Mexico. Duke writes about the
challenges workers face, which resemble hardships found around the world
for migrant labourers: access to clean water, nutritious food, medical care and
proper housing. He found that Jamaican and Latino workers had different
conditions. The Latino workers saw the Jamaicans as privileged, and the
Jamaicans tended to see themselves as more hard-working. This led not only
to conflict but also to a general lack of willingness to advocate for themselves
and demand better labour conditions. Peter Benson (2012) has also written
about ethnic tensions in the US. The farmers he studied in North Carolina
often blamed immigration practices and policies, in addition to governmental
public health initiatives, for their financial difficulties, even though a significant amount of the downturn of the market is due to changes supported by
or initiated by tobacco companies (including the rise of contract farming and
switching to foreign sources of tobacco).

Jennie Gamlin (2016) wrote about indigenous Huichol migrant seasonal
workers in Mexico, pointing out nuances that make unilateral judgements difficult. The Huichol workers' conditions lead to suffering on many levels: families slept outdoors on chemical-saturated soil that their children play in. The
Mexican farmer owners treated the Huichol paternalistically through the lens
of cultural and racial superiority. Gamlin argued that both the farmers and
the workers take this structural inequality for granted, normalising social
suffering. She also pointed to the nuances of this Mexican farming situation.
The owners of the farms the Huichol work on contract with tobacco companies. While the tobacco companies provide seeds, they also dictate the type
and amount of pesticides they use and the amount they can pay their workers.
Farmers have no insurance against damaging weather, and profit margins are
often slim. Many of these same farm owners leave for the US each year and
work on farms as migrant labourers, enduring discrimination on the US side
as they do. As for the Huichol, they migrate to work on the Mexican tobacco
farms to subsidise the subsistence way of life, replete with ancestral ritual

traditions, they live during the rest of the year. Gamlin makes the point that we must pay attention to 'both individual and collective agency, and the local and cultural specificities through which structural forms of violence are mediated' (2015: 305).

Finally, Sikstrom (2020) points out that it is not just ethnicity that divides but also status as a migrant. She studied social determinants of health in a tobacco-growing region of Malawi and found that the migrant labourers were systematically discriminated against in access to healthcare, and specifically to ART treatment for HIV. Sikstrom found a generally accepted, normalised attitude among local residents that the migrants are not worthy of healthcare. They are seen as pitiable and treated with scorn as 'outsiders'. The migrants are not necessarily ethnically different from locals, but their status as migrants sets them apart. Interestingly, however, Sikstrom found that the migrants were actually often better nourished than some of the locals who rented farms and had higher social status. Furthermore, many of the migrants owned land in their home villages and planned to return after making some money.

Once again, we see the anthropological focus on ethnography as allowing access not only to broad patterns of experience but also to locally specific versions. This is important not only because it is interesting but also because knowledge of local dynamics is the only way to enact positive change.

Profitability and the Global Capitalist Economy

Other common experiences arise out of the role of tobacco as a commodity traded in the global capitalist economy. Singer (2008: 71) outlines 'several central tenets that define the tobacco industry reality', including the acceptance of tobacco as an integral part of the world economy, providing livelihoods to millions of people, the assumption that government regulation is harmful, the belief that advertising is an expression of rightful free speech, the stance that individuals are responsible for their decisions (e.g. to smoke or quit), and the commitment to protecting individual decision-making rights. These central tenets have shaped economic policy since WWII and especially since the increasing commitment to free trade and deregulation in the 1980s under neoliberal policy shifts. The profitability of tobacco has changed through the years, and the rise of Big Tobacco in the midst of the global capitalist economy has shaped this arc.

In the US, for example, tobacco was one of the first major cash crops grown by the colonists, beginning in the 1600s. In many cases, independent colonial farmers grew tobacco and by the 1860s, there were small cottage industries for processing it into snuff and chewing tobacco (Singer 2008: 63). By the early twentieth century, with the help of the automatic cigarette rolling machine, tobacco companies gained power and market share, paving the way for the monopolistic practices and low prices for tobacco (Kingsolver 2011). By the early 2000s, many farmers had become independent contractors with tobacco companies – a quasi-working class that favours farmers with more land and more capital with which to buy up more land (Griffith 2009: 436). Tobacco production has increased globally, despite decreasing quantities coming out of the US. As Griffith writes (ibid.): 'Large tobacco companies like Philip Morris had powerful economic interests in both dismantling the allotment system and converting from purchasing tobacco at auctions to entering into production contracts with individual farmers'.

The world's largest producer of tobacco is China. In 2019, China grew over 2.61 million metric tons of tobacco, as compared with the next closest country, India, where only 800,000 metric tons were produced. By comparison, the US grew just over 212,000 metric tons as the world's fifth largest producer.[2] China's Big Tobacco is under state control but operates globally. While most of China's tobacco is grown domestically, they have begun buying high-quality tobacco from around the world, including Brazil, Zimbabwe and even the US (Kohrman et al. 2018: 3).

Zimbabwe provides a fascinating case of how China's economic practices have led to a significant rise of tobacco farming globally. Zimbabwe has replaced the US as the world's fourth largest producer according to 2019 statistics, at 257,000 metric tons per year.[3] The first growers of tobacco were European colonists in the late 1800s when it was called Southern Rhodesia (Rupert 1998). European growers hired African labourers, many of whom lived on the plantations – even some with families. Although most of the workers were men, there were some women labourers, who worked for lower wages in most cases. The workers were paid poorly, and they suffered difficult conditions, including crowded residences, poor nutrition from a corn-rich diet, diseases including respiratory (from working tobacco) and contagious diseases from overcrowding, and lack of medical care.

Southern Rhodesia became Zimbabwe in 1980, when it achieved independence. Tobacco production plummeted when commercial land was seized and redistributed to Zimbabweans of African descent. China, however, stepped in to revitalise tobacco by contracting with individual farmers (similar to how it is done in other countries) and purchasing tobacco on the auction floor (Fang et al. 2020). In 2020, Zimbabwe exported 33% of its tobacco to China, accounting for 30% of its export for hard currency (Fang et al. 2020). The COVID-19 pandemic did not hinder tobacco production there.[4]

Across the globe, the size of tobacco farms varies. While some is grown on large farms, many smallholder family farmers continue to grow tobacco. The prevalence of smallholder farming is in part because tobacco can grow on marginal land, without irrigation. Some smallholder farms are as small as a hectare, and others may be several hectares. In Brazil, for example, about 200,000 smallholders grow 95% of Brazil's tobacco.[5]

Small-scale farmers have been the primary target of contract farming, because they traditionally lack capital and benefit from the seeds, fertilisers, equipment and training these arrangements often provide (Mazwi et al. 2020). Accounts differ as to the profitability of tobacco, with results being highly politicised because of the public health versus industry concerns. On the negative side, growing tobacco requires inputs of fertilisers and is labour-intensive. On the positive side, many farmers have experienced tobacco as attractive financially. While media portrayals present happy farmers, some nongovernmental organisation (NGO) reports say that some contracts have high interest rates, a poor safety record, inadequate training and insurmountable debt (Mazwi et al. 2020).

Risks and Opportunities for Livelihoods

As we have explored earlier, there is no simple answer to the relationship between tobacco growing and selling and livelihoods. Tobacco clearly contributes great amounts to GDP in the countries where it is grown. While it brings income to many people, it is not without a cost: farms of all sizes (but especially small-scale ones) increasingly must contract their land and labour, thereby losing autonomy over the process, and for lower prices. Many farm labourers endure incredibly harsh conditions. Bourgois (2018) raises the question: does this count as predatory accumulation? Others encourage us to ask whether and how our ideas about what is 'normal' may disguise structural violence.

Khat

Khat is a fascinating crop and commodity, in part because its legal status is highly ambiguous, or *quasi-legal* (Carrier and Klantschnig 2018), and it contrasts greatly with the case study of tobacco. This term derives from Lee Cassanelli's chapter on khat in the classic Appadurai volume on commodities, *The Social Life of Things* (1986). Khat is legal in countries like Ethiopia and Kenya, yet often illegal in other territories where it is popularly consumed – hence, its legal status varies greatly over space (and over time – for example, we discussed in the last chapter British attempts to control khat in colonial Kenya (as they feared it was addictive). The term is also apt in relation to khat as it is often treated with much suspicion in countries where it is legal according to the statute books: sometimes it is treated as if illegal even where it is legal. In Kenya and Madagascar, for example, for decades khat was treated with great suspicion by the state given international concerns that it was a noxious substance (Carrier 2014, Gezon 2016). This meant that the khat industry received little support from the state or multilateral institutions, and instead it grew as a mostly *informal* cash crop and commodity that was little taxed. This is similar to production for local consumption of coca in Bolivia, which also grew in the face of international suspicion of the crop, in that case as the source of cocaine (Grisaffi 2019). Despite this international- and national-level suspicion, the khat industry has grown to great significance in a number of countries, especially Ethiopia and Kenya. In the latter, it is very much the cash crop for the Nyambene Hills in Meru County, supporting a whole region economically, and its annual worth being valued at many millions of US dollars (Carrier 2014).

Production

Being 'quasi-legal', khat production is generally very different from that of tobacco. It has mainly developed outside the confines of state-led agriculture, and as a consequence owes very little to private corporations, being mostly grown by smallholder farmers. In Kenya, producing khat as a crop began in the colonial period as the development of road infrastructure allowed a highly perishable commodity to be sold further afield than its Nyambene home, a crop that the British colonial state was unaware of, at least initially (Anderson and Carrier 2009). It was soon being sold throughout East Africa, prompting great concern from the colonial authorities who tried to ban the substance unsuccessfully. In the later colonial period in Kenya, however, some British officials sought to exploit the great demand for the substance in places like Aden by promoting an export market for Kenyan khat. This was at a time when British colonies were expected to be more self-sufficient, and so colonies like Kenya were seeking ways to boost their economy. This plan to promote khat in this way was put on hold as the authorities worried about the international suspicion that had grown about khat as a 'drug'. In the postcolonial period, this concern continued and the authorities kept their distance from the crop. Despite this, production expanded as export markets in Somalia increased. The spread of the Somali diaspora around the world in the wake of the civil war in the 1980s and 1990s gave a further boost to khat production in Kenya to feed demand in places like the UK.

In all this, the skills and techniques used to produce khat were honed by the people of the Nyambenes, in contrast to more 'respectable' cash crops such as coffee and tea whose production in Kenya had been started by colonial settlers. Furthermore, khat in Kenya and elsewhere has on the whole proven more valuable to farmers. In the Nyambenes, farmers report that the crop gives a much higher return than coffee or tea (Carrier 2007: 57–62). Not only that, farmers receive more frequent payments through khat farming. While coffee and tea are generally sold through cooperatives that pay at only certain times of the year, khat farmers can harvest their khat every two to three weeks depending on rainfall and can sell that directly at wholesale markets. Such is the attraction of khat to farmers throughout East Africa that there have long been reports of farmers pulling up coffee bushes to plant khat instead. This is portrayed in the media as a worrying thing, even though it involves simply replacing one stimulant crop for another. Another concern much expressed is that khat production has replaced food production (Gebissa 2010, Gezon 2012a,b), although farmers report being more food secure thanks to income from khat, and food crops are intercropped between khat trees in Kenya.

Khat is grown in different forms. In the Nyambene Hills, khat is grown as a tree, and plantations resemble apple orchards. Older trees known as *mbaine* are reputed to produce the better khat so fetching farmers a premium (Carrier 2008). Older trees are also more drought resistant, giving farmers lucky enough to own trees of 50 years old or more a strong advantage. Elsewhere in Kenya, and in Ethiopia (Gebissa 2004), Yemen (Weir 1985) and Madagascar (Gezon 2012a,b), however, khat is mostly grown as a small shrub, more resembling coffee plantations. In all this production, there is much scope for variety (Carrier 2006), as khat from different parts of the tree or shrub, or khat stems of different lengths, become differentiated as distinct types, while the area where khat comes from also is seen as a guide to quality or otherwise. There are also different varieties of khat plants, according to farmers (Carrier 2007: Chapter 1), which produce differently coloured leaves and stems (though usually these are a mixture of purple and green). In Kenya, khat from the Nyambene Hills has been rivalled recently by a type known as *muguka* that comes from a region to the south (Mbeere). This variety is popular as it is sold much more cheaply than the Nyambene type and consists solely of the leaves and stem tips that are sold in plastic bags while Nyambene khat is sold in bundles tied up with banana fibre and wrapped in banana leaves. All this variety allows farmers to harvest and sell khat of different qualities targeting different consumers.

While generally considered a valuable crop for farmers – one that is often praised by farmers in places like the Nyambene Hills for supporting families with food and education – farmers are unlikely to become rich through the production of khat alone. However, khat also offers opportunities for off-farm income, and in the Nyambene Hills, many households diversify income through younger generations moving to other parts of Kenya to sell khat as wholesalers or retailers, while others tend to the khat farms. In both Ethiopia (Gebissa 2004) and Kenya, takings from khat are used to capitalise other businesses, from bars to small shops and hotels.

Trade and Trust

However, as with most commodity chains, money to be made increases as khat moves away from the farm. In Kenya, it is in demand throughout the country, and so there are retail kiosks in all towns and cities selling it, and often young Meru men are those operating the kiosks, relying on contacts back in the Nyambene Hills to speed the commodity to them. Khat is a highly perishable product (unlike coffee which can be warehoused for long periods) and this has many implications for its trade and transport, again showing how understanding the social life of such a drug requires attending to its materiality. After harvest, khat is reckoned to become less potent as its main compound cathinone degrades into the milder cathine (Carrier 2005), though there is some evidence that khat can keep its potency for longer than previously thought. However, consumers certainly prefer the taste and texture of fresh khat, and so a *need for speed* comes into being post-harvest. This means that traders need to be smart in business to ensure that they are not left with unsellable khat. Transporters often drive at breakneck speed to get the commodity to its markets, leading to some tragic accidents over the years.

Importantly, traders also need to have a reputation as trustworthy to operate in the khat business as its networks tend to be part of the informal rather than formal economy. The *informal economy* is now a much used concept having been initially coined by anthropologist Keith Hart in the 1970s (Hart 1973), and came into being as Hart noticed in fieldwork in Ghana that despite there being few opportunities in places like Accra for the types of work recognised by the state (work that became noted in official statistics and upon which tax was paid) – that is to say, work in the formal sector – many people were busy with work, only work that was less visible to the state: for example hawking vegetables or clothes on the streets, or even illegal activities. This work disconnected from the state (though how disconnected it is from the state is much debated) is the type that the concept of the informal economy attempted to capture. While formal work often offers some legal protection for workers in the form of labour rights, as well as legal protections for trade relationships through binding contracts, work in the informal sector offers little recourse to the law in cases of exploitation or deceit. Instead, relationships in the informal sector often rely on strong social underpinnings to ensure those involved are happy to *entrust* goods or money to people who could simply depart with them. Here anthropologists can bring insight into how *trust* is built up in such relationships allowing them to continue and even thrive, and ethnographers researching commodity chains focus much on these social underpinnings. Trust is seen less as a virtue possessed by participants in the trade (although reputation is very important in informal and illegal trades), but more as something that emerges in relationships over time: it is eminently social. Work by Parker Shipton on trust and what he terms *entrustment* (or the process of creating trust) in Western Kenya is important here (Shipton 2007).

In the case of khat in Kenya, trust is built through shared kinship and friendship (which gives knowledge of trustworthiness and a social foundation for trust), as well as through shared interests in ensuring a consignment of khat gets to its consumers. However, business relationships are often hierarchical, meaning that power can become more important than trust in understanding how the trade operates (Carrier 2007: Chapter 5). The commodity itself and its perishability have some agency here too, as the need to move the commodity on compels traders to pass it along the chain even in instances where trust in a business partner might not be solid: to hesitate might be to be left with dried-up, unsellable khat.

Risks and Opportunities

As khat went global in the 1990s and 2000s with the spread of the Somali diaspora across the world, these contract-free, informal trade relationships were stretched out over much greater distances, from Ethiopia and Kenya to the UK, US, and several other countries. Opportunities grew strong for farmers, transporters and exporters, as well as Somalis in places like the UK who set up establishments known as *mafrish* where khat could be bought and chewed. Areas of the Nyambenes where khat had previously not been grown saw trees being planted, and many tonnes of khat were exported each week to the UK market at the peak of this trade in the late 2000s (Anderson and Carrier 2011). However, this export trade was mostly operated by Somalis in Kenya who would source khat from the Nyambene Hills. This led to tension, with suspicions that Somalis were exploiting khat farmers for profit, especially through leasing arrangements Somalis made with farmers (Carrier 2007: Chapter 5). Such was the tension that some violence erupted, and farmers conducted strikes to gain leverage – although this proved difficult to manage as farmers ended up losing harvests. While this tension simmered back down, it showed some of the pitfalls of the informal nature of the khat trade. Farmers and others have benefitted from the informality of the trade in some ways through lack of government interference, allowing them to develop the trade in a way that suited their interests. Yet, there was a flipside to this, as when trouble emerged there was a lack of support from the state in resolving disputes.

There are other risks in producing and trading a quasi-legal crop and commodity, especially in how changing legal status can affect those involved. This was the case with the ban on khat in the UK in 2014. The khat trade had boomed with the growth of the UK market and the UK's role as a khat transit hub for onward trade to the likes of Scandinavia (Anderson and Carrier 2011), creating numerous opportunities in the Nyambenes and beyond. The ban reduced these opportunities greatly, especially for those in parts of the region that grew khat to supply the UK market. While all international commodities are subject to uncertainties as regulations and tariffs may change, ones viewed with suspicion on the international stage such as khat are yet more susceptible to disruption. Strangely enough, however, the UK ban on khat spurred the Kenyan government to finally recognise khat as an official cash crop, and to pledge support to help farmers and traders find new markets for their crop (Carrier 2014). Becoming illegal in the UK led to khat becoming more unambiguously legal in Kenya.

In general, khat has proven a popular source of livelihoods in East Africa and beyond, one that has allowed smallholder farmers to a greater income compared to tea and coffee, the more respectable stimulants in the eyes of many. In this, khat and the livelihoods it generates subvert typical ideas of development as the khat industry has developed without the need for the external assistance so commonly seen as required in helping the 'developing world'. As Susan Beckerleg – who wrote about khat in Uganda – put it:

> Khat is subversive because in East Africa it has improved the lives of millions of poor people who are not part of development programs. Khat, I contend, renders 'development' irrelevant to the lives and livelihoods of independent-minded producers and entrepreneurs.
>
> (Beckerleg 2010: 182)

Crops like khat are not the answer to all livelihood needs in East Africa, but they have certainly helped many survive hard times and even thrive. The same is true of cannabis, another crop grown throughout much of Africa that has helped people navigate hard times. It is another crop that can be seen as quasi-legal, especially as its legal status is changing so much as debates on its legalisation or decriminalisation grow apace (Carrier and Klantschnig 2016).

Opiates and Opioids

Our final case study is that of opium, the substance which sparked the first international moves to control and prohibit drugs (Chapter 3), and so a very different substance to khat and tobacco in terms of legal status. Opium comes from the poppy plant. Like tobacco, producing it is a labour-intensive process. It involves hoeing to prepare the soil, sowing the seeds, weeding, and harvesting. Sometimes farmers must sow several times if their plants die. They must begin weeding when the weeds are taller than the poppies, making it back-breaking work. Harvesters make incisions on the poppy pods shortly after the leaves fall off. Over the next few days, sap oozes out and thickens to resin. Farmers collect this by hand, package it into bricks and sell it to traders. Because of its distinctive smell, it must be processed into a morphine base before being exported. It may be processed into heroin or other opiate products immediately or later. It may pass through several traders' hands before arriving at a processing facility (Cooley 2002, Ko-lin 2009). In Myanmar, Ko-lin reported that there are multiple layers of traders, including low-level ones who buy from farmers either in their villages or in a market. Traders purchasing in the market tend to be women. While these low-level traders earn about twice as much as farmers, their cut is considerably smaller than that of the higher level traders, who tend to be authorities, members of the military, or their associates. Most of the opium is sold for cash or trade goods and very little is consumed in farming villages. Dependency on opium that disrupts community life (addiction) is rare. In many farming communities in Southeast Asia, people have developed cultural traditions for consuming it that do not generally lead to abuse, including uses for ritual, healing and pain management (particularly in the elderly) (Fadiman 1997, Gillogly 2008).

Most opium farmers are smallholders, often with fields less than a hectare. A report on farm size in Afghanistan in 2002–2003 states that 73%

of the farms are less than 5 hectares (Greenfield et al. 2015). Most of the producers in the Golden Triangle (where Thailand, Laos and Myanmar meet) farm small plots in mountainous terrain. Many farms are on marginal land, because poppies grow well on hilly terrain in low-quality soils with low rainfall. They do better, however, with good soils and ample water, and some farmers in Myanmar (Regional Report on Southeast Asia and China 2015) and Afghanistan (Cooley (2002) have increased their production with irrigation. Most farmers grow food crops in addition to poppies, but most do not grow enough to be self-sufficient in food and so rely on opium sales for food security. A report on opium in Myanmar from 2019 states that 80% of people used money from opium to buy food (UNODC 2019).

Although opium poppies are grown in many parts of the world (including eastern Europe), the main production areas of opium poppies have been in China (Yunnan Province), India, the Golden Triangle, the Golden Crescent (Afghanistan, Iran and Pakistan), and, starting in the early twentieth century, in Columbia and Mexico. In the 1980s and 1990s, opium production rose significantly in the Fertile Crescent nations (Afghanistan, Pakistan and Iran), associated with the US-Russian war. Opium production in that region has been saturated with aiding and abetting by military CIA-enabled drug cartels. By the late 1990s, Afghanistan was the world's largest producer of opium, surpassing the Golden Triangle countries. In 1999, Afghanistan produced 70% of the world's crop (Cooley 2002: 107).

Eradication

There have been serious eradication campaigns in Thailand, Vietnam and Laos. Governments have partnered with United Nations agencies as well as with NGOs in a variety of approaches, including coercive military interventions and development initiatives designed to help farmers find alternative crops and otherwise make up for the lost income from opium. Eradication campaigns have had success. In each country, production was down and remained down over 96% since peak production (Windle 2018). Thailand and Laos were declared 'poppy-free' by the United Nations Office of Drugs and Crime (UNODC) in the early 2000s. Governments in Thailand, Laos and Vietnam supported opium eradication for political, economic and security-related reasons.

In addition to concern for international reputation and fear of sanctions, they also embraced the measures because it allowed an opportunity to extend state control into marginal regions and because it coincided with a religious and ideological anti-drug sentiment. Anti-drug attitudes have been tied up in stereotypes of the highland farmers and ethnic anxiety surrounding it. Throughout the Golden Triangle and Vietnam, most opium cultivation is done by ethnic minorities that have been isolated and relatively autonomous. In her account of opium eradication in Thailand, Gillogly (2008) noted that lowland Thai people do not see the ethnic highland dwellers as full citizens because of their religious, cultural and linguistic differences. Called 'hill tribes', they are reputed to be dirty, to be sexually promiscuous and to be poor. They are also seen as dangerous because of their association with opium and the related need for self-protection.

Despite these stereotypes, Gillogly (2008) reported that the Thai government partnered with local people in developing sustainable alternatives to opium in a gradual reduction approach. While Gillogly reported instances of local resistance, she noted that both sides – government and local people – negotiated for their own interests in the process. Local people were looking for secure access to land, subsidies for opium substitutions and freedom from state surveillance. What the local people lost, however, was considerable: the effects of their overall loss of income from opium reverberated through their social structure: it meant men had to marry later because of lack of bride price. It meant a strengthening of patrilineality and patrilocality, since sons could no longer move away to look for new land for growing opium. In fact, land became scarce: although they needed more (and higher quality) land for the substitute crops, the state was also simultaneously cracking down on people deforesting land to turn it into fields.

In Myanmar, the other country in the Golden Triangle, eradication has been less successful, and it retains its status as a top world producer (second after Afghanistan). The lack of success has not been for lack of trying: despite a governmental commitment that began in 1999, help from international agencies and regional governmental commitments to impose prohibition, the end does not appear in sight. At the height of prohibition in the mid-2000s, there was a sharp decline in opium production, followed by a resurgence in the mid-2010s. Reasons for their lack of success may be associated with security issues, as there are armed groups and occasionally conflict in the opium-growing areas. It may also be because there is a long history of government and military officials collecting opium taxes (Ko-lin 2009), and there may not have been the political will to give that up (Kaplan and Win 2020). Opium production has gone down again in recent years. In 2020, less than half the amount was produced as in the height in 2013 (United Nations 2021).

Risks and Opportunities

It would be simplistic to talk about opium eradication without also discussing its caveats. First, the role of imperialist European nations and the United States in allowing if not pushing opium use must be noted (see Chapter 3). Bourgois' predatory accumulation may perfectly describe the way that imperialistic nations enriched themselves at the expense of the Chinese. And since then and in our current times, politically dominant nations have tolerated if not outright promoted drug production in economically and politically dominant nations. The countries where opium is produced are all former colonies and remain some of the poorest countries on earth. Real change can only come about with full commitment to the end goal of improved livelihoods, with all parties fully on board. Critical analysts will look not simply at surface solutions but also at the contradictions and hypocrisies that surround them. Some argue that legalisation may in fact be the best way to counter abuses related to drug use.

That aside, a second point is about where and how to stop the flow of heroin. While some argue for stopping it at the farm gate, others point out that it is narrow-sighted to do so. Windle (2018) argues that there is not sufficient evidence that lower supply in one farming district results in lower supply in consumer countries, since production can easily be increased elsewhere. Furthermore, Windle reports 'the price mark-up for heroin between the Afghan farm gate and British streets as 15,800%' (2018: 366). Attacking farm-level production, while not without merit if done humanely and sustainably, may not be as effective as tackling higher level players, including the banking industry that permits the transformation of illicit into licit money (money laundering) and governments who turn a blind eye to the elements of it that tolerate and encourage drug production.

Finally, we must recognise that the farmers have much to gain and lose from drug production. Many would lose their entire livelihood. Ko-lin (2009: 62) identified one opium grower as saying, 'other people might be able to survive without growing opium, but I know if I don't, I can't make it'. To bring it around to the larger question of livelihoods, it is clear that opium has provided a substantial living to many farming communities for centuries. It is also clear that many people have suffered from heroin addictions and overdoses, and that there are still legal, pharmaceutical uses of farm-grown opiates. Farmers relying on illicit opium surely have a range of living situations, with many situations that are highly dangerous, surrounded by drug-related armed conflict or under threat of coercive law enforcement.

But again, we must ask if the threats to quality livelihoods are because of the nature of the drug or because of the nature of the political economy surrounding it: the fact that it is illegal. It is difficult to impossible to parse that out, but these are the questions we invite you to ask as you evaluate context-specific situations. The drug trade offers critical insight into the economic structures of our contemporary world, and its ambiguities.

Review of Production and Distribution Issues: Risks and Opportunities

Drug crops bring out many hypocrisies in the world of development. Certain crops are seen as legitimate even when highly harmful (tobacco) both in terms of health harms and in how they promote labour exploitation through their corporate capitalism; a crop like khat, on the other hand, would not be regarded by many in the west as a legitimate basis of development, yet has brought livelihoods and other forms of development to many in the 'developing world' on its own terms, as have cannabis and even opium. As Beckerleg suggests earlier, they subvert normative ideas of development. Nevertheless, we cannot will away decades and centuries of the global drug economy. While drug farming can be an important source of livelihoods for many of the world's agrarian communities, we must also consider the wider consequences of illegal drug production, including violence, corruption, addiction and its disproportionate impacts on youth (Singer 2008). These dangers are particularly salient with drugs that have global flows (opium, cocaine, cannabis) rather than ones that are locally or regionally traded (khat and sometimes cannabis).

All cash crops provide both opportunities and risks: they bring in hard currency when formally recognised (coffee, tea, sugar), but they leave farmers dependent on global pricing and restrictive industry protocols. On the other hand, small-scale production of drugs and other commodities at the local level can contribute to a stable local economy, although it does not contribute to GDP (and therefore would qualify as an 'alternative to development'). Recall that many of the problems with psychoactive substances have occurred since they have been global commodities, de-coupled from local contexts of use and subject to international regimes of prohibition. This is a segue to the next chapter, which digs deeper into the War on Drugs and its sequelae.

Anthropological perspectives are important in the study of drugs because of the focus we bring to understanding lived experiences as they are shaped by the political, economic, social, historical and cultural contexts that frame them. This makes it easier to understand benefits and risks that may lie in unexpected places, as people choose to become and remain involved in activities that, from the outside, do not appear to make sense. Working with local people to understand these dynamics is critical when developing initiatives to increase the quality of livelihoods in the highly charged arena of drugs.

Notes

1 Report by the Organized Crime and Corruption Reporting Project available online: www.occrp.org/en/loosetobacco/china-tobacco-goes-global/china-tobacco-very-discreetly-becomes-leaf-buying-powerhouse-in-brazil (accessed December 2022).
2 Statistics available online: www.statista.com/statistics/261173/leading-countries-in-tobacco-production/ (accessed December 2022).
3 See previous footnote for source.
4 See this online report: https://tobaccoreporter.com/2021/01/07/zimbabwe-earns-763-million-from-tobacco/ (accessed December 2022).
5 See this online article: www.ipsnews.net/2011/12/brazil-providing-alternatives-for-small-scale-tobacco-farmers/ (accessed December 2022).

Works Cited

Adeyanju, Collins G. 2020. "Drug Trafficking in West Africa Borderlands: From Gold Coast to Coke Coast." *Journal of Liberty & International Affairs* 6 (1): 70–86.
Anderson, David, and Neil Carrier. 2009. "Khat in Colonial Kenya: A History of Prohibition and Control." *The Journal of African History* 50 (3): 377–397.

———. 2011. *Khat: Social Harms and Legislation: A Literature Review*. Great Britain: Home Office.

Appadurai, Arjun. 1986. *The Social Life of Things: Commodities in Cultural Perspective*. New York, NY: Cambridge University Press.

Beckerleg, Susan. 2010. "'Idle and Disorderly' Khat Users in Western Uganda." *Drugs: Education, Prevention and Policy* 17: 303–314.

Bell, Kirsten, and Simone Dennis. 2013. "Towards a Critical Anthropology of Smoking: Exploring the Consequences of Tobacco Control." *Contemporary Drug Problems* 40 (1): 3–19.

Benson, Peter. 2012. *Tobacco Capitalism: Growers, Migrant Workers, and the Changing Face of a Global Industry*. Princeton, NJ: Princeton University Press.

Bodley, John H. 2014. *Victims of Progress*. Washington, D.C.: Rowman & Littlefield.

Bourgois, Philippe. 2018. "Decolonising Drug Studies in an Era of Predatory Accumulation." *Third World Quarterly* 39 (2): 385–398.

Carrier, Neil. 2005. "Under Any Other Name: The Trade and Use of Khat in the UK." *Drugs and Alcohol Today* 5 (3): 14–16.

———. 2006. "Bundles of Choice: Variety and the Creation and Manipulation of Kenyan Khat's Value." *Ethnos* 71 (3): 415–437.

———. 2007. *Kenyan Khat: The Social Life of a Stimulant*. Leiden: Brill.

———. 2008. "Is Miraa a Drug?: Categorizing Kenyan Khat." *Substance Use Misuse* 43 (6): 803–818.

———. 2014. "A Respectable Chew?: Highs and Lows in the History of Kenyan Khat." In *Drugs in Africa: Histories and Ethnographies of Use, Trade, and Control*, edited by Gernot Klantschnig, Neil Carrier and Charles Ambler, 105–123. New York, NY: Palgrave Macmillan US.

Carrier, Neil, and Gernot Klantschnig. 2012. *Africa and the War on Drugs (African Arguments)*. London: Zed Books.

———. 2016. "Illicit Livelihoods: Drug Crops and Development in Africa." *Review of African Political Economy* 43 (148): 174–189.

———. 2018. "Quasilegality: Khat, Cannabis and Africa's Drug Laws." *Third World Quarterly* 39 (2): 350–365.

Chin, Ko-lin. 2009. *The Golden Triangle: Inside Southeast Asia's Drug Trade*. Ithaca, NY: Cornell University Press.

Cooley, John K. 2002. *Unholy Wars: Afghanistan, America and International Terrorism*. London: Pluto Press.

De Lorenzo, Daniela. 2021. Ending Tobacco Farming Could Free Over 4 Million Hectares Across 120 Countries. *Forbes*.

Duke, Michael. 2011. "Ethnicity, Well-Being, and the Organization of Labor Among Shade Tobacco Workers." *Medical Anthropology* 30 (4): 409–424.

Escobar, Arturo. 1995. *Encountering Development: The Making and Unmaking of the Third World*. Princeton, NJ: Princeton University Press.

Fadiman, Anne. 1997. *The Spirit Catches You and You Fall Down: a Hmong Child, her American Doctors, and the Collision of Two Cultures*. New York: Farrar, Straus, and Giroux.

Fang, Jennifer, Lauren De Souza, Julia Smith, and Kelley Lee. 2020. "All Weather Friends': How China Transformed Zimbabwe's Tobacco Sector." *International Journal of Environmental Research and Public Health* 17 (3): 1–13.

Ferguson, James. 1994. *The Anti-Politics Machine: "Development," Depoliticization, and Bureaucratic Power in Lesotho.* Minneapolis, MN: University of Minnesota Press.

Frank, Andre Gunder. 1967. *Capitalism and Underdevelopment in Latin America.* New York, NY: Monthly Revew Press.

Gamlin, Jennie. 2016. "Huichol Migrant Laborers and Pesticides: Structural Violence and Cultural Confounders." *Medical Anthropology Quarterly* 30 (3): 303–320.

Gebissa, Ezekiel. 2004. *Leaf of Allah: Khat and Agricultural Transformation in Harerge, Ethiopia 1875–1991.* Oxford: James Curry.

———. 2010. *Khat in Ethiopia: Taking the Place of Food.* Trenton, NJ: Red Sea Press.

Gezon, Lisa L. 2012a. "Drug Crops and Food Security: The Effects of Khat on Lives and Livelihoods in Northern Madagascar." *Culture, Agriculture, Food and Environment* 34 (2): 124–135.

———. 2012b. *Drug Effects: Khat in Biocultural and Socioeconomic Perspective.* Walnut Creek, CA: Left Coast Press.

———. 2016. "The Loud Silence of 'Green Gold': Khat, Poverty, and an Alternative Economy in Northern Madagascar." *General Anthropology* 23 (2): 1–8.

Gillogly, Kathleen A. 2008. "Opium, Power, People: Anthropological Understandings of an Opium Interdiction Project in Thailand." *Contemporary Drug Problems* 35: 679–715.

Greenfield, Victoria A., Keith Crane, Craig A. Bond, Nathan Chandler, Jill E. Luoto, and Olga Oliker. 2015. *Reducing the Cultivation of Opium Poppies in Southern Afghanistan.* Santa Monica, CA: RAND Corporation.

Griffith, David. 2009. "The Moral Economy of Tobacco." *American Anthropologist* 111 (4): 432–442.

Grisaffi, Thomas. 2019. *Coca Yes, Cocaine No.* Durham, NC: Duke University Press.

Hansen, Helena, and Mary E. Skinner. 2012. "From White Bullets to Black Markets and Greened Medicine: The Neuroeconomics and Neuroracial Politics of Opioid Pharmaceuticals." *Annals of Anthropological Practice* 36 (1): 167–182.

Hart, Keith. 1973. "Informal Income Opportunities and Urban Employment in Ghana." *The Journal of Modern African Studies* 11 (1): 61–89.

Hofmeister, Naira, and Luiz Fernando. 2021. "China Tobacco 'Very Discreetly' Becomes Leaf-Buying Powerhouse in Brazil." *Organized Crime and Corruption Reporting Project.*

Kaplan, Karyn, and Khine Su Win. 2020. *Farmers in Myanmar Call for Justice.* Open Society Foundations. www.opensocietyfoundations.org/voices/farmers-in-myanmar-call-for-justice

Kingsolver, Ann E. 2011. *Tobacco Town Futures: Global Encounters in Rural Kentucky.* Long Grove, IL: Waveland Press.

Klantschnig, Gernot. 2016. "The Politics of Drug Control in Nigeria: Exclusion, Repression and Obstacles to Policy Change." *International Journal of Drug Policy* 30: 132–139.

Kohrman, Matthew, and Peter Benson. 2020. "Tobacco Reconsidered: Ongoing Omissions, Original Outlooks in the Slipstreams of Experience, Global Health, and Critical Industry Studies." *Annual Review of Anthropology* 49: A1-A-5.

Kohrman, Matthew, Quan Gan, Wennan Liu, and Robert N. Proctor. 2018. *Poisonous Pandas: Chinese Cigarette Manufacturing in Critical Historical Perspectives*. Stanford, CA: Stanford University Press.

Mazwi, Freedom, Walter Chambati, and George T. Mudimu. 2020. "Tobacco Contract Farming in Zimbabwe: Power Dynamics, Accumulation Trajectories, Land Use Patterns and Livelihoods." *Journal of Contemporary African Studies* 38 (1): 55–71.

Munro, William, and Steven C. Rubert. 1998. "A Most Promising Weed: A History of Tobacco Farming and Labor in Colonial Zimbabwe, 1890–1945." *International Journal of African Historical Studies* 31: 637.

Nichter, Mimi. 2015. *Lighting Up: The Rise of Social Smoking on College Campuses*. New York: New York University Press.

Otañez, Martin G., and Stanton A. Glantz. 2009. "Trafficking in Tobacco Farm Culture: Tobacco Companies' Use of Video Imagery to Undermine Health Policy." *Visual Anthropology Review* 25 (1): 1–24.

Peterson, Kristin. 2014. *Speculative Markets: Drug Circuits and Derivative in Nigeria*. Durham, NC: Duke University Press.

Rasmussen, Jacob. 2017. *Sweet Secrets: Sugar Smuggling and State Formation in the Kenya-Somalia Borderlands*. Copenhagen, Denmark: Danish Institute for International Studies (DIIS).

Rupert, Steven. 1998. *A Most Promising Weed: A History of Tobacco Farming and Labor in Colonial Zimbabwe, 1890–1945*. Athens: Ohio University Press.

Russell, Andrew, Megan Wainwright, and Hadii Mamudu. 2015. "A Chilling Example? Uruguay, Philip Morris International, and WHO's Framework Convention on Tobacco Control." *Medical Anthropology Quarterly* 29 (2): 256–277.

Shipton, Parker. 2007. *The Nature of Entrustment: Intimacy, Exchange, and the Sacred in Africa*. New Haven, CN: Yale University Press.

Sikstrom, Laura. 2020. "Dirty Like a Tenant': Migration and Embodied Dispositions in Malawi." *Medical Anthropology* 39 (6): 474–490.

Singer, Merrill. 2008. *Drugs and Development: The Global Impact on Sustainable Growth and Human Rights*. Long Grove, IL: Waveland Press.

Stebbins, Kenyon Rainier. 2001. "Going Like Gangbusters: Transnational Tobacco Companies "Making a Killing" in South America." *Medical Anthropology Quarterly* 15: 147–170.

Tucker, Catherine M. 2017. *Coffee Culture: Local Experiences, Global Connections*. New York: Routledge.

United Nations 2021. "UNODC Report: Opium Production Drops Again in Myanmar as the Synthetic Drug Market Expands." UNODC Regional Office for Southeast Asia and the Pacific. www.unodc.org/roseap/2021/02/myanmar-opium-survey-report-launch/story.html

United Nations Office on Drugs and Crime. 2019. *Opium Poppy Cultivation and Sustainable Development in Shan State, Myanmar: Socio-economic Analysis*. www.unodc.org/documents/crop-monitoring/Myanmar/Myanmar_Socio-econo mic_Survey_2019_web.pdf

van Schendel, Willem, and Itty Abraham. 2005. *Illicit Flows and Criminal Things: States, Borders, and the Other Side of Globalization*. Bloomington, IN: Indiana University Press.

Wallerstein, Immanuel. 1974. *The Modern World-System: Capitalist Agriculture and the Origins of the European World-Economy in the Sixteenth Century.* New York, NY: Academic.

Weir, Shelagh. 1985. *Qat in Yemen: Consumption and Social Change.* London: British Museum Publications Limited.

Windle, James. 2018. "Why Do Southeast Asian States Choose to Suppress Opium? A cross-case comparison." *Third World Quarterly* 39 (2): 366–384.

World Health Organization. 2019. *Report: Global Tobacco Epidemic.* World Health Organization. www.who.int/publications/i/item/9789241516204

8   The Drug War and Its Effects

The topic of this chapter is drug policy, and in particular the policy approach encapsulated by the term the *war on drugs*. In general, this approach focuses on restricting and policing production and trade as well as consumption, usually through criminalisation – or treating people involved with drugs as criminals and punishing them as such. More specifically, the term has referred to the militarised drug policies of the US and elsewhere from the 1980s onwards. The war on drugs has become hegemonic (that is a powerful, dominant ideology) and has affected almost all aspects of the policing and regulation of drug production, trade and use. Because of the violence and repression that has escalated around the policing of drugs, critics of the war on drugs assert that this approach has been more harmful than the drugs themselves.

This chapter will begin by tracing the origins of the war on drugs, considering a historical timeline of how drugs became objects of international legal and militarised concern. It will also explore how this so-called war has been conceptually/discursively framed. It will assess its outcomes, evaluating its success in its own terms, as well as raising questions of who wins and who loses in the wake of this violence. In addition to a general description of the war on drugs, the chapter will present some of the ways that anthropologists have engaged this 'war' in their research and writing, their engagement with the contrasting drug policy approach of 'harm reduction'. We also consider how anthropologists might respond to the current fracturing of international consensus around drug policy (Bewley-Taylor 2012).

Introducing the 'War on Drugs'

We discussed the history of prohibition in Chapter 3, exploring how, before the twentieth century, drugs were commodities often more-or-less freely traded in much of the world, until the temperance movements of the 1800s around the world encouraged prohibitionist approaches. These were mainly focused on alcohol (and of course led to the attempt to suppress alcohol through prohibition in the US in the 1920s), but they expanded to cover

DOI: 10.4324/9781003109549-8

other intoxicants of concern, such as opium (see also Chapter 6). Throughout the West, drug panics and policy in the 1800s and 1900s were linked to racialised fears, with opiates being associated with Chinese labourers, cannabis with Mexican immigrants and African Americans in the US with heroin. The Opium Wars of the 1800s between China and the West (especially England and France, with the US lending support) were an initial spark leading to national and international drugs treaties. This included the Hague International Opium Convention of 1912, which sought to control manufacture and trade of opiates and cocaine through export restrictions rather than outright prohibition. The Single Convention on Narcotic Drugs in 1961 superseded the Hague Convention and strictly prohibited unauthorised sale or use of listed drugs.

The effort to control drugs gained its status as a 'war' in the mid-twentieth-century US around the time of the Vietnam War in the 1960s and 1970s. Before then, drugs (not including alcohol) were a fairly marginal issue in the public eye. People tended to see addiction of any kind (including alcohol) as a problem for only a few. Fear of broader drug use increased with counter-culture anti-war movements and with heroin use in inner cities. US President Richard Nixon introduced the concept of a war on drugs in a speech in 1971 where he declared drug abuse as 'America's public enemy number one'. Nixon declared that 'It is necessary to wage a new all-out offensive', 'a world-wide offensive' (Farber 2021). It is important to note, however, that Nixon's approach focused more on treatment, rehabilitation, education and research than on a militarised control of supply (Pembleton 2021: 895). This is evident in his choice of Dr. Jerome Jaffe, a psychiatrist who promoted methadone for treating heroin addiction, to lead the interagency initiative. Under Nixon's administration and Jaffe's leadership, methadone clinics were widely established to treat heroin addiction. Like heroin, methadone is an opiate, but it is longer acting and therefore avoids the dramatic highs and lows experienced with heroin. While methadone treatments have been criticised for being ineffective or enabling continued drug use, the point is that Nixon sought to rehabilitate and treat, taking a public health approach to addiction (Raz 2016). His approach was more in line with what is referred to as a 'harm reduction' than a 'criminalization' approach (see later).

In addition to the methadone programme, Nixon also promoted research into drug addiction. He enlisted a Commission on Marihuana and Drug Abuse to assess dangers and recommend policies. Commission members found little danger of harm to self or society from intermittent use of cannabis and recommended against criminalising drug users in favour of education and treatment where necessary. The report was controversial even at the time (Nahas and Greenwood 1974) and did not result in the legalisation of cannabis. President Jimmy Carter, who followed Nixon as president from 1977 to 1981, supported the elimination of all federal criminal penalties for the possession of up to one ounce of cannabis. He is quoted in a speech for saying that

[p]enalties against possession of a drug should not be more damaging to an individual than the use of the drug itself ... . Nowhere is this more clear than in the laws against possession of marijuana in private for personal use.

(Kleinman and Hawdon 2011)

Cannabis did not end up being legalised under Carter and talk of war became less and less metaphorical under the next US President, Ronald Reagan (1981–1989). Reagan ended methadone treatment programmes and began spending large amounts with the goal of reducing the supply of illegal drugs from foreign sources. The war expanded beyond the US, evident in the international 1988 Convention against Illicit Traffic in Narcotic Drugs. This convention sought to enhance international cooperation in supply-side policies (aimed at penalising suppliers) and enshrined a war of drugs approach internationally.

The drug war became ever more militarised, especially in Colombia and Mexico, and the US military and CIA (Central Intelligence Agency) became ever more involved in drug interdiction beyond the US. Drug suppression became intertwined with and indistinguishable from US imperialist and political Cold War ambitions around the world. A poignant example of this is in the US support of an Andean programme designed to eradicate coca production. Chien et al. (2000) report that at least 50% of US drug eradication aid actually went to train and support Colombian military in their war against leftist insurgents. The same happened in Mexico, where funds sent from 1988 to 1992 that were supposed to be used to combat drug traffickers were instead used to massacre indigenous peasants, including the Zapatistas (Chien et al. 2000: 299). On the other side of the world, the US's CIA made alliances in Afghanistan with opium producers after 1979 and the fall of the Shah of Iran. The US also used narcotics control to economically subject minority populations in Burma in the early 1970s (Singer 2008a,b: 76).

It is important to note that earlier in the twentieth century, the US already relied heavily on drug production to fund its overseas military campaigns. One of the most egregious examples was during the Vietnam War, when the US worked with and even paid Hmong opium producers and smugglers in Laos in their offensive against North Vietnam (Fadiman 1997: 130). Many Hmong fought against the communists, including youth as young as 13, while civilians died by 'cannon and mortar fire, bombs, land mines, grenades, postwar massacres, hunger, and disease' (Fadiman 1997: 133). The Hmong refugee crisis of the 1970s was a direct result of that. Case after case points to policies that were not even about drugs, but where drugs served as an excuse for or otherwise promoted foreign policy.

A militarised approach to drugs was not restricted to the US. In 1988, the United Nations passed a Convention against Illicit Traffic in Narcotic Drugs. It enhanced international cooperation in cracking down on drug suppliers and enshrined the war of drugs approach internationally. On the UN Office on Drugs and Crime (the title itself presents a crime-focused approach) website, we read a list of components that comprise this approach: the Convention includes 'measures against drug trafficking, including provisions against money laundering and the diversion of precursor chemicals. It provides for international cooperation through, for example, extradition of drug traffickers, controlled deliveries and transfer of proceeds'.[1]

In some countries, there is a death penalty for drug-related crimes. President Duterte of the Philippines has tried to introduce the capital punishments for drug crimes, and he has been widely condemned for his endorsement of extrajudicial killing of drug users (Holden 2021). There have also been documented extrajudicial punishments for drug offenses in Mexico, El Salvador, Honduras, Guatemala and Thailand (Fleetwood and Seal 2017). A publication in *The Lancet* (a British medical journal) reported that 87% of death sentences globally were related to drug crimes in 2020 (Burki 2021). The nongovernmental organisation Harm Reduction International (2021) reported that in at least five countries people were executed for drug crimes (including China, Iran, Saudi Arabia, Singapore and Vietnam) in 2020 or 2021, and that at least 237 death sentences were reported in 16 countries in 2021.[2] About 600 people were executed for drug crimes in 2014 (Fleetwood and Seal 2017). Criminologists Fleetwood and Seal (2017) argued that the war on drugs is 'profoundly gendered' in portraying men as evil traffickers and women and youth as victims. In reality, around 30% of drug trafficking arrests are for women and up to ¾ of prison populations in Latin America and southern Europe are women convicted of drug offenses (Fleetwood and Seal 2017: 363). Many of these women work as in low-level roles as mules who transport drugs (see the TV show *Orange Is the New Black* 2013 for a fictionalised depiction of a memoir about such an incarceration).

War on drugs policy in the US has been particularly racialised in its effects. Indeed, statistics reveal that the US domestic war on drugs has consistently had negative racialised effects, targeting people of colour disproportionately. The Sentencing Project is a nongovernmental organisation in the US that aims to eliminate racial inequality in the criminal justice system. In 2018, they wrote a report to the United Nations on racial disparities in the US criminal justice system that calls for an end to the war on drugs (The Sentencing Project 2018). The report stated that while rates of illegal drug use are similar across ethnic groups, 'More than one in four people arrested for drug law violations in 2015 was black' and that 'of the 277,000 people imprisoned nationwide for a drug offense, over half (56%) are African American or Latino'. The reasons for this are many, including both explicit and implicit bias and allocation of policing resources to heavily populated, minority-dominant low-income areas.[3] The take-home message is that drug stereotypes and policies have racialised effects, no matter what the explicit intention of laws.

The war on drugs remains in full force globally, despite a lack of evidence of its effectiveness at curbing drug use or related criminal activity. We will explore this point at the end of the chapter.

Anthropological Approaches

We now turn to how anthropologists have engaged with the 'war on drugs' in their research, both thematically and conceptually. In general, anthropological approaches – as with those of other academic disciplines studying drugs – have primarily been critical of war on drugs-type policy and the harms that the policy itself has brought.

Drug War as a System of Meanings

Conceptually, anthropologists analyse it not simply as a matter of law and policy but also as a set of practices that are shaped by cultural constructions of drugs and their effects. The drug war requires the naturalising of certain perspectives on drugs. It involves ways of seeing and understanding causality, morality, danger and risk. It involves articulations of our experiences of fear, joy, pleasure and pain. In a word, it involves culture. The drug war has created a potent discourse linking 'drugs' to criminality and illegality. This discourse about drugs has become a part of our collective consciousness through films, media and the like. The logic of illegality and criminalisation has been naturalised.

In analysing cultural meanings of drugs, anthropologists have studied how the drug war and its 'goodies' and 'baddies' are constructed through imagery and other forms of representation. Ethan Sharp (2014) has written a visual anthropology of the Museum of Drugs run by the Mexican military. He examined how, in visualising *narcocultura*, the museum builds a contrast between the evil trafficker and the noble police and military. Mannequins depict various kinds of people involved, including a peasant guarding his poppy fields from theft by drug traffickers and a drug trafficker dressed as a sophisticated cowboy, meant to depict their penchant towards showing off in ways that verge on the ridiculous. The decadence and backwardness of traffickers is put in contrast with depictions of the military as sophisticated and in keeping with a modern national identity.

Howard Campbell (2014) looks at *narcopropaganda* (videos, songs, blogs, graffiti and violence) for the other side – the Mexican cartels – arguing that this is a form of political discourse for increasingly state-like organisations that have taken over some of the functions of government and become the major opposition forces in some of the country. As Campbell puts it:

> As cartels have assumed economic and political power in specific territories, they have begun to broadcast their quasi-ideological/political perspectives, recruit new members, and position themselves through various media including banners, newspapers, web sites, and YouTube. Thus, the Mexican drug war is not only about extracting the profits of the narcotics trade but also about influencing or coercing public opinion.
>
> (ibid. 64)

Some of the propaganda entails spectacles of extreme violence and brutality that can convey the power of a cartel, while other propaganda comes in the form of *narcocorridos*, a popular genre of music in parts of Mexico that celebrates famous traffickers. Narcoculture in Mexico – including this genre of music – is also studied by anthropologist Shaylih Muehlmann (2013).

In a very different cultural context, Paul T. Cohen (2013) showed how opium is associated with poverty through official communications both by the Laotian government and international agencies. In one example of many, the UN country profile states: 'The cultivation and production of opium is closely associated with poverty and opium abuse' (United Nations Office on Drugs and Crime [UNODC] 2013: 6). Within Laos, there have been educational campaigns that have included evocative visual images. One poster, captioned 'the danger of opium addiction', included images of a man both before and after becoming an addict. It depicts opium as a seductive woman, enticing the innocent man. In the next image, the woman has turned into an angry aggressor, hitting the helpless man on the head with an opium pipe. This image portrays opium as an actor that seduces and destroys the will. Statements and images reinforce the lens through which people evaluate opium production and consumption. Systems of meanings matter, because they shape how people associated with drugs get treated legally, in healthcare systems, and in terms of moral condemnation. Such imagery has been of course potent in much popular culture depictions of drugs, including in films such as *Reefer Madness*, as well as in campaigns against consumption of the likes of methamphetamine, which often depict the changing appearance of people using drugs.

Drug War as Assemblage

Given the variety of forms it takes, it makes sense to analyse the drug war as an *assemblage* rather than as a static, homogeneous, monolithic form. We introduced the term assemblage in Chapter 2 to refer to the intricate meshes of relationships that come together at particular times and places, a term inspired by the work of philosophers Deleuze and Guattari (1987) that has gained popularity in anthropology as it captures much of the flux and complexity of the social worlds in which we live. Zigon elaborates the concept in describing the war on drugs, arguing that the drug war is not a singular issue or totalised strategy. The drug war is not a thing in itself, but 'rather assembled aspects of other assemblages that together create a widely diffused situation that is differentially distributed and has very real effects in worlds' (2015: 503). For him, 'situation' captures how people become entangled in localised manifestations of this assemblage. Examples include military engagements, surveillance and control by governments, border security, legal and prison systems, structural inequalities and therapies designed to address drug use (including harm reduction and addiction treatment). Assemblic ethnography identifies global flows of these processes that are linked but manifest differently. Importantly, Zigon argues, seeing drug involvements as assemblages also allows for a theory and understanding of political change: he identifies assemblic situations as moments of paradox and conflict, which open up opportunities for confrontation, experimentation and play – and potentially, change. Zigon identifies an activist approach to scholarship, exploring processes of political change.

Zigon's theories of global interconnectedness are not new in anthropology, nor in the analysis of the war on drugs. Howard Campbell (2009), for example, in studying the effects of the war on drugs on the US/Mexican border, referred to it as a drug war zone that spans multiple countries and requires historical perspectives to understand. His book includes testimonies of people from multiple walks of life, including drug dealers, a Mexican police officer, a musician and a US Border Patrol agent. This allows him to reveal the complexity of the micro-politics as well as the rich cultural generativity (such as the emergence of new musical forms) of this space. An important contribution to understanding the war on drugs is to disrupt facile dichotomies between legal and illegal, law enforcement and criminality, and even borders between countries. In the end, it is impossible to assume who the 'good guys' and 'baddies' are.

Anthropologists have thus recognised the war on drugs as complex, transnational cultural space that is impossible to isolate either thematically or geographically. The contribution of the 'assemblic' approach is to assign a label that captures how vastly complex the drug war is.

Drug War Ethnography

From Global to Local

Relatedly, anthropologists contribute meaningfully to scholarship on the drug war because of our contemporary emphasis on seeing both the big, global picture and the ways that it plays out in different ways at local levels. Any attempt to understand, and change, the way drug policies affect people must be attuned to local dynamics. This discourse of the war on drugs is a global one: it is true that drugs have colonised statute books the world over through global treaties, enshrining the drug war into law, but this logic gains or loses momentum in different locales. Khat provides a good example. As we discussed in relation to the history of khat in colonial Kenya (Chapter 6, and see also Anderson and Carrier 2009), khat has long been seen through a lens of prohibitionist drug policy, as something 'addictive' that should be suppressed. Yet local desires to control or prohibit it are not just a result of drug war logic. Indeed, concern among earlier generations to restrict access of youth to khat in khat-producing parts of Kenya (Anderson and Carrier 2009), even in pre-colonial times, has motivated moves to prohibit khat in East Africa, while concerns among the Somali community about perceived social harms of khat (e.g. high rates of divorce and unemployment among UK Somalis) provided much of the impetus for the UK ban.

The campaign to eradicate opium in Laos provides another example. Cohen (2013) pointed out that political explanations of the origins of this campaign focus on external pressures to conform to the global war on drugs. However, this explanation ignores internal processes of creating a Laotian cultural identity based on marginalising ethnic minorities who are associated with opium production and poverty, in part because of opium's reliance on shifting cultivation (considered backward) rather than permanent, irrigated agriculture. Cohen argues that 'Opium has become a fetish and, as such, objectified into a potent force that, as a form of shifting cultivation, destroys the nation's forest and, as a drug, weakens the individual, the family and the nation' (p. 188).

Anthropologists studying the war on drugs thus reveal local dynamics that are critical for understanding how the war on drugs works on the ground, in ordinary spaces.

Drug Commodity Chains

Reprising the theme of Chapter 7, we turn to how anthropologists have studied the drug commodity chains impacted by the war on drugs. A range of ethnographic accounts of various processes in the commodity chain, including drug production, trade and consumption, have revealed local manifestations of the drug war. Our study of the *quasilegality* of khat in Madagascar and East Africa provides an example of how global regulation of drugs has effects on local economies of drug production. In Kenya, the khat industry developed without much support of the Kenyan authorities given that internationally it was seen as suspect as a 'drug' (Carrier and Klantschnig 2018). This meant that it had an ambiguous position in terms of legality, being legal according to the statute books, yet often treated as illegal. Because of this, it developed as an informal industry (see Chapter 7), meaning that farmers and traders found little state interference in their endeavours. This was beneficial in some ways, as they could develop its trade networks on their own terms, but it was less beneficial in others as the state was less likely to step in to protect people when things went wrong. In Madagascar, the situation is similar: khat is tolerated as part of the informal economy, but it is not formally recognised as legal. This reluctance to recognise khat production as legitimate is because the government of Madagascar relies heavily on international aid, and global power brokers (the World Health Organization and the United Nations) have identified khat as a Schedule I drug, along with heroin and cocaine – and therefore potentially subject to control in the war on drugs. Khat farmers in Madagascar feel the effects of this quasilegality in that they do not qualify for governmental or international aid to support agricultural developments related to khat farming.

Similarly, cannabis production in various African countries has been analysed as quasi-legal in an opposite way to khat, as in most African countries it is illegal according to the statute books, yet often treated as legal and apparently freely grown and traded in several regions (Carrier and Klantschnig 2018). This has resulted in a situation where farmers and traders can benefit from high prices (cannabis illegality means prices are kept high due to the risks in growing it), and the lack of involvement of corporate interests in the trade; yet, the risk of arrest and police harassment is still present and potentially could become salient at any moment. The war of drugs logic and its policies have thus created much ambiguity, especially where substances are still seen as socially *licit* even if *illegal*. This is the case for cannabis in many parts of Africa given its long history of production and uses in many different contexts, including in healing.

Drug Production

Anthropologists have studied the effects of the drug war on farmers and other producers. Harry Sanabria (1993), for example, examined what the war meant for Bolivian peasants who grow coca. He examined the local dynamics of coca expansion in the early 1980s, considering not only growing foreign demand but also local dynamics of migration and inequality where local migration patterns increased wealth differentials and restricted access to land and productive resources. Conzelman (2006) studied coca cultivation in the Yungas region of Bolivia, where coca had been cultivated for at least a millennium and had long been a mainstay in local livelihoods. She identified the agrarian reforms of 1953 as pivotal in casting off hierarchical colonial forms of organisation in favour of a *sindicato* form, based on Western labour unions and the pre-colonial indigenous Aymara *ayllu* system. Conzelman wrote that indigenous Aymara coca farmers used the *sindicatos* as a democratic counterbalance to state and international interests, including efforts at eradicating coca cultivation in the name of the war on drugs.

More recently, Lyons (2016) studied how small-scale Colombian farmers in Putumayo faced the war on drugs. When Plan Colombia, the US-Colombia militarised antinarcotics policy, went into effect in 2000, this region supplied about 40% of the nation's illicit coca. Under the Plan, the US paid for military training and equipment for the Colombian military. They enacted forced eradication by spraying herbicides from planes (aerial fumigation programme), with significant negative impacts on human health. The police and military also arrived to manually rip out whatever crops remained. Despite these massive efforts, the region still supplies about 20% of the country's coca. What struck Lyons, however, is that despite this devastation, she witnessed overwhelming vitality and resilience among people determined to find alternative livelihoods. In particular, she observed that instead of adopting the cash crops recommended by the United States Agency for International Development (USAID), farmers developed subsistence-based biodiverse farming based on Amazonian practices. Lyons also examines the structural factors that led people to settle in the rural frontier coca growing zones in the first place, including mining and urban poverty.

Drug Trade

Anthropologists have also explored the dynamics of the drug trade. One major area of focus is on international, wholesale transshipment of drugs from producer to consumer countries. African countries serve as stop-over points for drugs going into Europe (see, e.g., Henrik Vigh on the trade trafficking of cocaine through Guinea-Bissau to Europe [Vigh 2019]), and Latin American countries for drugs going into North America. This results in many forms of devastation to those countries of transshipment. Consequences of this include 'spill-over' effects, where drug traders develop local markets for the drugs to cover their costs. Thus, paradoxically, the war on drugs has resulted in the spread of drug consumption and addiction around the world as smugglers seek routes to evade law enforcement.

Merrill Singer (2008) argues that the problems associated with drug trade include organised crime and the repression associated with it, including gangs and violence, problems very much linked to the war on drugs and the criminalisation of drugs. Sometimes governments themselves become involved in the illegal trade because of the amount of profit that can be gained, and the need to pay their debt burden. But even states that wish to remain drug-free have a difficult time resisting the tyranny of the drug cartels. Singer's point is that to understand the transshipment dynamic, it is critical to trace historic roots related to colonialism, and to contemporary structural political and economic constraints that leave former colonies at the economic mercy of financial institutions created by and for colonising countries (see also Chapter 7). A result has been weak states that cannot provide basic services to their populations and that owe vast amounts of money: drug trafficking helps with the latter of these problems. Singer (2008: 15) argues that the results on the ground include the violation of the human rights and civil liberties of populations, the reduction of quality-of-life-oriented worker productivity and education, increase in poor health from violence and disease, the corruption of government officials and the disintegration of social institutions.

Ethnographic research has revealed the lived experiences of people living amid drug trafficking. Sarah Luna (2020) studied both sex worker migrants and US missionary expatriates on the Mexican side of the border, across from Texas, in a town in the crosshairs of the drug trade. Similar to Campbell's research, Luna found that the entrenched narcoeconomy blurred lines between taken-for-granted categories of legal and illegal, virtue and vice. Luna discovered where and how people forged intimacies and moral economies of reciprocal obligations amid the violence and inequalities that characterise the region.

As in every aspect of the drug economy, drug trafficking is highly gendered. In his study of drug traffickers in a *favela* (often translated as shanty town) in Rio de Janeiro, Brazil, Penglase (2010) argued that traffickers use a culturally recognised form of masculinity that justifies the use of violence in response to perceived threats. This patriarchal notion, whereby men are expected to control their family and possessions, is not the only model of Brazilian masculinity. Nevertheless, it is the one that many drug traffickers use in seizing control over, and in protecting, people (including other men) and communities from the police, among other threats. In exchange for the protection of their neighbourhood 'family', people owe them 'respect'.

In addition to studies of drug trafficking, some examine drug dealing, focusing on the retail trade. Yolanda Martín (2015) also takes a gendered perspective. Although drug dealing is commonly associated with men, Martin (2015) followed a female heroin dealer in her 70s in the Dominican Republic. La Dona's activities disrupted not only gender stereotypes (positing men as dealers and women as victims) but also those that assume that drug dealers have purely negative effects on their communities and lack a code of moral ethics. On the contrary, La Dona, the 'Queen of Heroin', is a strong matriarchal actor who embodies traditional family values and who works to monitor the consumption of those who buy from her. For example, she would not sell drugs to some people, including those who had said they want to go to rehab. She would also occasionally give a free dose to regular customers who were going through withdrawal but had no money. Aside from drug dealing, La Dona gave charitably in the community and helped watch neighbourhood children. She did this in the face of a repressive and corrupt Dominican government that does not hesitate to use force on people.

One of the most ground-breaking studies was of crack dealing in East Harlem by Philippe Bourgois (1995). He revealed the subculture of crack dealing, including internal moral codes, modes of operation and dealing as a source of masculine identity and 'respect'. He also examined forces, such as the school system, that socialise people into those roles. He linked analysis of everyday lives with a structural analysis of the persistent poverty that plagues the neighbourhood, tracing it to such factors as racism and deindustrialisation that resulted resulting in the loss of jobs and middle-class opportunities. He explains drug dealing as a logical option in the face of those circumstances.

Drug Consumption

Some studies have examined how the war on drugs has shaped experiences associated with drug consumption. Klein (2008) identified Western influences in the spread of drug use in countries of transshipment and the local economic problems that accompany it. Western tourism, for example, brought heroin to Kenya on a large scale and powdered and crack cocaine to Jamaica. Along with these came an increase in crime and health problems and a decrease in general well-being. Taking a different angle, Tobias Brandner (2020) studied community life in Philippine prisons, which have seen a surge in prisoner numbers, without a corresponding increase in funding, in the wake of President Duterte's war on drugs. Brandner examined the role of religious activities in prison to show how prisoners are not merely victims of prison hardships but also are actively creating meaning as they suffer privations.

Others study how the drug war affects experiences of drug users. In their study of female sex workers who inject drugs in the border town of Tijuana, Mexico, Syvertsen et al. (2017) discovered how these drug users and their intimate partners find meaning amidst the repressions and ferocity of the drug war. Specifically, they created communities of care. People let others stay in their apartments when their makeshift homes in the canal were destroyed by police sweeps or unlivable due to unsanitary conditions. They established injection sites where people could go in relative safety. They participated together in an informal economy, since, with prison records, many could not find formal sector employment. Intimate couples helped each other find drugs while navigating the precarious conditions of their existence. In all, they found 'hope amidst the horror of war' (p. 577).

Some themes that run through anthropological studies of the war on drugs are: (1) that, at the local level, people adapt and show resilience in the face of devastating and oppressive conditions; (2) that commonly accepted dichotomies, such as those between 'good' and 'bad', moral and immoral, are difficult to discern on the ground since lines become blurry in real-life situations; (3) the war on drugs is best thought of as a complex *assemblage* of policies, practices and worldviews that manifest themselves differently depending on the context and time; and (4) that many people experience great physical and social suffering as a result of war on drugs policy.

The war on drugs can also have paradoxical effects on drug consumption and consumers, making drugs appear more attractive and glamorous than would otherwise be the case. This is certainly true for khat, the substance we have both studied. Many consumers resist the conflation of khat alongside other drugs, preferring to think of it as a 'stimulant' as for them the category of 'drug' suggests stigma (Carrier 2008). However, for some – especially young men – there is an allure in the thought of consuming a 'drug', something seen as daring and defiant, something 'cool' (Carrier 2005). Indeed, consuming something considered a drug is a source of 'respect' (in a 'street' sense as referred to also by Bourgois [1995]), even if not 'respectable' (in a genteel sense).

Who Pays the Price? Violence, Structural Violence and Marginality

In key ethnographies we have already encountered, we can see how the prohibition and criminalisation resulting from war on drugs approaches has disproportionately affected the already marginalised. The war on drugs can be seen as war that generates poverty and entrenches those who are already poor. More than a war on drugs, it is an offensive against the poor. Bourgois (2018) traced the historical dynamics of colonialism and capital accumulation that lay the framework for the predatory dynamics of the war on drugs. The work by Garcia (2008) on addicts in a marginalised part of New Mexico speaks to hardships resulting from structural violence. Being labelled a criminal compounds and reinforces this structural violence.

The war on drugs has racialised effects as well as class effects. Disproportionately more people of African American descent in the US are imprisoned for drug offences than whites (Lowry 2018). Anthropologists have studied these dynamics. In a study of suburban versus street drug dealing, David Crawford (2016) contrasts the economic activities of a suburban dealer of powder cocaine with a Latino crack dealer on an urban street. Crawford argues that the suburban model is less hazardous, partly because business is conducted indoors. He argues that ethnicity and class have affected these two men's lives significantly, with the middle-class white man facing fewer threats by the criminal justice system.

The opioid crisis in the US also brings into relief the racialised dynamics of public perceptions of addiction and criminality. Sonia Mendoza et al. (2019) identify a culture of blame in the opioid epidemic in New York City. They found that dominant discourses about opioid users, who are predominantly suburban and white in their study area, lay blame not on the user but on prescribers and dealers/suppliers outside the control of the user. This public health lens contrasts with rhetoric commonly applied to users of crack cocaine and heroin users, who are held up as the 'other', and vilified. They also happen to be poorer and more non-white. Mendoza and colleagues trace how

a white suburban community works to invert the meaning of addiction such that addicted members are not othered, and to blame systemic factors, rather than opioid users, for addiction, by means that do not articulate race but are selectively applied to Whites.

(245)

Outside of the US, the drug war also preys on the already-marginalised. Hernandez Castillo (2019) explored the effects of the war on drugs on women and indigenous people in Mexico. Women suffer sexual violence at the hands of military and paramilitary groups, and indigenous women have been disproportionately incarcerated. Castillo argued that this punitive invasion, violation and incarceration of women's bodies serve to extend and reinforce territorial control in the name of drug control. Based on her study of women in prisons, her goal is to show that racialised effects are also gendered. The intersectionality of the war of drugs – how its impacts stretch across axes of class, race and gender mentioned in this section – is more fully developed in a review article on gender and the war on drugs by Shaylih Muehlmann (2018).

The drug war not only preys on the poor but also creates poverty: in one example, Dannemiller presented a visual exposé of Ciudad Juárez, another Mexican border town that he describes as 'a city at war with (its own idea of) itself' (2010: 136). In his piece, Dannemiller juxtaposed the aspired-for *maquiladora* miracle town with the drug-saturated drug war cartel cross-roads, where violence, and fear of it, has permeated civic life and dashed hopes of an increased quality of life associated with global participation in the capitalist economy.

Studying Up

Anthropologists have not just focused on the margins, but they have also 'studied up' in the words of Laura Nader who encouraged anthropologists to study the powerful as well as the apparently powerless (1972). In one example, the anthropologist Winifred Tate (2015), who herself worked in the US government, conducted extensive fieldwork in Colombia and interviews among policy makers and activists. Her ethnography of drug war policy focused on the US Plan Colombia policy that was signed into law by President Clinton in 2000, where the US government provide military aid to Colombia to be used for counter-narcotics activities, particularly towards the eradication of coca production and cocaine trafficking. Tate demonstrates different motivations and aims of many actors driving forward this policy. On the one hand, the military-industrial complex sought to boost weapons sales, and selling them for counter-narcotics was an easy pitch. President Clinton's administration was trying not to be outflanked by hawkish Republicans, and the US Southern Command had an interest in raising their profile. On the other hand, the Colombian army needed military supplies, not necessarily for counter-narcotics, but to fight against counter-insurgent rebels so that they could shore up their power. The result was that these varied interests coalesced to produce policy that went against commitments to human rights in US foreign policy. Tate's is an ethnography of policy in the making, rather than an ethnography of the implication of the policy.

Tate's work is an important anthropological contribution to 'studying up' in the field of drug research, something urged by Axel Klein in his overview of the anthropology of drugs (2012). Klein describes how 'Organizational studies are needed to understand the practical workings of national agencies, the Advisory Council on the Misuse of Drugs, and international agencies – like the UNODC and INCB (the International Narcotics Control Board)' (ibid. 372). Indeed, additional 'studying up' is necessary to understand the logic and decision-making processes of power holders in the war on drugs. Alex Stevens (2021), a criminologist, has recently published an insightful article using the method of 'autoethnography' – where the researcher foregrounds their own experiences as material to analyse – to explore the workings of the UK's Advisory Council on the Misuse of Drugs. He investigated in particular the role of 'experts' on the council, which included Stevens himself, as he has served on the council. Such research brings ethnographic light to how policy is constructed and by whom.

A Failed War?

One key question to ask about the drug war is why it persists when in many ways it appears inhumane and a colossal failure even by its own terms. Despite the tremendous increase in resources used to combat illegal drugs, consumption and supply rates have not lessened, and violence has escalated around the world. The result has been a growth of organised crime globally, prisons full of drug-related criminals, and increasing rates of overdose deaths (see Coyne and Hall 2017). So, why does the war on drugs continue? We must start by asking what constitutes failure and for whom. The short answer is that many people and agencies have and continue to profit from drugs. This is not just the smugglers and traffickers, though they do profit greatly from the illegality of drugs which makes their trade lucrative. Indeed, a much wider range of people make livelihoods from the drug war, including those working for government agencies tasked with applying the law, including the likes of the Drug Enforcement Administration and equivalent bodies around the world, such as Nigeria's National Drug Law Enforcement Agency (Klantschnig 2013). They owe their continued existence and funding streams to the drug war. Chien et al. argue that the drug war protects elite interests generally (2000). Also, as we saw earlier, the drug war has served foreign policy interests, providing a cover for potentially objectionable military goals, as in the case of Tate's account. The agenda of eradicating drugs also serves domestic interests, including for the likes of President Duterte and other authoritarian leaders for whom the drug war provides distractions and scapegoats in the stereotyped figures of 'drug dealers' and 'addicts'.

In short, taking the purported aims of the drug war – to rid the world of drugs – at face value is perhaps rather naïve, both as such an aim is exceedingly unrealistic, and because of all the vested interests that coalesce around drugs. The drug industry thus does not just involve smugglers and dealers, but a much wider array of people. This is similar to the lucrative infrastructure that has been built up around illegal immigration between northern Africa and Europe, as analysed by anthropologist Ruben Andersson (2014). In this analysis, Andersson shows how the migrant industry revolves not just around smugglers, but also others, including those charged with keeping migrants out of the EU who have received great budget boosts in recent years with talk of a migration 'crisis'.

Countercurrents: Anti-War on Drugs

As with every dominant perspective, there are and have been countercurrents, sometimes in parallel, and sometimes in opposition to the War on Drugs. In fact, the War on Drugs was actually never universally accepted. There have been alternative discourses of drug use being a public health problem and of the economic benefits of legalising drugs. Some countries have decriminalised drugs. Portugal, for example, decriminalised all drugs, including heroin and cocaine, in 2000, although penalties remained in place for producing or moving large quantities of them. Other countries, including the Czech Republic, the Netherlands, Colombia and Argentina, have also decriminalised drug possession of at least some drugs in small amounts for personal use. There are shifting and sometimes inconsistent discourses and policies about drug use even within a given country. Because decriminalisation tends to be paired with 'harm reduction' approaches, many international organisations support decriminalisation, including the World Health Organization, Human Rights Watch and the Organization of American States. We will return later to current debates around drug policy, and the significant policy changes of recent years.

Harm reduction focuses on reducing the negative impacts of drug use and drug policies. It is based on the goals of upholding human rights and promoting social justice. It encourages drug safety rather than drug abstinence. Examples of interventions include creating public spaces where people can take drugs, needle and syringe exchange programmes, housing and employment that does not require abstinence, overdose prevention and reversal, mental health support, and social support services. Specific interventions are tailor-fit to each specific context, as there is no one-size-fits-all. Initiatives can also include educational campaigns encouraging people to drink water while consuming alcohol, or to consume nicotine through a patch instead of smoking it. In addition to creating programmes, harm reduction focuses on providing appropriate health services and supporting legislation that decriminalises drugs. This includes a revisitation of the official classification of drugs through the Schedules of the UN Commission on Narcotic Drugs. A number of US anthropologists have received government funding to study drug use patterns in order to inform effective programme development, implementation and assessment. In the late 1980s, J. Bryan Page, for example, directly observed self-injecting and needle-sharing behaviour of users in Miami (Page and Singer 2010: 77). The published results of this study revealed specific risky behaviours and pointed to possible harm reduction interventions.

The rise of HIV/AIDS in the 1980s also gave way to a reformed way of thinking about drug policy, since cases of HIV spread through intravenous drug users (IDU). Indeed, the spread of blood-borne diseases through unsafe needle-sharing practices has become a core example of how war on drugs-type policy can lead to ever-increasing harms, especially where injection equipment itself has been criminalised. As Reinarman and Granfield (2015: 13) suggest:

The spread of HIV/AIDS and hepatitis C among injection drug users stems from the criminalisation of injection equipment, which makes it artificially scarce and thereby encourages unsafe injection practices such as syringe sharing. This sort of policy reflexivity is particularly acute in the broader context of extreme poverty, inequality, and socio-cultural dislocation from which so much problematic drug use arises. In short, over time our drug control policies are in some measure self-ontologizing, that is, they help bring into being the very outcomes that are then invoked to justify those policies.

Some anthropologists have studied existing harm reduction programmes. In a study of recreational drug use in Amsterdam, Hardon et al. (2020) found that users demonstrated an ethic of care and self-responsibility that manifest itself in an evolving set of practices to minimise risk. They found, for example, that the drug users took precautions: in concern for dosing, users shared information with each other about trusted sources. The harm reduction initiative helped them by offering facilities to test the content and quality of the drugs. Attention to dosing is a concern shared by both users and health practitioners. Users are concerned about having a positive environment, and harm reduction literature reinforced this by encouraging drinking water, staying out of the sun and wearing comfortable clothing.

In another example, Uzwiak (2021), an applied anthropologist working on a project in collaboration with the Philadelphia Department of Public Health, did interviews with next-of-kin of people who died from opiate drug overdoses. While working within the paradigm of harm reduction, Uzwiak calls for a politicised approach to harm reduction that recognises the need to attend to 'structural conditions that conspire to make the process of "recovery" unattainable and proximity to death (the threat of overdose) a condition of care' (p. 15). These structural conditions include 'experiences of institutional neglect, interpersonal violence, and the realities of living in a resource poor urban area in which choices may be truncated by lack of employment opportunities, housing instability, and economic insecurity' (p. 6).

There are some important criticisms of harm reduction, many of which come from applied anthropologists and other practitioners who are committed to some version of harm reduction as an antidote to the harmful war on drugs, yet at the same time are aware of some of the pitfalls. Some have criticised harm reduction for being complicit in a neoliberal approach that does not question structural violence but rather focuses on the control of individual behaviour (determined by outsiders to be 'risky') and self-governance (Campbell and Shaw 2008). A related argument is that 'harm reduction' increases surveillance of drug users through a Foucauldian lens of biopower and governmentality (Bourgois 2018). This argument holds that, despite the guise of moral neutrality, people's behaviours become monitored through a public health lens that creates a sense of a moral self within the framework of authoritative power (Pereira and Scott 2017). Bourgois (2018) noted that harm reduction 'is capable of melding scientific therapeutic efficiency and empathetic ethical tolerance with ideological righteousness and even brutal repression' (387). Harm reduction approaches have also often denied the role of pleasure and rational choice in drug use (Watson et al.

2020). Acknowledging the role of pleasure in drug use opens opportunities for developing practical interventions that resonate with people's experiences (Race 2008).

In response to these criticisms, some harm reduction discourses reject drug use as pathological and seek to reframe it in terms of well-being. Portuguese scholars Rego et al. (2021) explain the importance of affirming the dignity, agency and self-termination of users. They embrace an approach that respects human rights, and in particular, the right to informed choice, including the right to risk-taking behaviour. Another reframing emphasises the need to involve drug users themselves in designing interventions: Uzwiak goes beyond simple criticism to propose the importance of a critical harm reduction approach, writing: 'In the spirit of the radical potential of harm reduction, people who use drugs and those who care for them need to be involved in redirecting public resources to this end' (p. 15). Hardon et al. concluded their study in Amsterdam, writing that 'harm reduction strategies will be more effective when they engage with the collective, material, and affective practices constantly evolving within drug-using communities' (Hardon et al. 2020: 213).

A harm reduction approach is in many ways the opposite of that of the war on drugs, and yet both approaches are practiced side by side within the same countries. This contributes to structural vulnerabilities, as practices of care exist alongside those of incarceration. Moral condemnation of drugs that fuels the war on drugs and related 'institutional mechanisms mark persons who use drugs as underserving, thereby subjecting them to death and its anticipation even as they attempt to access care' (Uzwiak 2021: 15). Paradoxically, the violence of governmental approaches to the war on drugs coexists with a harm reduction approach that embraces care.

Conclusion: Summary and Future Directions

Understanding drugs and the social worlds that revolve around them would scarcely be possible if the context of the war on drugs was not also considered, such is its power in defining drugs and their consumers, and in naturalising certain forms of policy towards them as right and proper. Yet things are changing in this regard. Drug policy is in a state of flux globally, as cracks have been growing wider in the former consensus around drugs and drug policy (Bewley-Taylor 2012). This is most evident in the trend towards the liberalisation of cannabis law around the world, whereby countries and states – including Canada, Jamaica, Colorado, California and many others – have moved away from criminalisation in relation to that substance. Furthermore, harm reduction has become much more embedded in drug discourse and policy. This is not a one-way process; however, as while the likes of cannabis become more legal, substances such as khat are becoming more illegal, the recent UK ban being a case in point. Also, several countries – including China and Russia – still remain highly repressive in relation to drugs.

There is much further work for anthropologists to do in all this policy flux. For example, while there are many ethnographies of prohibition, it will be important to apply the ethnographic eye to the socio-cultural impacts of decriminalisation and legalisation too. Of particular importance in this regard will be studying the form taken by legal businesses stepping into the previously illegal industry of certain drugs, something already undertaken by the likes of Marty Otanez and David Vergara in exploring the role of corporate social responsibility in the cannabis industry (2021). There is fear of 'corporate capture' of such industries, and anthropologists will be well-placed to study such dangers, not just in regard to the cannabis industry but also to the growing industry around psychedelics. Prohibition and the war on drugs have underpinned so much of contemporary understandings of drugs, yet there still will be much to study in a post-prohibition world, should one emerge out of the current fracturing consensus.

Notes

1 Website available here: www.unodc.org/unodc/en/treaties/illicit-trafficking.html?ref=menuside (accessed May 2022).
2 See report by Harm Reduction International available here: https://hri.global/flagship-research/death-penalty/the-death-penalty-for-drug-offences-global-overview-2021/ (accessed December 2022).
3 See The Sentencing Project website available here: www.sentencingproject.org/publications/un-report-on-racial-disparities/ (accessed December 2022).

Works Cited

Anderson, David, and Neil Carrier. 2009. "Khat in Colonial Kenya: A History of Prohibition and Control." *The Journal of African History* 50 (3): 377–397.

Andersson, Ruben. 2014. *Illegality, Inc.: Clandestine Migration and the Business of Bordering Europe*. Oakland, CA: University of California Press.

Bewley-Taylor, David R. 2012. *International Drug Control: Consensus Fractured*. Cambridge: Cambridge University Press.

Bourgois, Philippe. 1995. *In Search of Respect: Selling Crack in El Barrio*. New York: Cambridge University Press.

———. 2018. "Decolonising Drug Studies in an Era of Predatory Accumulation." *Third World Quarterly* 39 (2): 385–398.

Brandner, Tobias. 2020. "The Room is Small, But the Heart is Big – Religion and Community Life in Philippine Prisons." *Asia Pacific Journal of Anthropology* 21 (4): 295–314.

Burki, Talha. 2021. "The Death Penalty Continues Unabated Globally." *The Lancet* 397 (10284): 1531–1532.

Campbell, Howard. 2009. *Drug War Zone: Frontline Dispatches from the Streets of El Paso and Juárez*. Austin, TX: University of Texas Press.

Campbell, Howard. 2014. Narco-Propaganda in the Mexican "Drug War": An Anthropological Perspective. *Latin American Perspectives*, 41(2), 60–77.

Campbell, Nancy D., and Susan J. Shaw. 2008. "Incitements to Discourse: Illicit Drugs, Harm Reduction, and the Production of Ethnographic Subjects." *Cultural Anthropology* 23 (4): 688–717.

Carrier, Neil. 2005. "'Miraa Is Cool': The Cultural Importance of Miraa (Khat) for Tigania and Igembe Youth in Kenya." *Journal of African Cultural Studies* 17 (2): 201–218.

———. 2008. "Is Miraa a Drug?: Categorizing Kenyan Khat." *Substance Use Misuse* 43 (6): 803–818.

Carrier, Neil, and Gernot Klantschnig. 2018. "Quasilegality: Khat, Cannabis and Africa's Drug Laws." *Third World Quarterly* 39 (2): 350–365.

Castillo Hernández, and Rosalva Aída. 2019. "Racialized Geographies and the 'War on Drugs': Gender Violence, Militarization, and Criminalization of Indigenous Peoples." *Journal of Latin American & Caribbean Anthropology* 24 (3): 635–652.

Chien, Arnold, Margaret Conners, and Kenneth Fox. 2000. "The Drug War in Perspective." In *Dying for Growth: Global Inequality and the Health of the Poor*, edited by Jim Yong Kim, Joyce V. Millen, Alec Irwin and John Greshman, 293–327. Monroe, ME: Common Courage Press.

Cohen, Paul T. 2013. "Symbolic Dimensions of the Anti-Opium Campaign in Laos." *Australian Journal of Anthropology* 24 (2): 177–192.

Conzelman, Caroline S. 2006. "Fieldwork in Coca Country: Investigating Democracy and development in the Bolivian Andes." In *Dispatches from the Field: Neophyte Ethnographers in a Changing World*, 119–136. Long Grove, IL: Waveland Press, Inc.

Coyne, Christopher J., and Abigail R. Hall. 2017. "Four Decades and Counting: The Continued Failure of the War on Drugs." *Policy Analysis* 811: 1–28.

Crawford, David. 2016. "Suburban Drug Dealing: A Case Study in Ambivalent Economics." In *The Economics of Ecology, Exchange, and Adaptation: Anthropological Explorations*, edited by Donald C. Wood, 197–219. Bingley, UK: Emerald.

Dannemiller, Keith. 2010. "Juarochos: Fleeing Ciudad Juárez." *Visual Anthropology Review* 26 (2): 136–143.

Deleuze, Gilles, and Felix Guattari. 1987. *A Thousand Plateaus: Capitalism and Schizophrenia*. Minneapolis, MN: University of Minnesota Press.

Fadiman, Anne. 1997. *The Spirit Catches You and You Fall Down: a Hmong Child, her American Doctors, and the Collision of Two Cultures*. New York: Farrar, Straus, and Giroux.

Farber, David. 2021. "The Advent of the War on Drugs." In *The War on Drugs: A History*, edited by David Farber, 17–36. New York: New York University Press.

Fleetwood, Jennifer, and Lizzie Seal. 2017. "Women, Drugs, and the Death Penalty: Framing Sandiford." *Howard Journal of Crime and Justice* 56 (3): 358–381.

Garcia, Angela. 2008. "The Elegiac Addict: History, Chronicity, and the Melancholic Subject." *Cultural Anthropology* 24 (4): 718–746.

Hardon, Anita, Takeo David Hymans, Inge van Schipstal, Swasti Mishra, Moritz Berning, Hayley Murray, Daan Kamps, and Tait Mandler. 2020. "Caring for 'Hassle-Free Highs' in Amsterdam." *Anthropology and Humanism* 45 (2): 212–222.

Harm Reduction International. 2021 "The Death Penalty for Drug Offences: Global Overview 2021." Harm Reduction International. https://hri.global/flags hip-research/death-penalty/the-death-penalty-for-drug-offences-global-overv iew-2021/

Holden, William. 2021. *President Rodrigo Duterte and the War on Drugs: Fear and Loathing in the Philippines.* Washington D.C.: Lexington Books.

Klantschnig, Gernot. 2013. *Crime, Drugs and the State in Africa: The Nigerian Connection.* Leiden: Brill/Republic of Letters.

Kleiman, Mark A.R., and James E. Hawdon. 2011. *Encyclopedia of Drug Policy.* Thousand Oaks: SAGE Publications.

Klein, Axel. 2008. *Drugs and the World.* London: Reaktion Books.

———. 2012. "The Anthropology of Drugs." In *The SAGE Handbook of Social Anthropology,* edited by Richard Fardon, Olivia Harris, Trevor H.J. Marchand, Mark Nuttall, Chris Shore, Veronica Strang, and Richard A Wilson, 365–376. Thousand Oaks: SAGE Publications.

Lowry, David Shane. 2018. "Redpilling: A Professional Reflects on White Racial Privilege and Drug Policy in American Health Care." *Journal of Ethnicity in Substance Abuse* 17 (1): 50–63.

Luna, Sarah. 2020. *Love in the Drug War: Selling Sex and Finding Jesus on the Mexico-US Border.* Austin, TX: University of Texas Press.

Lyons, Kristina. 2016. "Decomposition as Life Politics: Soils, Selva, and Small Farmers under the Gun of the U.S.-Colombian War on Drugs." *Cultural Anthropology (Society for Cultural Anthropology)* 31 (1): 56–81.

Martín, Yolanda C. 2015. "The 'Queen of Heroin': Gender, Drug Dealing, and Zero-Tolerance Policies in the Dominican Republic." *Dialectical Anthropology* 39 (4): 443–451.

Mendoza, Sonia, Allyssa Stephanie Rivera, and Helena Bjerring Hansen. 2019. "Re-Racialization of Addiction and the Redistribution of Blame in the White Opioid Epidemic." *Medical Anthropology Quarterly* 33 (2): 242–262.

Muehlmann, Shaylih. 2013. *When I Wear My Alligator Boots: Narco-Culture in the U.S. Mexico Borderlands.* Oakland, CA: University of California Press.

———. 2018. "The Gender of the War on Drugs." *Annual Review of Anthropology* 47: 315–330.

Nader, Laura. 1972. *Up the Anthropologist: Perspectives Gaines from Studying Up.* Washington, DC: ERIC Clearinghouse.

Nahas, Gabriel, and Albert Greenwood. 1974. "A Critique of the First Report of the National Commission on Marihuana and Drug Abuse (1972)." *Psychiatric Annals* 3 (4): 94–106.

Orange Is the New Black (OITNB). 2013. American comedy-drama series created by Jenji Kohan for Netflix. www.netflix.com/title/70242311

Otanez, Mary, and David Vergara. 2021. "Cannabis Corporate Social Responsibility: A Critical and Mixed-Method Approach." In *The Routledge Handbook of Post-Prohibition Cannabis Research,* edited by Dominic Corva and Joshua Meisel, 183–191. New York: Routledge.

Page, J. Bryan, and Merrill Singer. 2010. *Comprehending Drug Use: Ethnographic Research at the Social Margins.* New Brunswick, NJ: Rutgers University Press.

Pembleton, Mark R. 2021. "Revising the Drug War: A Genealogical and Historiographical Sketch." *Diplomatic History* 45 (5): 890–902.

Penglase, Ben. 2010. "The Owner of the Hill: Masculinity and Drug-Trafficking in Rio de Janeiro, Brazil." *Journal of Latin American & Caribbean Anthropology* 15 (2): 317–337.

Pereira, Margaret, and John Scott. 2017. "Harm Reduction and the Ethics of Drug Use: Contemporary Techniques of Self-Governance." *Health Sociology Review* 26 (1): 69–83.

Race, Kane. 2008. "The Use of Pleasure in Harm Reduction: Perspectives from the History of Sexuality." *International Journal of Drug Policy* 19 (5): 417–423. https://doi.org/10.1016/j.drugpo.2007.08.008

Raz, Mical. 2016. "Treating Addiction or Reducing Crime?: Methadone Maintenance and Drug Policy Under the Nixon Administration." *Journal of Policy History* 29 (1): 58–86.

RÊGo, Ximene, Maria João Oliveira, Catarina Lameira, and Olga S. Cruz. 2021. "20 Years of Portuguese Drug Policy: Developments, Challenges and the Quest for Human Rights." *Substance Abuse Treatment, Prevention, and Policy* 16 (1): 59.

Reinarman, Craig and Robert Granfield. 2015. Addiction Is Not Just a Brain Disease: Critical Studies of Addiction. In *Expanding Addiction: Critical Essays*, edited by Robert Granfield and Craig Reinarman, 1–21. London: Routledge.

Sanabria, Harry. 1993. *The Coca Boom and Rural Social Change in Bolivia*. Ann Arbor, MI: University of Michigan Press.

Sharp, Ethan. 2014. "Visualizing Narcocultura: Violent Media, the Mexican Military's Museum of Drugs, and Transformative Culture." *Visual Anthropology Review* 30 (2): 151–163.

Singer, Merrill. 2008. *Drugs and Development: The Global Impact on Sustainable Growth and Human Rights*. Long Grove, IL: Waveland Press.

Singer, Merrill, and J. Bryan Page. 2014. *The Social Value of Drug Addicts: Uses of the Useless*. New York: Routledge.

Stevens, Alex. 2021. "The Politics of Being an 'Expert': A Critical Realist Auto-Ethnography of Drug Policy Advisory Panels in the UK." *Qualitative Criminology* 10 (2). www.qualitativecriminology.com/pub/v10i2-p4/release/1

Syvertsen, Jennifer L., Angela Robertson Bazzi, and María Luisa Mittal. 2017. "Hope Amidst Horror: Documenting the Effects of the 'War on Drugs' Among Female Sex Workers and their Intimate Partners in Tijuana, Mexico." *Medical Anthropology* 36 (6): 566–583.

Tate, Winifred. 2015. *Drugs, Thugs, and Diplomats: U.S. Policymaking in Colombia*. Stanford: Stanford University Press.

The Sentencing Project. 2018. "Report to the United Nations on Racial Disparities in the U.S. Criminal Justice System." The Sentencing Project. www.sentencingproj ect.org/reports/report-to-the-united-nations-on-racial-disparities-in-the-u-s-crimi nal-justice-system/

United Nations Office on Drugs and Crime (UNODC). 1988. "United Nations Convention Against Illicit Traffic in Narcotic Drugs and Psychotropic Substances, 1988." United Nations. www.unodc.org/unodc/en/treaties/illicit-trafficking. html?ref=menuside

United Nations Office on Drugs and Crime (UNODC). 2013 "Lao PDR Government: National Drug Control Master Plan 2009–2013." United Nations. www.coursehero.com/file/176670092/NDCMP-Engpdf/

Uzwiak, Beth A., Anastasia Hudgins, and Lia N. Pizzicato. 2021. "Legacies of the War on Drugs: Next of Kin of Persons Who Died of Opioid Overdose and Harm Reduction Interventions in Philadelphia." *International Journal of Drug Policy* 97: 1–22.

Vigh, Henrik. 2019. "Life in the Ant Trails: Cocaine and Caustic Circuits in Bissau." *Focaal* 2019 (85): 15–25.

Watson, Tara Marie, Gillian Kollab, Emily van der Meulend, and Zoe Dodd. 2020. "Critical Studies of Harm Reduction: Overdose Response in Uncertain Political Times." *International Journal of Drug Policy* 76: 1–6.

Zigon, Jarrett. 2015. "What is a Situation?: An Assemblic Ethnography of the Drug War." *Cultural Anthropology* 30: 501–524.

9 Postlude
Engagements and Future Directions

This book has presented a broad coverage of scholarship in the anthropological study of drugs. In this last chapter, we want to look to contemporary trends, the future of drug studies and ways to become engaged beyond the classroom. Before we do, and as a way of framing our conversation about the future, we take a moment to reflect on why we got into the project of writing this book in the first place.

Why Study Drugs?

We each came to the study of drugs from different perspectives, and we both started by studying khat. Gezon (2006) had been studying conservation and protected area management in Madagascar, in the northern province of Antsiranana, or Diego Suarez. It came to her attention that one of the problems related to land cover change was that people were cutting down the forest inside and near the protected rainforest to grow khat. Satellite image analysis confirmed that there had been patches of deforestation in the areas where we knew people were growing khat. Local people were well-aware of the increase in khat production and consumption locally, and there were vastly divergent opinions about it. Khat growers and traders were enthusiastic about it. Some called it 'green gold' because of its positive effects on household incomes. Consumers enjoyed chewing it in the company of others or by themselves for the energy boost. Others considered it a menace not only because its effects on the rainforest but also because they were afraid that farmers were abandoning food crops in favour of khat, that consumers were draining family resources to purchase it, that consumers were becoming addicted and that consumers would rather sit around all day and chew than take on productive employment. What started as a study in conservation became a holistic study of the entire commodity chain of khat production, trade and consumption, as well as khat's pharmacology and the rhetoric that surrounds it. Gezon realised that, because of the charged dynamics of drugs, she could not understand the forest without understanding drugs more

DOI: 10.4324/9781003109549-9

broadly. She learned that khat's effects are complex and nuanced, as was discussed earlier in this book.

Carrier began his career with doctoral research into khat in Kenya, having been drawn to the field of ethnobotany through earlier studies of ancient Greek and Roman use of various medicinal plants, and through a study of tobacco. Initially, he set out to study khat consumption in a particular town in northern Kenya (Isiolo), but, as is often the case with anthropological research, his project changed with the dynamics 'on the ground' and began tracking the substance as it moved from farmer to consumer within Kenya, as well as beyond. Indeed, his research was at a time when khat production and trade was expanding greatly through the spread of the Somali diaspora and consequent growth in demand for khat in places as far afield as Manchester and Minneapolis, and Kenya was the main production centre supplying these expanded networks. Following khat – following its 'social life' – thus led him to a wider study of the social underpinnings of such an informal trade network, as well as underscoring how the meanings the substance had for people changed radically along the networks it followed: from a substance culturally and economically validated in the production zone of Meru, Kenya, to a source of much controversy in the context of the UK where many Somalis were pushing for a ban on the grounds that it was causing harm to their communities. As with Gezon, khat and those who animate its social life taught him much about how one substance can mean so many different things, and how it can be caught up in so many debates and transnational webs of significance. It also led him to further research into drugs in the East African context, including a current project on cannabis and its links to development and livelihoods.

For both of us, studying khat revealed the poignancy of drugs and underscored their centrality in human experiences cross-culturally. It motivated us to write a text that would bring together anthropological perspectives on drugs, considering multiple topics, methods and theoretical approaches.

Engaged Anthropology

Engagement in the world outside of academia is critical. Given that the odds of dying from an overdose exceed those of dying by a car accident (in the US), for example, anthropological insights into accidental death by overdose can help shape effective responses to this crisis. One way that anthropologists engage is by making their voices known in the public sphere through media outlets, where they link everyday experiences (desires, perceptions, cost-benefit calculations) with the structures that shape them. In calling attention to harmful effects, Friedman and Bourgois (2022) have, for example, written about novel synthetics (including Xylazine and Fentanyl) for *Time* magazine. Their piece combines attention to pharmacological toxicity and health risks, laboratory production, and the appeal of these drugs to consumers.

They also explain harm reduction as an important way to increase the safety of using them. Another way of engaging the public is through blogs, such as that written by Hilary Agro, a PhD student at the University of British Columbia. In her blog, *Raving Anthropology*, she argues for the end of prohibition and for harm reduction. Some scholarly work is reviewed in public media. For example, physician/anthropologist Kimberly Sue's (2019) book advocating against incarceration for people with substance use disorders was reviewed by National Public Radio in the US.

Anthropological perspectives are important for contributing to critical thinking in public understandings of the ways that drug effects disproportionately negatively affect people of colour, the poor, women and sexual minorities and other marginalised groups in many different contexts. In addition to calling attention to drug harms, anthropological voices can help with deconstructing moral panic around drugs that may not be as pharmacologically or socially dangerous, but around which there is social ambivalence and even fear. According to Tim Ingold, anthropology's strength is not in providing pre-packaged information, but about listening, learning *with* people and questioning assumptions. He writes that what drives anthropologists 'is not the demand for knowledge but an ethic of care' (Ingold 2018: 131).

Anthropologists have long been concerned not only with generating knowledge but also with forging understandings that lead to just and equitable action. Franz Boas was actively involved in condemning scientific racism and the eugenics movement early in the twentieth century. Roy Rappaport (1993: 297) charged anthropologists with developing 'conceptions of what it is that constitutes "troubles"'. He warned against seeing symptoms as the ultimate root cause of social and environmental problems. In particular, he pointed to the effect of language in shaping conceptions, which in turn shape actions. He wrote that

> naming also tends to blur the distinction between *symptoms*, such as widespread substance abuse ... and underlying disorders that generate such symptoms, for instance poverty or, at a yet deeper level, whatever it is that generates and perpetuates that poverty.
>
> (Rappaport 1993: 298, emphasis in original)

Kozaitis (2022) highlighted Rappaport's call 'for an engaged anthropology: a value-laden holistic "corrective science" to determine the root causes of maladaptations'. Kozaitis (2000: 46) called for anthropological praxis, which she defined as 'a way of work by anthropologists engaged in intellectually mediated, ethically sound, and socially responsible work'. Kirsch (2018) specified that engaged anthropology seeks 'to address larger concerns about social justice, structural violence, and environmental degradation that are often rooted in colonial history and exacerbated by globalization and contemporary forms of capitalism' (2018: 3).

Some professionals, scholars and activists become involved in processes of problem-solving, sometimes called applied anthropology. Going back at least to Radcliffe-Brown in the early twentieth century, many anthropologists have identified an unfortunate divide between anthropology that is primarily concerned with problem-solving ('applied anthropology') and those contributing to theoretical frameworks ('pure anthropology') (Kozaitis 2000: 47). More recently, however, the dichotomy has become increasingly dismantled because of the inherent interconnections between knowledge production and application to real-world circumstances.

Many have found engagement inescapable for themselves as anthropologists. Many feminist anthropologists, and Black feminist anthropologists in particular, have maintained a commitment to scholar-activism. Irma McClaurin (2001) wrote that Black feminist anthropology is necessarily linked with 'praxis informed by identity, social race, discriminatory practices in the academy and society, and field encounters influenced by colonialism' (p. 11), with the goal of helping 'ameliorate the oppressive/subordinate conditions to which Black women historically have been and continue to be subjected' (p. 16). In a monograph focusing on engaged anthropology, Kirsch (2018) wrote about having found himself engaged in the challenges of the people he was working with in Papua New Guinea, as he helped them in a lawsuit against the Ok Tedi copper and gold mine that was polluting their rivers and threatening their very existence. Sometimes engagement takes the form of sharing research findings with local communities. Gezon shared her community-based research on khat with local leaders in Madagascar, for example. Many of the recipients of the research report were also interviewed and helped shape the direction of the research.

Kirsch's work demonstrates that we become enmeshed within our worlds of research whether they are in our home countries or not. We do that by, according to Carole McGranahan (2022), grounding our theories in collaboration with the lived experiences of the people we work with ethnographically. In this way, ethnography is also theoretical. She wrote that 'relationships are what build ethics, build theory, build community, build family' (2022: 294). These relationships build compassion and the will to correct injustices. The study of drugs is ripe for this engaged theoretical relationship-building, because of the powerful effects on people's lives.

Some anthropologists engage directly in work that applies their anthropological tools and understandings to specific troubles. J. Bryan Page and Merrill Singer (2010) tell of the history of funding for drug research by the National Institute on Drug Abuse in the US. Through that funding, many anthropologists contributed not only to understanding the nature of street drug consumption and accompanying dangers but also to designing, implementing and evaluating the success of programmes meant to meet the needs of drug users using mixed methods approaches that include substantial ethnographic components. Anthropologists and anthropological perspectives continue to contribute to efforts to comprehend such phenomena as the intertwined epidemics of opioid-related overdose and HIV risk (Wolfson-Stofko et al. 2016), opioid risk generally (Mendoza et al. 2019, Caroll 2020), supervised injection programmes (Small 2016), tobacco cessation (Nichter et al. 2017), harm reduction strategies in various contexts (Hardon et al. 2020) and clinical uses of psychedelic drugs (Schleim 2022).

Current and Future Directions: Topics and Approaches

Studying drugs fits with many contemporary theoretical and methodological directions in anthropology, including biocultural syntheses (Lende 2005, Singer et al. 2017), as well as critical and systemic studies of inequality and structural violence that affect individual experiences (Bourgois 1995, Singer and Baer 2018). Anthropologists of drugs also engage in studies considering the agency of things (new materialism) (Hardon and Sanabria 2017, Dennis 2018). There are opportunities for multi-species ethnographies of drugs, as anthropologists work to capture interactions and hierarchical relations between humans and nonhumans in a more powerful way (Ji and Cheng 2021).

Drug scholars have also explored innovative methods, including digital research into internet communities and knowledge formation around drugs (Krieg et al. 2017, Hupli et al. 2019). Furthermore, drug studies have the potential to be on the forefront of feminist and postcolonial methods, ethics, and question formulation (notice that methods and theory cannot be separated) (Smith 1999; Harrison 2007), as voices of colonised and marginalised people are critical for understanding effects of drugs on individuals and their communities that are invisible to those on the outside. Indeed, what has been termed 'necropolitics', or the politics of death (Mbembe 2003), is ridden through with drugs in the aftermath of colonialism, including the deadliness of their dosing as well as the lethality of the politics that make some more vulnerable to those deadly experiences.

We hope you feel inspired to delve into questions and engagements of your own, adding to the creative ways in which anthropological approaches shine light on what it means to experience mind-altering substances in academic, applied, political or simply everyday life contexts.

Works Cited

Agro, Hilary. "Raving Anthropology." https://hilaryagro.wordpress.com/

Bourgois, Philippe I. 1995. *In Search of Respect: Selling Crack in El Barrio.* New York: Cambridge University Press.

Carroll, Jennifer J., Marlene C. Lira, Karsten Lunze, Jonathan A. Colasanti, Carlos del Rio, and Jeffrey H. Samet. 2020. "Painful Subjects: Treating Chronic Pain among People Living with HIV in the Age of Opioid Risk." *Medical Anthropology Quarterly* 35 (2): 141–158.

Dennis, Simone. 2018. "Research Paper: Becoming Enwinded: A New Materialist Take on Smoking Pleasure." *International Journal of Drug Policy* 51: 69–74.

Friedman, Joseph, and Philippe Bourgois. 2022. "Xylazine, a Dangerous Veterinary Tranquilizer, is Showing Us the Future of the Overdose Crisis." *Time*. 6 April 2022.

Gezon, Lisa L. 2006. *Global Visions, Local Landscapes: A Political Ecology of Conservation, Conflict, and Control in Northern Madagascar*. Lanham, MD: AltaMira Press.

Hardon, Anita, and Emilia Sanabria. 2017. "Fluid Drugs: Revisiting the Anthropology of Pharmaceuticals." *Annual Review of Anthropology* 46 (1): 117–132.

Hardon, Anita, Takeo David Hymans, Inge van Schipstal, Swasti Mishra, Moritz Berning, Hayley Murray, Daan Kamps, and Tait Mandler. 2020. "Caring for 'Hassle-Free Highs' in Amsterdam." *Anthropology and Humanism* 45 (2): 212–222.

Harrison, Faye. 2007. "Feminist Methodology as a Tool for Ethnographic Inquiry on Globalization." In *The Gender of Globalization: Women Navigating Cultural and Economic Marginalities*, edited by Nandini Gunewardena and Ann E Kingsolver, 23–31. Santa Fe: School for Advanced Research (SAR) Press.

Hupli, Aleksi, Moritz Berning, Ahnjili Zhuparris, and James Fadiman. 2019. "Descriptive Assemblage of Psychedelic Microdosing: Netnographic Study of Youtube™ Videos and On-going Research Projects." *Performance Enhancement & Health* 6 (3–4): 129–138.

Ingold, Tim. 2018. *Anthropology: Why It Matters*. Cambridge: Polity Press.

Ji, Ruobing, and Yu Cheng. 2021. "Thinking Global Health from the Perspective of Anthropology." *Global Health Research and Policy* 6 (47): 1–3.

Kirsch, Stuart. 2018. *Engaged Anthropology: Politics Beyond the Text*. Oakland, CA: University of California Press.

Kozaitis, Kathryn A. 2000. The Rise of Anthropological Praxis. *NAPA Bulletin*, 18(1), 45–66.

———. 2022. *Primacy of the Human: General Anthropology in Times of Crisis*. American Anthropological Association, Seattle, WA.

Krieg, Lisa Jenny, Moritz Berning, and Anita Hardon. 2017. "Anthropology with Algorithms? An Exploration of Online Drug Knowledge Using Digital Methods." *Medicine Anthropology Theory* 4 (3): 21–52.

Lende, Daniel H. 2005. "Wanting and Drug Use: A Biocultural Approach to the Analysis of Addiction." *Building Biocultural Anthropology* 33 (1): 100–124.

Mbembe, Achille. 2003. "Necropolitics." *Public Culture* 15 (1): 11–40.

McClaurin, Irma. 2001. "Introduction: Forging a Theory, Politics, Praxis, and Poetics of Black Feminist Anthropology." In *Black Feminist Anthropology: Theory, Politics, Praxis, and Poetics*, 1–23. New Brunswick, NJ: Rutgers University Press.

McGranahan, Carole. 2022. "Theory as Ethics." *American Ethnologist* 49 (3): 289–301.

Mendoza, Sonia, Allyssa Stephanie Rivera, and Helena Bjerring Hansen. 2019. "Re-Racialization of Addiction and the Redistribution of Blame in the White Opioid Epidemic." *Medical Anthropology Quarterly* 33 (2): 242–262.

Nichter, Mimi, Asli Carkoglu, Mark Nichter, Seyda Ozcan, and M. Atilla Uysal. 2017. "Engaging Nurses in Smoking Cessation: Challenges and Opportunities in Turkey." *Health Policy* 122: 192–197.

Page, J. Bryan, and Merrill Singer. 2010. *Comprehending Drug Use: Ethnographic Research at the Social Margins*. New Brunswick, NJ: Rutgers University Press.

Rappaport, Roy. 1993. "The Anthropology of Trouble." *American Anthropologist* 95 (2): 295–303.

Schleim, Stephan. 2022. "Grounded in Biology: Why the Context-Dependency of Psychedelic Drug Effects Means Opportunities, Not Problems for Anthropology and Pharmacology." *Frontiers in Psychiatry* 13: 1–5.

Singer, Merrill, and Hans Baer. 2018. *Critical Medical Anthropology* (2nd ed). New York: Routledge.

Singer, Merrill, Nicola Bulled, Bayla Ostrach, and Emily Mendenhall. 2017. "Syndemics and the Biosocial Conception of Health." *The Lancet* 389 (10072): 941–950.

Small, Dan. 2016. "Cultural Alchemy and Supervised Injection: Anthropological Activism and Application." *Practicing Anthropology* 38 (2): 26–31.

Smith, Linda Tuhiwai. 1999. *Decolonizing Methodologies*. London, England: Zed Books.

Sue, Kimberly. 2019. *Getting Wrecked: Women, Incarceration, and the American Opioid Crisis*. Oakland, CA: University of California Press.

Wolfson-Stofko, Brett, Ric Curtis, Faustino Fuentes, Ed Machess, and Alexis Del Rio-Cumba. 2016. "The Portapotty Experiment: Neoliberal Approaches to the Intertwined Epidemics of Opioid-Related Overdose and HIV/HCV, and Why We Need Cultural Anthropologists in the South Bronx." *Dialectical Anthropology* 40 (4): 295–410.

Index

Actor Network Theory (ANT) 28
Adderall drug 32, 96, 126, 131
addiction 113; agency/power
    109–10; anthropology of 126–7;
    brain disease 116; complicating
    addiction 114; cultural meaning/
    social interaction model 116–17;
    drugs potency 126–7; ethnographies
    119–21; hijacking, metaphorical
    usage 115; history of 110–14; khat,
    case studies 123–4; medical model
    of 114; neurobiological/disease
    models 114–16; opioids, case studies
    125–6; pathologizing view of drugs
    108; political-economic model of
    117–19; political economies 121–2;
    socio-cultural/political-economic
    determinants of 109; structural
    model of 119; substances harm 108;
    sugar 7; tobacco, case studies 124–5;
    treatment, as cultural constructions
    122–3; United States (US), sociological
    theory of 3; Vietnam, signs of 4
Afghanistan, opium farmers in 146,
    147, 157
Agar, Michael 11, 120, 121
alcohol: banned, in United States 56;
    beverages 45; consumption 99–102,
    112, 118–19, 170; cross-cultural
    study of 11; disinhibitor 4; drinking
    see drinking alcohol; fruit-eating
    animals 41; movements prohibiting
    102; potent effect 19; prohibition 111;
    societies loss 19
alcoholism 18, 112, 118, 120;
    Alcoholics Anonymous 11, 112, 119;
    in Central America 17; self-fulfilling
    prophecies 113; violence and
    anti-social behaviour 4

Alderete, Ethel 70, 86
Alexander, Bruce 117–119
Allen, Catherine 12, 22, 90
Alpert, Richard 79
Amanita muscaria (Fly Agaric) 48, 64,
    67, 68
American Anthropological Association
    21; Principles of Professional
    Responsibility 32
American Psychiatric Association (APA)
    113
Andersson, Ruben 169
Anti-Politics Machine 135
anti-social behaviour, drug users 4, 22
anti-war on drugs: counter-currents
    169–72; harm reduction 171–2
Argonauts of the Western Pacific, 1922
    8
armchair anthropology 30
Asad, Talal 33
assemblages 5, 21, 79, 108, 122, 124–5,
    160–1, 166
Attention Deficit Hyperactivity Disorder
    29
Australia 1, 65, 102, 134
ayahuasca 7, 10, 43, 63, 64, 71–2,
    76–8, 80, 81; *Banisteriopsis caapi* 71;
    mixtures of different ingredients 43;
    'psychologization' of 77; tourism 77,
    80; *yagé* 7
Aymara *ayllu* system 163
Aymara coca farmers 163

Barleycorn, John 109
Barnard, Mary 40, 43
Barratt, Monica J. 79, 80
Bateson, Gregory 11, 119, 120
Becker, Howard 4
Beckerleg, Susan 12, 121, 146, 149

beer 7, 10, 18–20, 26, 43, 51, 100–2
Bell, Kirsten 98
Bemba of Zambia 10; *ubwalua* 10
Benedict, Ruth 20
Benson, Peter 136–8
Bergschmidt, Viktoria B 23
Big Tobacco 137, 139–40
biopower 23, 171
biosocial 5, 113, 124
blood-borne diseases 57, 122, 170
Boas, Franz 18, 20, 180
Bouayad, Aurelien 9
Bourdieu, Pierre 88
Bourgois, Philippe 12, 20, 21, 22, 24, 29, 31, 32, 132, 141, 148, 165, 179
Boyer, Paul 77
Brazil 76; Members of Brazil's Landless Rural Workers' Movement (MST) 100; tobacco cultivation in 137, 140
Bretton Woods agreement 134
Briggs, Daniel 78
British: China, opium to balance trade 24; East India Company 91
Brown, Michael 64
Brunton, Ron 13
Burroughs, William S. 114
Burton, Richard 8
Bwiti religion 66, 75

caffeine-bearing plants, globalization of 51
Camba, drinking patterns 4, 100
Campbell, Howard 27, 159, 161
Campbell, Nancy 115
cannabis 3, 50, 56, 157; African countries 41, 162, 179; archaeological origins of 41–3; dizziness feelings 4; globalization of 51; Mexican policy 57, 156; Nixon's Commission on Marihuana and Drug Abuse 156; psychoactive use of 49; Rastafarian spiritual use of 45; smoking overdose 29; United States (US) 56; usage 4; younger generations 19; Zulu warriors 97
Capone, Al 56
Carneiro, Henrique S. 65
Carr, E. Summerson 122
Carrier, Neil 7, 109, 123, 179
cartels 126, 147, 164
Carter, Jimmy 156, 157
Casey, John J. 31
cash crops 27, 64, 72, 135, 139, 141–2, 145, 150, 163

Castillo, Hernandez 167
Central Intelligence Agency (CIA) 73, 147, 157
ceremonial/ritualised consumption 88; ayahuasca tourism 77–8, 80; Mexico 67–70; Santo Daime 76; shamanic 72; Stimulants 89–91
China: Big Tobacco 140; economic practices 55, 140; immigration 55; opium consumption in 55; Opium Wars 24; producer of tobacco 140; trade advantage 54
Chin, Ko-lin 146, 149
chronic relapsing disease of the brain (CRDB) 114
Church of Jesus Christ of Latter-day Saints 89
Ciudad Juárez 167
coca: in Bolivia 141; globalization of 51; psychoactive crops 46
cocaine 1, 3, 6, 26, 29, 42, 71, 87, 114, 141, 150, 162, 165, 167, 170; crack cocaine 11, 12, 89, 94, 98, 125; export restrictions 156; penalties for convictions 57; practice of consuming 22; in restaurants 96; as Schedule II drug 56; trafficking 164, 168; United States (US) 56
coffee 1, 5, 27, 28, 52–4, 81, 89–92, 94–7, 142, 143, 145, 150; drinking of 89; as exotic drugs 53; 'fair trade' models 135; psychoactive substances 132
Cohen, Paul T 160, 162
commodities, drug as 26–7, 51, 131–2, 134–5, 141, 150, 155
community, building 93–4
Confessions of an English Opium Eater, The (1822) 109, 112
Constructive Drinking (1987) 11, 20
consumers' mental health 78
Convention against Illicit Traffic in Narcotic Drugs 157
Conzelman, Caroline S 163
Counterblaste to Tobacco, A 52
Courtwright, David 26, 50, 51, 54, 55
COVID-19 pandemic 140
Crawford, David 167
crime 111, 133; anti- social behavior 22; death penalty, 158; drug trade 133, 164; drug users 22; growth of 169
Critical Medical Anthropology (CMA) 12, 23, 24, 80, 119, 121

cultural constructs 23, 81, 108, 109,
    113, 122, 159
cultural institutions 13
cultural relativism 20, 21
culture: blame 167; drug consumption
    39, 45, 47, 52, 80; materiality 27–30,
    43; Mayan cultures 44; meanings/
    values 20–2; non-indigenous drug 76;
    prohibition 24; social stimulation
    88–9; stimulating culture 88–9;
    tobacco smoking 92; Western popular
    culture 73
Cusicanqui, Silvia Rivera 92
Cypriot juglets 44–5

d'Abbs, Peter 91
Dai, Bingham 11
Datura stramonium 42, 66
decolonising movements 34
decriminalisation: harm reduction 170;
    socio-cultural impacts of 173
deer-maize-peyote complex 69
Deleuze, Gilles 5, 160
Dennis, Simone 98
De Quincey, Thomas 109, 111, 112
de Rios, Marlene Dobkin 64, 81
*Diagnostic and Statistical Manual of
    Mental Disorders* (DSM) 113
digital technology, importance of 32
N,N-dimethyltryptamine (DMT) 63
dizziness, cannabis usage 4
Donner, William W. 100
Doors of Perception, The (1954) 73,
    74
dopamine 29, 87, 125
Douglas, Mary 11, 20, 88, 89
drinking alcohol: anthropological
    approach 18; cultural/social contexts
    of 99–100; Europe 110; harms 103;
    identity, marker of 100–1; Iran 95;
    MST membership 100; stress *see*
    stress relieving, drinking
drug policy: internationalisation of 7;
    social effects of 2
drugs, definition of 6–8
Drug, Set and Setting (1984) 4, 63, 116,
    124
drug traffickers 157–9, 164, 165
Drug Use for Grown-Ups (2021) 122
drug users 3, 11, 26, 31–3, 54, 112,
    116, 121, 158; crime and anti-social
    behaviour 22; criminalising 156;
    drug war affects 166; HIV/AIDS and

hepatitis C 170; needs of 172, 181;
    precautions 171
drug war: anthropological approaches
    159; anti-war *see* anti-war on drugs;
    assemblage 160–1; as assemblage
    160; commodity chains 162–3;
    consumption 165–6; effects 155;
    ethnography 161; failed war 169;
    global to local 161–2; marginality
    166–8; overview of 155–8;
    production 163; structural violence
    166–8; studying up 168; system
    of meanings 159–60; trade 164–5;
    violence 166–8
drunken behavior 4, 18, 56, 100, 110,
    111
Drunken Comportment (1969) 99
'drunken monkey' hypothesis 40, 41
Dumit, Joseph 114
Duranti, Alessandro 21
Duterte, Rodrigo 22, 158, 164, 169
Duvall, Chris 50, 53

East Africa: alcohol and power 57; khat
    2, 26, 162
economies, drug: consumption 131;
    crops/commodities 131–2; dangerous
    commodities 133–4; economic
    development 134; khat 141–6;
    livelihoods 134–6; opiates/opioids
    146–9; production/distribution issues
    149–50; tobacco *see* tobacco, drug
    economies
Edgerton, Robert B. 99
Electric Kool-Aid Acid Test, The (1968)
    74
Elegiac Addict, The (2008) 122
emic/etic analyses 23, 168
Encountering Development (1995)
    135
Ephedra altissima 41
Ephedra plant 41, 42, 48
epidemics, addiction 55; heroin 4; HIV/
    AIDS epidemic of 1980s 11; opioids
    125, 126, 167, 182
epistemologies 23, 33, 119, 120
Escobar, Arturo 27, 135
ethics, drugs anthropological themes:
    ethical considerations 32–3;
    ethnography 30–2; postcolonial
    perspectives 33–4
Ethiopia, trade routes 1, 13, 26, 43, 53,
    123, 141, 143, 145

ethnic minorities 100, 147, 162
European colonialism 22, 52, 65

Fabian, Johannes 32
Fadiman, James 79
fake medicines 132
Faris, Suzanne B. 110, 113
Farmer, Paul 23
faulty wiring 81
'feel-good' compound 87
Ferguson, James 135
Fernandez, James 66
Fikes, Jay Courtney 77
Fitzpatrick, Scott 41
Foucault, Michel 23
Framework Convention on Tobacco
    Control (FCTC) 136
Friedman, Joseph 179
functionalism 17–20
Furst, Peter T. 63, 65, 68, 70

Gamlin, Jennie 138, 139
Garcia, Angela 31, 122, 123, 166
Garriott, William 26, 114, 122
Geertz, Clifford 20, 22, 30, 88, 89
Gell, Alfred 28
Germany, drug isolation
    pharmaceuticals 3
gerontocracy 18, 19
Gezon, Lisa L 96, 123, 178, 179, 181
Ghost Dance, The 75
Gillogly, Kathleen A 55, 147, 148
Glantz, Stanton A. 136
global economy 25, 28, 133, 135; free-
    market society 117; interconnections
    52; markets 117, 132
global nomads 78
Golden Triangle, opium farmers 1, 55,
    147, 148
Gosden, Chris 41
Gow, Peter 71
Granfield, Robert 115, 170
Grisaffi, Thomas 12
Gross Domestic Product (GDP) 134,
    141, 150
Guattari, Felix 160
Gurr, Mel 100

Hague International Opium Convention
    (1912) 55, 156
hallucinogen 10, 42, 44, 78, 80–1, 87;
    in ancient Greek Eleusinian Mysteries
    48; consumption of 74; Datura 49;

defined 62–3; effects of 73, 74, 79; as
    entheogens 62; flashbacks 63; fungi,
    use of 44, 66–7; henbane 49; Ibogaine
    66; international search for 77;
    microdosing 79; mushrooms 40,
    66–8, 97; old and new world use
    of 65; as psychedelics 62; public
    enthusiasm for 73; ritualised use
    of 64; role in human evolution
    40; shamanic use of 45, 46, 71;
    substances associated with 63;
    synthetic 73; tobacco 69–70; wine
    with 49; *yagé* (ayahuasca) 7
haram, for Muslims 87
hard drugs 122
Hardon, Anita 7, 99, 171, 172
harm reduction 34, 57, 79, 98, 112,
    122, 155, 156, 160, 170–2, 180, 182;
    approaches 170, 172; criticisms of
    171; strategies for 98, 172, 182
Harm Reduction International (2021)
    158
Heath, Dwight 4, 11, 100
Hendy, Katherine 79
Herodotus 8, 49, 50
heroin 3, 94, 97, 114, 146, 149, 165,
    167; addiction to 4, 12, 20, 23, 29,
    31, 55, 117, 121, 126; consumption
    of 11, 121; decriminalisation on use
    of 170; economy 120; as hard drug
    122; lives and experiences of heroin
    users 120; life and livelihoods of
    heroin users 11; Nixon's drug war
    55, 156; Opium Wars of the 1800s
    156; overdose 122; poppy plants 125;
    supply of 120; treatment for addiction
    of 156; use in pharmaceutical industry
    6; used by US soldiers 124
Herskovits, Melville 21
Hickman, Timothy 109, 110, 115
hijacking, metaphorical usage 115
historical studies , drugs anthropology:
    ancient literature 47; deep time
    41–5; domestication 45–51; human
    ancestors, use of drugs 57–8; human
    transformation 39–41; inequality
    45–51; presentism 39; prohibition
    54–7; society and culture 39
HIV/AIDS: ART treatment 139; blood-
    borne diseases 170; epidemic, of
    1980s 11; intravenous drug 24;
    intravenous drug users (IDU) 170;
    levels of education 24

Hofmann, Albert 48, 67, 73
Hold Life Has, The (1988) 12
Homo sapiens 40, 42
Horton, Donald 11, 18
Hugh-Jones, Stephen 6, 7
Huichol of Mexico 68
human dispersion 69
Human Relations Area Files 90
human rights 172; goals of 170;
    recognition of 21; US foreign policy
    168; violation of 21, 164
Human Rights Watch 170
hunter-gatherer societies 46, 65
Huxley, Aldous 73, 74
hybrid vigour 6
Hyoscyamus niger 42
hypertension 24
hyper-traditionalisation 77

ibogaine 66
iboga, Bwiti religion 75; pre-colonial use
    of 66
identity 25, 48, 49, 72, 78, 117, 165;
    cultural messages 91, 162; drinking
    100–1; drugs, social stimulation 91–3;
    ethnic/national 92; gendered 93
illegal drugs 24, 25, 33, 95, 112, 115,
    126, 131–3, 150, 157, 158, 169
illegal substances 78
illicit commodity 133, 134
illicit flows 26
Immortality Key, The (2020) 48
inequalities 12, 78, 127; criminal justice
    system 158; critical/systemic studies
    182; domestication 45–7; formal/
    informal structure 94; poverty 23;
    power/intersecting 22–3, 25; social
    stimulation disintegration 89, 93–5
informal economy 120, 144, 162, 166
Ingold, Tim 180
International Narcotics Control Board
    (INCB) 56, 168
International Opium Commission (IOC)
    55
intoxicants 6, 8, 32, 40, 48, 50, 51, 53,
    156
intravenous drug users (IDU) 170;
    blood-borne diseases 170; HIV/AIDS
    170
Isherwood, Baron 88
Isolating, drug 3
Israel, brewing from stone mortars
    43

Jaffe, Jerome 156
Jay, Mike 68, 73, 77
Jellinek, Elvin Morton 112

karam 92, 94
Kenya 13, 142–5; heroin addicts 12,
    121, 165; khat ban 123; khat, from
    Catha edulis tree 1, 92, 161, 162,
    179; khat legal/ illegal 141; Meru
    people of 19, 90; Nico 109; Somali
    community, about social harms 161;
    trade routes 1
Kesey, Ken 73
ketamine 63, 73
khat, from *Catha edulis* tree 1, 179;
    addiction, case studies 123–4; ban
    123; from Catha edulis tree 1, 92,
    161, 162, 179; chewing of 93, 94,
    97–9, 124; drug economies 141–2;
    green gold 178; harmful drug, in UK
    2; industry 162; in Kenya 1, 144,
    179; khat-free environment 124;
    legal/ illegal 141; in Madagascar 1,
    96; Meru identity 92; muguka 143;
    production 142–3, 161; quasi-legality
    of 162; in Somalia 1; trade/trust
    143–6; in Yemen 1t
Klein, Axel 165, 168
Kohrman, Matthew 137
Kozaitis, Kathryn A 180
Kula ring 9, 88

La Barre, Weston 9, 63, 65, 68, 74, 75,
    77
labour 11, 100, 121, 141; African 140;
    Chinese 156; disciplined bodies
    95–7; exploitation 149; immigrant 56,
    92, 139; labour-intensive crop 137;
    legal protection 144; on sugar cane
    and tobacco plantations 52, 137–8;
    Western 163
Lancet, The 158
Langill, Jennifer C. 100
Leary, Timothy 73
Lende, Daniel 115
Levine, Harry G 111, 113
Lewis-Williams, David 44
Life magazine (1957) 67, 76
Lighting Up (2015) 137
Lindesmith, Alfred 3
Liu, Ting 92, 93
Lophophora williamsii 9, 68
Lukasz, Kamienski 97, 98

Luna, Sarah 164
Lyons, Kristina 163

MacAndrew, Craig 4, 99
Macaulay, G. C. 49
MacRae, Edward 76
Madagascar 13, 27, 42, 93, 96–7, 123, 141, 143, 178, 181: khat, from *Catha edulis* tree 1; khat, quasi-legality of 162; trade routes 1
mafrish 94, 124, 145
magic mushrooms 44, 67
Mak, Veronica Sau-Wa 91
male superiority, Han Confucian cultural notions of 93
Malinowski, Bronislaw 8, 9, 30, 31, 88
market economy, of drugs 18, 134
Marshall, Mac 6, 11, 24, 90, 93, 102, 103
Marxist 23
Marx, Karl 23, 27
masculine identity 100, 165
material culture, of drugs 27, 28, 41, 43
Mauss, Marcel 88, 120
McGranahan, Carole 181
McKenna, Terence 40, 63
Mendoza, Sonia 126, 167
Mescalero Apache 68
mescaline 63, 68–9, 73
Mescaline: a global history of the first psychedelic (2019) 73
methodological relativism 21
Mexico 1, 9, 27, 68–70, 74, 75, 122, 138, 147, 157, 158, 160, 166, 167; drug war 159; heroin addiction 31; immigrant labourers 56; psychoactive mushrooms 67
Michaud, Jean 100
microdose 79
Miller, Daniel 27
Mintz, Sidney 26, 52
missionaries 30, 66, 67, 68, 72, 90, 164
Moerman, Daniel 5, 80
molacas 72
Mooney, James 9
moral economy 120–1, 164
Morales, Evo 12, 71
moral judgement 7, 110, 115
Mother Earth (*Pachamama*) 70
Muraresku, Brian 48, 49
Murray, A. T. 47
mushrooms 29, 40, 44, 48, 63, 65–8, 74, 97

Myanmar, opium 93, 97, 146–8
Myerhoff, Barbara 69

Nader, Laura 25, 168
narcocorridos 160
narcoculture, in Mexico 160
narcopropaganda 159
National Institute on Drug Abuse in the US 181
neolithicization 45
Neolithic transitions 45, 46
neuroanthropology 115
New York Academy of Sciences 63
New Zealand 1, 102
Nichter, Mimi 92, 98, 125, 137, 182
Nicotine 116; admixture plants 71; brain activity 125; patch 170; pipe smoking 69; replacement therapies 136; in tobacco 28, 87, 125
Nigeria's National Drug Law Enforcement Agency 169
Nixon's drug war 56
non-governmental organisation (NGO) 141
Norton, Marcy 53
Nyambene Hills 1, 142, 143, 145

obesity 24
Ohler, Norman 98
Oklahoma Area Indian Health Service 70
ontologies 23, 171
opiates 29, 44, 47, 51, 112, 113, 118, 124; Chinese labourers 156; cold turkey 114; drug overdoses 171; globalization of 51; medical purposes 111; natural opiates 125; and opioids, 146–7; OxyContin/buprenorphine 132; trade of 156
opioids 56, 114, 117, 125–6; abuse 126; crisis in North America 1, 167; drug addiction 126; drug economies 146; epidemic 126; eradication 147–8; and opiates 146–7; overdose 182; risks/ opportunities 148–9; semi- synthetic 126; tramadol/fentanyl 126
opium 8, 24, 42, 44, 45, 47, 48, 54–6, 109, 111–12, 123, 136, 146–50, 156–7, 160, 162; addiction 160; case studies 125–6; in China 54; consumption 112; crisis in US 1, 56, 167; cultivation 55; farmers 146; morphine 3; overdose 182; semi-synthetic 126; usage 111

Opium Wars of 1800s 54, 55, 112, 156
Ortner, Sherry 25, 30
Osmond, Humphrey 62
Otañez, Martin G. 136, 173
overheating 96
Oxford Handbook of Global Drug History, The, 2022 51
OxyContin 114, 126, 131, 132

Page, J. Bryan 7, 8, 22, 30, 31, 33, 121, 170, 181
Papaver somniferum 42
participant observation method 2, 30, 31
Patterns of Culture, 1934 20
Pen-ts'ao Ching 50
Per Capita Income 134–5
Peterson, Kristin 132
peyote cactus *(Lophophora williamsii)* 9, 63, 68
Peyote Cult (1938) 9, 68, 74
pharmacological determinism 3, 99, 116, 118, 124
pharmacology, social stimulation 86–7
Pharmakon 47, 50
Philip Morris International (PMI) 137
physiological reliance 113
Piper methysticum 13, 99
Pitt Rivers Museum, Oxford 28
pharmacology 2–6, 27–30, 63, 69, 86–87, 178
placebo effect 5
plastic shaman 77
pneuma enthusiastikon 49
Po, June Y. T. 100
political-economic 23, 110, 114, 122; addiction 117, 121; drug effects 109; moral economy of 22, 121
postaddiction model 113
Preble, Edward 11, 31, 120
premodern quasi-ethnography 8–10
'pro-social' behaviour 46
Psilocybe hispanica 44, 66–7
psilocybe mushrooms, use of 44, 74
Psilocybe semilanceata 67
psilocybin (mushrooms) 40, 44, 63, 64, 68, 73, 79; toxic substances 29; use of 67
Psychedelic Explorer's Guide: Safe, Therapeutic, and Sacred Journeys, The 79
Psychedelic psychotherapy 78–81

psychedelics, in cultural contexts 62–6, 73–5, 78–81, 182; ayahuasca 71–2; ibogaine 66; mescaline 68–9; mushrooms 66–8; synthetic hallucinogens 73; tobacco 69–70
psychoactive crops 46
psychoactive substances 3, 6–8, 18, 28, 29, 39, 41, 45–7, 81, 103, 125, 132, 135, 150
Psychotria viridis 71
psychotropic plants 10
Pythia 49

Race, Kane 98, 99, 172
racial disparities, in US criminal justice 158
Radcliffe-Brown, A. R. 17, 181
Raikhel, Eugene 114, 122
Raving Anthropology 180
Reefer Madness, 1936 3, 160
Reinarman, Craig 3, 113, 115, 170
religious change 75
respectability 53, 54, 91
Righteous Dopefiend 120
Rig Veda 48, 68
Rinella, Michael 50
Ripping and Running (1973) 120
River Thames 43
Robbins, Michael C 101
Room, Robin 19, 103, 118
Rosenthal, Richard J. 110, 113
Royal Fort gardens 43
Rudgley, Richard 6
Rush, Benjamin 111
Russell, Andrew 52, 125, 137

Sahara Desert 67
Sakha of Siberia 64
Sanabria, Harry 30, 99, 163, 182
San Pedro cactus *(Trichocereus pachanoi)* 68, 81
Santo Daime 76, 77
Schedules of the UN Commission on Narcotic Drugs 170
Schonberg, Jeff 20, 32, 120
Schultes, Richard Evans 10, 63–65
Search of Respect: Selling Crack in El Barrio, In 21
self-identification, ethnic 71
self-medication 94
Serpent and the Rainbow, The (1985) 63
Sertürner, Friedrich 3

shamanism 62, 64–5, 69, 71, 72, 77, 78, 80
Shanghai, International Opium Commission (IOC) 55
Sharp, Ethan 159
Sherratt, Andrew 6, 7
Shryock 91, 92, 94
Siberia: intoxicants 48; shamanic rituals 97; Tungus language of 64
Siff, Stephen 76
Singer, Merrill 7, 8, 12, 22, 30, 33, 80, 103, 134, 138, 139, 164, 181
Smith, Huston 40
Smith, Linda Tuhiwai 34, 182
Smith, Woodruff 53
smoking: cigarette 100; European 70; gendered 93; MST membership 100; Nichter's study 92; nicotine 170; opium 55; pipe 69; public health campaigns 93; social relationships 98; tobacco consumption 69, 70, 92; toxic 29; try to quit 124; women 92
social gathering 9, 94
social inequality 25, 46
social integration 17–20, 76, 94, 100, 101
Social Life of Things, The (1986) 26, 132, 141
social movements: anthropology/ psychedelics 81; Castaneda, Carlos 74–5; counterculture 74–5; counterculture/new age contexts 73–4; globalisation/change 75; Native American Church 75–6; Santo Daime 76, 77
social problems 113, 121
social relationships 77, 87, 88, 93, 98, 108, 110, 117, 120
social stimulation: alcohol 86; building community 93–4; consumption 87–8; drug harms/anthropology 103; drugs, as identity 91–3; Incan workers, efficiency of 95; inequalities/disintegration 94–5; labour, disciplined bodies 95–7; pharmacology/toxicology 86–7; pleasure 98–9; rationality 95; ritual, to everyday practice 89–91; stimulating culture 88–9; war 97–8
Social Value of Drug Addicts, The (2014) 22, 121
social violence 136
societal attitudes, drug's production trade and consumption 2

socio-cultural model 114, 117; anthropology 1; drug effects 109
Soma: Divine Mushroom of Immortality (1968) 40, 48
Somalia: export markets 142; khat-chewing 98; khat, from Catha edulis tree 1; Somali community, about social harms 161; sugar 134; trade routes 1
Sora of India 64
Spicer, Edward H. 74
Spicer, Paul 101, 102, 118, 119
Spirits 64, 71; distilled 100; exchange in trade 24; globalization of 51
Stebbins, Kenyon Rainier 137
Stoned Ape theory 40
street ethnography/addiction 11–12, 121
stress relieving, drinking 98–101; cultural/social contexts of 99–100; identity, marker of 100–1
structural violence 23, 125, 126, 138, 141, 166, 167, 171, 180, 182
substance abuse 7, 180
Sue, Kimberly 180
Suggs, D 100, 101
syndemics 24

Tabernanthe iboga 66
Tate, Winifred 168
tea 1, 13, 27, 28, 52–54, 68, 71, 81, 89, 90, 91, 93–6, 100, 132, 142, 145
Teachings of Don Juan: A Yaqui Way of Knowledge, The (1968) 74
Tilki, Mary 101
Time magazine 74, 179
tobacco 7–9, 24, 28–30, 42, 43, 51–3, 63, 64, 69–70, 81, 86, 87, 90, 92, 93, 95, 96, 98, 121, 124, 131, 132, 134, 136–42, 146, 149, 179, 182; addiction 125; archaeobotanical traces of 42; case studies 124–5; cigarettes 70; consumption 70; drug economies, farming 137–9; ethnic tensions 138; globalization of 51; legal status and public health 136–7; livelihoods, risks/opportunities 141; nicotine 28; Philip Morris 140; pre-Colombia 70; production 136; profitability/global capitalist economy 139–41; psychoactive crops 46; ritual use of 70; smoking 70
tourism 76–8; psychedelic psychotherapy 78–81; recreational contexts 76–8

toxic drugs 29, 87
toxicology: social stimulation 86–7;
    toxicologists 29
trafficking 158, 159, 164, 165
*Tribal College: Journal of American
    Indian Higher Education* 77
tuberculosis: levels of education 24;
    treatment 23
Turner, Sarah 100
Turner, Tim 78

ubwalua 10
United Kingdom (UK): khat, banned
    1; khat, from *Catha edulis* tree 1–2;
    social anthropology 20; social harms
    20
United Nations Office of Drugs and
    Crime (UNODC) 147, 157–8, 160
United Nations Universal Declaration of
    Human Rights (UDHR) 21
United States (US) 148, 163; addiction,
    sociological theory of 3; Central
    Intelligence Agency 73; cocaine
    trafficking 168; cultural anthropology
    20; Drug Enforcement Administration
    115; opioid crisis 167; opium, cocaine
    and cannabis 56; prison-industrial
    complex 22; street ethnography 11
United States Agency for International
    Development (USAID) 163
Uzwiak, Beth A. 171, 172

Valium 114, 131
Vedas 48
vegetalismo 77
Vietnam, addiction signs 4; drug crimes
    158; eradication campaigns 147;
opium cultivation 147; post- WWII
    anxiety 74; US soldiers 4, 124; war
    156, 157
Vuh, Popol 70

Wakeman, Stephen 120
Wang Xiaochuan 92
war on drugs 22, 54, 57, 150, 155, 156,
    158–73
Wasson, R. Gordon 40, 48, 67, 68, 76
Weir, Shelagh 13, 123, 124, 143
Western influences, spread of drug use
    165
Western labour unions, *sindicato* form
    163
Willis, Justin 19, 57
Wilson, Monica 18, 19
wine 5, 19, 27, 42, 43, 45, 47, 49–51,
    89, 92, 94: Catholic sacrament of 45;
    globalization of 51
Women's Petition against Coffee, The 53
work ethic 96, 111
World Health Organization (WHO) 24,
    29, 93, 113, 126, 136, 162, 170
Writing Culture (1986) 33

yawarapu 9
Yemen 13, 96, 99, 123, 124, 143;
    khat, from *Catha edulis* tree 1; trade
    routes 1

Zapatista democracy movement 102–3
Zigon, Jarrett: theories of global
    interconnectedness 161; war on drugs
    160
Zinberg, Norman 4
Zulu warriors 97

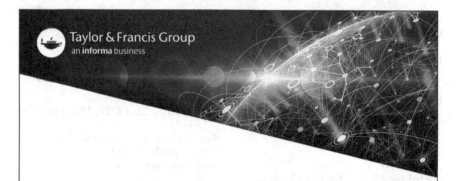